MAKING WAVES

Making Waves

READING B.C. AND PACIFIC NORTHWEST LITERATURE

TREVOR CAROLAN, EDITOR

Carolyn Zonailo * George McWhirter * Judith Copithorne
Susan McCaslin * Hilary Turner * Michael Barnholden
Joseph Blake * Colin James Sanders * Mike Doyle
Frances Cabahug * Paul Falardeau * Chelsea Thornton
Martin VanWoudenberg * Ron Dart

UFV PRESS – ANVIL PRESS

Anvil Press Publishers Inc.   University of the Fraser Valley (UFV Press)
P.O. Box 3008, Main Post Office   33844 King Road
Vancouver, B.C. V6B 3X5   Abbotsford, B.C.
www.anvilpress.com   V2S 7M8

Library and Archives Canada Cataloguing in Publication

Making Waves : Reading B.C. and Pacific Northwest Literature / edited by Trevor Carolan.

Includes bibliographical references and index.

ISBN 978-1-897535-29-5

1. Canadian essays (English)—21st century. 2. British Columbia—Literary collections. I. Carolan, Trevor, 1951-

PS8367.B7P38 2010   C814'.608032711   C2010-901063-9

Printed and bound in Canada
Cover design by Derek von Essen
Interior design by HeimatHouse

Represented in Canada by the Literary Press Group
Distributed by the University of Toronto Press

The publisher gratefully acknowledges the financial assistance of the Canada Council for the Arts, the Canada Book Fund, and the Province of British Columbia through the B.C. Arts Council and the Book Publishing Tax Credit.

For Jim Andersen, a Viking who loved books

and for Kuldip Gill,

In Memory

There is something bigger than fact: the underlying spirit,
all it stands for, the mood, the vastness, the wildness, the
western breadth of go-to-the-devil-if-you-don't-like-it, the
eternal big spaceness of it...the West!

—EMILY CARR
Hundreds and Thousands, 1927

CONTENTS

Introduction

Tracking the young, still evolving literary history of North America's West Coast is fascinating, if idiosyncratic work. Canadian and U.S. nationalist considerations aside, in 1985 American poet, eco-essayist and generational sage Gary Snyder wrote of a "new world" culture that he identified arising jointly from the West Coast of North America and the Asia-Pacific region—what a Canadian term from the period broadly imagined as the North Pacific Rim. Its new-world symbolism acknowledged and encompassed British Columbia, intimating a culture more sympathetic to environmental, spiritual, and economic practices, and to social justice. Geographically, this larger terrain can be thought of locally as extending roughly from the Alaska Panhandle through British Columbia, Washington, and Oregon, and into Northern California.

Intercultural linkages up and down this long coastline are long and deep, including millennia of aboriginal trading and raiding along well-established routes, reputed Chinese Buddhist missionary voyages under Hui-Shin, European square-rigger explorations by Drake, Cook, and Spanish adventurers, and the Klondike Gold Rush steamship trade that provided Robert Service with fertile story material. In 1891, beloved B.C. painter Emily Carr would journey south from Victoria to study art in San Francisco. In reverse migration, poets Robin Blaser, George Stanley, and author Stan Persky would head northward during the 1960s, from the San Francisco Bay Area to settle in Vancouver.

For many readers, locating books of an interpretive or critical nature about literature from British Columbia and the adjacent U.S. Pacific Northwest can take some digging. My hope is that the fifteen essays which follow will be a constructive addition to the field and might serve as a kind of "nurse log" compendium, fertile in archival memory, critical thinking, creation myths, and homage to some celebrated elders of the region's literary tribe. Ideally, other writers, scholars, and commentators can benefit from the research here and build upon it in the future.

In gathering this material, the natural impulse was to shape the collection around representational themes such as landscape, self, and intercultural narratives. This would offer, one reasoned, a broad horizon of literary terrain to draw upon. Distinguished in part by its attention to language of place, literature from this stretch of North America's West Coast has long been mindful of land and seascapes, the particulars of local flora and fauna, and the cultures of its aboriginal forebears. Traditionally, much of the region's literature has also been informed by cross-border and multicultural perspectives, notably in terms of the North-South sympathy that B.C. writers and artists have often shown for San Francisco Bay and Seattle-area culture. In a more contemporary light, and one that is hardly surprising given the influence of significant population migrations from East Asia, there has been a further shift and B.C.'s literary self-identity now demonstrates an increasing disposition toward trans-Pacific cultural ecologies.

Within the context of the region's written history—a history that only begins seriously during the late 1700s with the accounts of English mariners like Cook, Vancouver, Meares, John R. Jewitt, the Spaniards Crespi, Quadra, and Malaspina, and the overlanders Simon Fraser and David Thompson—the attunement of West Coast writers with the unconscious natural rhythms of the land and sea has remained constant. In many ways it is expected of writers here that they be familiar with such fundamental elements of natural science. Combined with knowledge of the region's human geography the result is a set of vivid signifiers that effectively constitute a previously undefined "literacy of place."

The material that follows is diverse; it arrived through a public call for submissions. Contributors were invited to focus on a broad spectrum of topics including regional perspectives, frontier and colonial legacies, nationalist and post-nationalist traditions, Beat and Black Mountain poetry and cross-cultural linkages, First Nations groundings, and shifting definitions in community identity. The arrivals reflected something of the music of what is happening in our deepening appreciation of literature from B.C. and the nearby U.S. Pacific Northwest—an area sometimes jointly referred to, with considerable emotional accuracy, as Cascadia. Yet more will be needed to thicken our foundational knowledge and scholarship of the region's literature, thus the hope that further explorations will be encouraged by this volume.

Hilary Turner's insightful reading of two important books by Elspeth Cameron and Sandra Djwa probes the thorny Earle Birney-Roy Daniells politics within UBC's English Department that gave impetus to the rise of Canada's renowned first university program in Creative Writing— a program that has had major influence during the past forty years especially. A searching analysis by Susan McCaslin investigates the meaning and relevance of contemporary ecopoetics in the works of three challenging nature-based poets, while appreciations of George Woodcock, Robin Blaser, and a salty interview with the late eminence of Canadian poetry, P.K. Page, bring historicity and a fuller sense of what the fundamental nature of the West Coast writing project has been about for the past sixty years.

Veteran Vancouver poet Judith Copithorne and editor Michael Barnholden provide essential new archival information regarding the structural development of Vancouver's literary community—necessary research in the building up of critical mass upon which subsequent discourse can be based. Of similar value are several personal essays where the subject matter comprises or includes original source-text material upon which future research can be undertaken. Poet, publisher and arts administrator Carolyn Zonailo and former Head of UBC Creative Writing program George McWhirter contribute memoirs that address the foundation myths of organizations and events, without which there would be no substantial West Coast literary community.

Accordingly, as a number of essays reveal in addressing the fractious relations between Nationalist and Internationalist literary and academic schools in Vancouver during the 1960s and onward, challenges to the unfolding intellectual story of late-20th-century literature in B.C. have been common in these parts. To these diverse trajectories are added actual border-crossing contributions which consider affiliations between writers and writing from B.C. and the U.S. Pacific Northwest—a geographic region of subtle, but important influence upon ideas of East-West hybridity in contemporary multiculturalism. To this concern with diversity and cultural pluralism add the work of Seattle-area-raised Gary Snyder, work that for forty years has been central to global environmental thought and which helped inspire early Greenpeace action during its founding days in Vancouver. Younger writers are also featured in several of the essays that follow, inquiring promisingly into the state of trans-genomic literary perspectives from Vancouver and writing from the rugged Northern British Columbia region, while a third surveys the contribution of polymath Robert Bringhurst to our knowledge of Haida and West Coast First Nations mythology.

Because a series of books is properly needed to provide a comprehensive view of B.C. and Pacific Northwest literature—its fiction, drama, non-fiction, poetry, children's writing and various sub-genres of each—realistically this collection does not attempt to be representative of the whole field. Fiction is only lightly addressed and properly deserves its own critical volume. Perhaps a companion anthology to this edition, one addressing fiction from the region, is already underway. If not, there is argument for Volume II and further collaboration between Anvil Press and UFV Press. Similarly, readers will find that to consider writing from such areas as the Kootenays, the Thompson-Okanagan, the Gulf Islands, or for a substantial gathering of critical portraits of mentors like George Ryga, Ethel Wilson and others central to the region's story, a whole series of books is needed.

Inevitably, much of the work here, especially that addressing poetry and poetics, has a Vancouver focus, although this was not a preoccupation but rather a matter of what inspired the contributors whose work you are about to encounter. It may be that poetry, with its usual lack of heed for proprietary interpretations by this or that school of thought, is more in the air that critical writers breathe of late: the death of Robin Blaser and a recent colloquium at Simon Fraser University's Harbour Centre commemorating the historic 1963 Vancouver Poetry Conference have generated renewed interest in the linkages between Vancouver writing and Beat and Black Mountain legacies. The flourishing spoken word and slam poetry scenes among younger and newer writers share obvious genetic affiliations with both. Yet as personal essays by Carolyn Zonailo, Colin James Sanders, and the invaluable chronology compiled by Judith Copithorne confirm, within Vancouver's poetry scene there has always been more than one game in town.

Within these essays, interviews, memoirs, and critiques there are some provocative revelations. Accounts of how the literary world has worked hereabouts, about the awarding of prizes and how they may be determined, the role of teaching and the utility of Creative Writing programs, articulations on how university English departments in Vancouver and Victoria have exerted particular intellectual influence for decades on literary production in the region—all this is grist for the mill in helping forge new and renewed patterns of interpretation regarding literature from B.C. and the Pacific Northwest. Accordingly, these essays bring to light the extensive layerings of interconnectivity that are part of the subject region's literary history, ongoing traditions, and active community of practitioners. With the emergence of interconnectivity as the new meta-narrative for the 21st century, might any idea be more appropriate for the future of writers, literature and literacy in this place we call home?

In compiling a book of this nature, much help was necessary. In addition to the authors whose work appears here, and to whom grateful thanks are offered, many individuals contributed to this project. Ken Fernstrom extended the original invitation to begin compiling the edition for the *UFV Research Review*, 3:1. For their invaluable editorial readings, special aloha to Hilary Turner and Helene Littman in particular, and to the following international readers who helped give the collection its final shape: Gregory Dunne, Miyazaki International College, Japan; Charlotte Franson, Canterbury University College, U.K; Lach Loud, State University of New York, Stony Brook; and Hillel Wright, Keizi University, Tokyo. Also contributing important editorial readings were Stephen Morrissey, Champlain College, Montreal; Sanja Garic Komnenic, British Columbia Institute of Technology; and Lorette Clement-Smith, University of the Fraser Valley. Paul Falardeau provided faithful research assistance throughout. Thanks also to Marlene Roseboom for her care in final editorial inspections. Fred Wah, Jamie Reid and John Carroll lent an encouraging ear at an early stage. Yvon Dandurand and Brad Whittaker of the Research Office at University of the Fraser Valley contributed valuable support, and Brian Kaufman at Anvil Press had the steady nerve to consider publishing the project. Indefatigable B.C. literary historian Alan Twigg offered a rigorous critique of the work in its late production phase that was essential in pointing out necessary revisions. For her forbearance, many thanks also to my wife Kwangshik, whose patience was undeservedly tested during many overly long editing sessions. Fair play to all who put their shoulder to the wheel.

Nine Bows,
Trevor Carolan
North Vancouver, B.C.

Creators versus Embalmers:
POETS AND SCHOLARS AT THE UNIVERSITY OF BRITISH COLUMBIA, 1954-1963

HILARY TURNER

One of the threads in the plot of Robertson Davies's novel of manners *Leaven of Malice* (1954) is devoted to the scholarly career of young Solomon Bridgetower, newly hired as a lecturer in the English Department at the fictional Waverley University. With a degree from Cambridge and an innocent heart, he is directed by his head of department, Dr. Darcy Sengreen, to make a name for himself in the burgeoning field of American and Canadian literary studies. (Davies dubs this "Amcan"—the more specific term "Canlit" had presumably not yet come into currency). Solly is to build his reputation as an annotator, biographer, and interpreter of the all-but-forgotten Canadian poet and playwright Charles Heavysege (1816-1876). An unwilling recipient of this dusty task, Solly is immediately possessed by "a sudden nausea" and a "fit of gagging."[1] But after many twists in the plot and in perhaps his finest moment, Solly finds it in him to give Heavysege "the heave-ho."

"I met Dr. Sengreen this morning quite by chance," he says, "and told him I wanted to be a creator of Amcan, not one of its embalmers."[2] This spoof of literary scholarship and its relation to creative activity will strike many readers, particularly those who have spent time in English departments, as only too accurate.

In the very year that Davies's novel was published, the wheels were set in motion in the English Department at the University of British

Columbia for a similar but very public and dramatic schism between the professors and the poets. The rift was symptomatic of a general upheaval in literary studies in the 1950s and early 1960s, and of two other widespread cultural phenomena: the professionalization of academic disciplines and careers, and the coming-of-age of Canadian poetry—both of which were taking place in the same eventful decade. The specific agency of change in this case, however, can be found in the personality clash between Roy Daniells, who had become head of the department in 1948, and his old friend and rival, Earle Birney, who was then emerging as Canada's most prominent poet. Two books provide a blow-by-blow account of the events and decisions that led to the creation of the Department of Creative Writing at UBC, now a venerable institution in its own right, separate from and decidedly independent of the Department of English. Birney's point of view as the rupture occurred is represented in Elspeth Cameron's biography *Earle Birney: A Life* (1994), while Daniells' perspective is recorded by Sandra Djwa in her book *Professing English: A Life of Roy Daniells* (2002). Both authors were enrolled in English courses at UBC in the 1960s. Both works are well researched, and rich in anecdotal and archival detail. They deserve to be read side by side.

The English Department at UBC has functioned for most of its eighty-five years as a sort of Ellis Island for the literary scholars and creative writers of this province. It has always been large; and, given its mandate to provide a course in composition to most UBC undergraduates, its huge enrolment has made it influential within the university. That influence also extends well beyond the institution. Not only have hundreds of thousands of undergraduates passed through its portals, but also many thousands of graduate students, writers, visiting scholars, and teachers of various ranks.[3] It is therefore both of immediate local interest, and part of a wider cultural discussion, to study the political maneuvering (as well as the ideas and principles behind that maneuvering) by which the English Department, in 1963, brought forth the Department of Creative Writing.

When Roy Daniells assumed the role of head of department in 1948 he was stepping into a position that had been occupied by Garnett Gladwin Sedgewick for the previous three decades—ample time for anyone, let alone a man of Sedgewick's personal flamboyance, to leave an imprint. Daniells had Sedgewick's blessing in the succession, though other members of the department, notably Earle Birney, may have thought otherwise. As Djwa reports, Sedgewick communicated his satisfaction in a private letter, describing Daniells, in contrast to himself, as "puritanically conscientious." "[T]hat," he went on to say, "is a virtue surviving from the Plymouth Brethren...He will be *good*."[4]

Indeed, in Djwa's account, conscientiousness and a scrupulous moral fairness seem to characterize Daniells' approach to the handling of departmental affairs and personalities. His agenda was transparent and timely. He undertook reform of the curriculum, scraping away the patina of genteel Edwardian literary appreciation that had been the legacy of Arnoldian criticism in English departments everywhere, and encouraged an emphasis on close reading and scholarship, stressing in particular the psychological and mythological brands of criticism that were then current. Recognizing that the longstanding practice of sending UBC's best graduates off to the University of Toronto was counterproductive, he began to build an in-house graduate program. This would of course entail a more serious attitude towards research and publication, and faculty members were directed to keep their scholarship up to date. Finally, he went some distance toward democratizing the department: he inaugurated a policy of voting in department meetings, and consulted widely, especially among the younger faculty. In short, it was under Daniells that the department began to resemble the efficient engine of scholarly research that it is today.[5]

It is not difficult to see that reforms like these have the practical effect of subordinating the creative aspects of the discipline to the more measurable ones of scholarship and research. On Daniells' part, the effect was unintentional—merely a by-product of his vision for the department—and, as became evident in the support he was to give to Warren Tallman and Robert Creeley, and in his own efforts to promote contemporary Canadian writing, he was very much the friend of poets and poetry. On the other hand, his new approach made the inner conflict that is endemic among academics in English both inevitable and stark. This is the conflict between one's "own" writing and one's professional work. When only the latter is rewarded in tangible ways—through salary, through promotions, through the scholarly prestige that goes with research grants—a working academic must be motivated by superhuman powers to devote much time to the former. In the absence of academic recognition for strictly literary productivity, the only other solution to the problem is to quit one's job and support oneself exclusively by writing. It is scarcely surprising that the occupations of "professor" and "writer" are understood to be distinct.

Few literary people can have experienced the inner division between scholar and artist more keenly than Earle Birney. Today, Birney's reputation rests almost exclusively on his poetry; his two novels are not much read; and his scholarly work is scarcely remembered. In the late forties, however, he was attempting to sustain an academic career that consisted of teaching courses and supervising honours students in Old English, Middle English, and Creative Writing—all the while keeping his own literary output steadily before the public. Cameron notes that "for Birney...at times the Chaucer scholar or expert on Canadian literature, at others the poet, and at others yet the mentor of students of creative writing—the issue was serious. If these various activities were diametrically opposed, he was self-cancelling, more or less his own worst enemy."[6] The expectation circa 1950 that he was now to add scholarly publications to his workload must have struck him as burdensome. Although he did eventually comply with the pressure to polish his credentials as a scholar, it was not until 1957-58 that he produced the series of six articles that were later edited and published in *Essays in Chaucerian Irony* by his former student Beryl Rowland. As he toiled "like a proper mole," Birney complained bitterly to friends about the aridness and confinement of the scholarly life and, mixing the metaphor slightly, spoke contemptuously of "the academic squirrel-cage."[7]

But long before this concession to the demands of the profession, the lines of battle between Birney and Daniells had been drawn. They had been drawn as early as the spring of 1948 when Birney instigated the first of many skirmishes in a campaign designed to depose Daniells as head and reshape the department in his own image. That their first confrontation as academic colleagues should concern the academic respectability of creative work indicates the centrality of this issue to all the conflicts great and small that Birney was to stir up. As Djwa tells the story,

> Birney had been talking to an honours graduate, Hilda Thomas, who proposed to write a book of lyrics for an M.A. in creative writing. Birney thought it a fine idea and nipped in to the next-door office to clear it with Daniells. After ten minutes, the voices in the adjoining office became louder and louder until finally Thomas heard a roar from Birney: "What the hell do you thinking I've been doing in my creative writing class all this time if you can't evaluate creative writing?" But Daniells was adamant. [8]

No doubt the show of resolve on Daniells' part was almost as irksome to Birney as the philosophical difference that is evident in the exchange. In any case, over the next few years, as their battle escalated, the tactics of both men came to resemble nothing so much as a naked struggle for power.

In 1954, in a series of events that Djwa characterizes as "the revolt of the dukes"[9] and "a watershed,"[10] Birney moved systematically to gather the senior professors into what Cameron calls "something remarkably like a Trotskyite cell."[11] His goal was, as he put it, "to organize a *coup d'état* and take dictatorial powers from the... Chairman."[12] The eleven men who rallied to Birney, all full professors, had had in addition to their individual grievances collective misgivings about the recent changes in the academic weather. This makes political sense: those who are already established in their careers will not necessarily welcome the. shift from a benign dictatorship to a democracy; the people more likely to benefit are those who lack power. According to Djwa, the senior professors "saw the end of Sedgewick's regime as the beginning of their freedom. They had expected Daniells (who, after all, had been taught by two of their number) to be their spokesperson rather than their head."[13] In a letter to Herman Singer, which is cited in part by Djwa and in full by Cameron, Birney explained his motivations as follows:

> *I returned from a year's leave to find all the senior men cleverly isolated, power shared with a crop of new faces, kids with a couple of years' experience, imported by the Head to be henchmen of the new order. It made things bad for us, especially for me. The Head has a particular grudge against me; he applied for the same fellowship I did and didn't get it. Also he is by way of being a poet who resents the fact that his executive duties interfere with his own writing. In fact, he wallows in executive detail to escape from the challenge of trying to write. Sooo, he's determined I shan't have time to write either. (Djwa 277; Cameron 351)*[14]

But Daniells had unwittingly played into the hands of the malcontents by making a tactical error in university protocol. His error in judgement had to do with the issue of faculty workload, which (because of the nature and number of the assignments that have to be marked) is generally heavier in the arts than in the sciences, and (because of the necessity of offering "service" courses in composition) is often heavier in English than in any other arts department. Daniells was undoubtedly well-intentioned in bringing the matter before the UBC senate, and if he had been successful in obtaining some concessions, he might well have regained the support of his senior staff. He was not successful, however; and his action was resented by the man to whom the matter should have gone in the first place—

Sperrin Chant, Dean of Arts and Sciences. As Djwa summarizes the situation,

> By simultaneously antagonizing his department and his dean, Daniells had placed himself between a rock and a hard place. The dynamics of academic departments are such that if the senior members of a department are not governed, or represented by their head to their satisfaction, they may object to his procedures and go over him to the dean and president and attempt to unseat him.[15]

Led by Birney, who had nurtured his connection with men at the highest levels of administration, this is precisely what they did.

The upshot was that Chant sanctioned the formation of a "Senior Committee" within the English department. This committee, nominally chaired by Daniells, consisted only of the full professors: those in the lower ranks, probably fearing the consequences upon their careers of entering the fray, had cooperated in their own exclusion.[16] Daniells did officially retain some of the prerogatives of department head, but he was now compelled to resolve matters of hiring, promotion, and departmental policy through the Senior Committee. It was an awkward division of power, as Djwa points out: "the Senior Committee had supplanted the head."[17] It was, moreover, anomalous: "this bifurcation of authority was not instituted in any other department at UBC."[18]

Birney found it easy to consolidate his gains that summer, for while Daniells was away in New Zealand delivering the prestigious de Carle lectures, he operated as acting head. Opportunistically, he seized on Daniells' seemingly harmless retention of Jan de Bruyn as his personal assistant: post-*coup*, as it were, this action was found to be "undemocratic"[19] and against the wishes of the Senior Committee. All through the summer of 1954, Birney flexed his muscles, subsequently crowing to Herman Singer that he had "had fun exercising power... fired the department secretary and hired another from Paris, a honey; hired an American poet, Melvin La Follette...hired Peter Marchant

[from] Cambridge...bought new office furniture; chiseled a small scholarship out of certain Bookstore profits; and generally played hare and hounds in the general faculty paperchase."[20] These actions are not quite as motiveless as they appear, however, for Birney was in the process of protecting his turf. His next act was to write directly to President MacKenzie and put the case for an increase in his salary. As Cameron reports, the request was a masterpiece of misdirection:

> He exaggerated what he had accomplished on leave: most of another novel (true), three short stories (he wrote one), eight articles (he did six) and a dozen poems (no previous mention of these anywhere). He applied pressure by stating that the universities of Oregon and Washington had sounded him out for jobs... In conclusion, he compared himself to Daniells: "To be quite frank I have for some time resented the fact that my salary is so far below that of Daniells ... though I have great respect for [him] as a teacher and a scholar, I do not think that his record or reputation surpasses mine."[21]

Once again, Birney was successful. "Two weeks later," says Cameron, "Birney's salary leapt from $7,200 to $8,000, making him the highest paid senior member in the department...aside from Daniells."[22] Djwa's account of the maneuver adds the following tidbit: "In 1955 Daniells was jolted to discover that he had received a raise of $100 in contrast to Birney's $800."[23]

During the next few years, Birney seems to have devoted his professional attention to the Creative Writing courses offered by the department. Yet despite his previous triumphs, and despite writing, in 1959, his best poem next to "David" ("The Bear on the Delhi Road," that is), he in all likelihood felt insecure. Styles in poetry were changing, and "despite his adaptability," says Cameron, "Birney could not quite keep pace with change."

> Language that was second nature to Birney was "square" to young listeners. Although he quickly mimicked the jargon of

a new Americanized generation…his letters were still pep-
pered with words (often British) like "motorcar," "batching,"
"hack," "snooty," "rather," "stuffed shirt," "fortnight, "stin-
keroo," "rascal," "welched," and—significantly—"oldster."
His poetry, too, was both in and out of the sixties' picture. He
was experimental and interested in other cultures, but he was
also reflective, and often detached.[24]

Fresh challenges to his ego may have existed within the
department as well. Warren Tallman had been hired in 1956, and as
Djwa reports, "Daniells and Tallman got along very well—for Tallman,
although a Maverick, was not political."[25] Originally a Henry James
scholar, Tallman was asked by Daniells to teach the third-year course
"Approaches to Poetry," and encouraged to broaden his knowledge of
Canadian poetry. Tallman was not long in transforming himself into
something of a guru to students interested in creative writing. He
was, says Djwa, "a mentor to a group of active young poets who
congregated at his home—the *TISH* poets—and he wanted to widen
their experience by bringing some of the chief figures of the new
Black Mountain poetics to Vancouver."[26] (Indeed, Robert Creeley was
to be taken on staff in 1962.) Birney professed enthusiasm for the
critical mass that seemed to be building within and around the
Creative Writing stream.[27] Nevertheless, another serious clash with
Daniells was in the offing, fuelled, as will be evident, by a measure of
paranoia on Birney's part.

In early 1962 Birney learned that he had received a Canada Council
grant that would support him "to travel, write, and lecture on
Canadian poetry for a year."[28] Aware that the Creative Writing courses
were staffed disproportionately by Americans, Birney took it upon
himself to find a Canadian poet to replace him while he was on leave.
He wrote to Irving Layton, who responded enthusiastically, adding
that he would be interested in a permanent position. Birney, says
Djwa, was "delighted" at the prospect; he went immediately to
Daniells who, Birney later reported, "clapped [his] hand to [his] head
and said, 'Not Layton!'"[29] Given that no position had been advertised,

and that no funding existed for a continuing appointment, Daniells' next move is puzzling: he agreed that Layton could submit an application. On 7 May, 1962, Layton did.

According to Djwa, in spite of his doubts about Layton's academic credentials, Daniells handled the application professionally, writing to Desmond Pacey, Northrop Frye, and Harold Files for their views of Layton, and soliciting their advice;[30] he then retired to consider the matter with the Tenure Committee, a newly-created body that somewhat limited the clout of the Senior Committee.[31] Meanwhile, Birney had drummed up enthusiasm for Layton's application among the Creative Writing Committee, which consisted of Jake Zilber, Warren Tallman, and John Hulcoop. Teaching assistants George Bowering, Lionel Kearns, Frank Davey, and Phyllis Webb also expressed their support.[32] At a meeting of the two committees on 8 May,[33] Daniells merely announced that there was no money to hire Layton. Birney retorted that Daniells must request funding from Dean Chant—who was, as it turned out, about to go away himself.[34] The ensuing silence from Daniells must have been alarming to Birney, for he now made a tactical error of his own, or at least a serious breach of decorum. Going over the heads of both Daniells and Chant, on 14 May he wrote directly to President MacKenzie strongly endorsing Layton's candidacy. According to Cameron, the letter was "long [and] carefully worded";[35] in Djwa's account, it "consisted of a covering letter, with a number of supporting letters from students taking creative writing courses, notably Bowering, Davey, and Kearns, and instructors such as Zilber, A.M. Friedson, Tallman, and Phyllis Webb."[36]

Now ensues a truly bizarre episode in academic politics—bizarre even by the standards of English departments, widely known for their internecine struggles over minutiae. Furious that Birney had once again contravened his authority, Daniells' "response was to wash his hands of the whole matter, and he sent all of Layton's application materials to the Dean, thus absolving the department of responsibility for the decision."[37] As Djwa goes on to say, Birney, hearing nothing

from Daniells, began to get impatient, and commenced a campaign
of stalking and pestering him about Layton's application:

> *In the following weeks, Birney attempted to corner Daniells*
> *in corridors, in front of his office, in the coffee room in front*
> *of colleagues. Daniells evaded him, refusing to discuss the*
> *matter. What Daniells wanted was for Birney to go away—*
> *far away—so that he could get on with English department*
> *business. But he had no intention of being boxed into a*
> *corner. One day, suffering from a severe migraine (probably*
> *the after effects of the decision) he bundled up in a scarf and*
> *overcoat and wore dark glasses to the office to protect his eyes*
> *from the strong light.*[38]

In Birney's version of these strange days, he had observed Daniells'
attempts to avoid him with hauteur. His account occurs in a six-page
letter to Daniells written from Mexico (where he had taken his leave)
and copied to MacKenzie, Chant, the Creative Writing Committee,
and the English Department's Executive Committee (that is, the
Senior Committee, slightly reconfigured). He says:

> *Two colleagues in other departments separately reported to*
> *me that they saw you once more tip-toeing to my office door*
> *while I sat working and waiting inside; this time, although*
> *it was a sunny day, you wore a raincoat buttoned up, a scarf*
> *around your chin, a hat pulled down over your face. I will*
> *spare you their speculations about your mental health.*[39]

This curious stand-off was not the end of the matter. With the decision left up to him, Dean Chant decided not to offer Layton a position.
According to Djwa, he based his decision on the materials provided by
Layton's referees. Birney, unaware of the contents of the letters Daniells
had solicited from Frye, Pacey, and Files, sent Layton his own account
of the process, in which he blamed Daniells for mismanagement of the
process, and the deliberate sabotage of Layton's chances. Layton then
wrote an abusive letter, which he sent directly to Daniells.[40]

Out of the undignified struggle that I have summarized, the Creative Writing Department at UBC was born. Defeated by what he perceived as the sinister machinations of Daniells, Birney burnt his bridges with the English department, accusing Daniells of intolerance, sectarian Puritanism, and intellectual sterility. As his catalogue of insults comes to a close, with a savage flourish, he tenders his resignation:

> As an alumnus and a long time senior staff member of this university I denounce you as a man unfit to hold administrative office, as a man whose humanism is a sham, who stoops to deceit, lie, [sic] and trickery to gain his ends—in sum, a moral and intellectual coward. You will not have Irving Layton in your department next year. Neither will you have me. I have endured your leadership of our department for fourteen years but this final piece of stupidity, arrogance, trickery and plain falsehood is more than I can take.[41]

Next, in a Machiavellian move, he solicited a job offer from the University of Oregon and, without mentioning that his salary there would be much lower than what he had been earning at UBC, he leveraged the separation of the Creative Writing program from the English department and extracted an informal agreement from Chant that he would hold the top administrative position in the newly constituted unit.[42] Birney was salvaging what he could from the situation, but unfortunately for him both Chant and President MacKenzie were approaching retirement. In the administrative lull that characterized their last few months in office, the new department—or whatever it was to be called—was left in limbo.

In a final irony, it was not Birney after all, but Robert Harlow, then working as a producer and programmer for the CBC who was chosen in 1965 as the first director of Creative Writing at UBC. Birney seems to have given up the struggle, or withdrawn from the fray. He took a year-long position as Writer in Residence at the University of

Toronto,[43] and retired shortly thereafter. As Djwa points out, however, his retreat was not without rancour. He put it about that he had left UBC in protest over Daniells' despotic ways;[44] and his physical departure was also conducted "in a great huff." He took with him the papers he had previously donated to the Special Collections of UBC library, "with the explanation that he needed to tidy them up. In 1966, he sold them to the University of Toronto for the equivalent of a year's salary."[45]

On the subject of Birney's outrageous conduct between 1963 and 1965, Cameron speculates that he was fearful of losing his status— not so much in relation to Daniells, or where his academic duties were concerned, but as a poet who might still be taken seriously.[46] With Warren Tallman then at the centre of the creative writing group at UBC, and with the Black Mountain school so much in the ascendancy, Birney may have begun to feel like yesterday's man. Certainly, he was dismissive of the poetry conference organized by Tallman in the summer of 1963. Though he must have known that the conference was an important landmark in the literary annals of the West Coast, he took care to stay away, writing sourly to Ron Everson that

> *[The] solid phalanx of Black Mt. hillbillies...did a good job in their way.... But they introduced cultism in its extreme form. Anything written unlike what they were writing was dubbed not just inferior, but Anti-poetry. How the Puritan mind is reborn in every new movement! Christ = Creeley, and anti-Christ = anti-Creeley.*[47]

Just as it is an oversimplification to claim that the Church of England came into being because Henry VIII wanted a divorce, it would be misleading to explain the existence of the Creative Writing department at UBC by pointing merely to the egotistical demands of Earle Birney. His actions are also related to—or, in part the expression of—an ideological divide that continues to polarize the academic delivery of "English." In the analysis of Hilda Thomas, an eye-witness of some of the interactions between Birney and Daniells, their different styles seemed to be directed by a sort of dialectical process. Daniells and Birney, she says,

> Became more and more separate in the paths they pursued because of their different temperaments. Everything in Daniells that said upright, respectable, disciplined, morally correct was reinforced as time went on until that became his métier if you like, and everything in Birney that said romantic, free, untrammelled, explorative, wide-ranging, developed until they completely diverged.[48]

Studying literature (as well as creating it) requires both approaches, of course. Discipline needs to be balanced by exploration, rigour by playfulness. Yet perhaps there is something to be said for the partition of these different habits of mind where the practical business of teaching and writing (not to mention the teaching *of* writing) is concerned.

The necessity for a separation of the two departments is perhaps the one thing on which Birney and Daniells were agreed. According to Djwa, in his capacity as the new president of UBC, John Barfoot Macdonald sought Daniells' views on the migration of the creative writing program to a department of its own:

> As he saw it, the primary purpose of the academic study of literature was to provide the student with historical and textual knowledge together with critical appreciation. However, the primary function of creative writing was to liberate individual experience. "It follows that academic people with reason resent the granting of formal English credits for poems and stories that seem emitted rather than composed, while creative writers find academic restrictions intolerable."[49]

There is a case to be made for the other side, however. A department that jointly houses artists and scholars from many backgrounds will avoid the dangers of parochialism and the development of a "house style." Moreover, writers who are learning their craft need to know the traditions that have gone before them, and to be steeped in the very genres and forms against which they might choose to hone their skills or, indeed, to rebel. Only if they are so steeped can budding poets recognize, for example, that the apparent formlessness of modernist poetry is only apparent. More abstractly, and perhaps too idealistically for the quarrelsome humans that populate academic departments everywhere, the interdependency of gnosis and praxis is usually understood to be a good and desirable thing.

Notes

1. Robertson Davies, *The Salterton Trilogy* (London: Penguin, 1986), 379.

2. Ibid., 458.

3. Like most North American academic departments, it grew rapidly and somewhat unevenly after 1945 (just to focus on the period in question) when returning servicemen poured back into the classrooms. By 1965, it had swelled to nearly one hundred faculty members (Djwa 354). After some shrinkage in the cash-strapped 1980s and 1990s, it currently stands at eighty-eight teaching faculty. Broken down by rank, the department currently employs twenty Full Professors, sixteen Associate Professors, thirteen Assistant Professors; three Senior Instructors; two Lecturers; and (with more members than any other rank) thirty-two Sessional Lecturers.

4. Sandra Djwa, *Professing English: A Life of Roy Daniells* (Toronto: University of Toronto Press, 2002), 263.

5. Ibid., 265-285.

6. Elspeth Cameron, *Earle Birney: A Life* (New York: Viking, 1994), 416.

7. Ibid., 403.

8. Djwa, *Professing English*, 266.

9. Ibid., 284.

10. Ibid., 293.

11. Cameron, *Earle Birney: A Life*, 352.

12. Ibid., 352.

13. Djwa, *Professing English*, 274.

14. Cameron, *Earle Birney: A Life*, 351.

15. Djwa, *Professing English*, 276.

16. Ibid., 282.

17. Ibid., 280.

18. Ibid., 282.

19. Ibid., 279.

20. Cameron, *Earle Birney: A Life*, 353.

21. Ibid., 358.

22. Ibid., 358.

23. Djwa, *Professing English*, 273.

24. Cameron, *Earle Birney: A Life*, 421-2.

25. Djwa, *Professing English*, 331.

26. Ibid.

27. Cameron, *Earle Birney: A Life*, 426.

28. Ibid.

29. Djwa, *Professing English*, 332.

30. Ibid.

31. Ibid., 333.
32. Cameron, *Earle Birney: A Life*, 427.
33. Djwa, *Professing English*, 333.
34. Cameron, *Earle Birney: A Life*, 427.
35. Ibid.
36. Djwa, *Professing English*, 333.
37. Ibid.
38. Ibid., 334.
39. Cameron, *Earle Birney: A Life*, 429.
40. Djwa, *Professing English*, 335.
41. Cameron, *Earle Birney: A Life*, 432.
42. Ibid., 439.
43. Djwa, *Professing English*, 336.
44. Ibid., 338.
45. Ibid., 337.
46. Cameron, *Earle Birney: A Life*, 452-5.
47. Ibid., 441.
48. Djwa, *Professing English*, 328.
49. Ibid., 337.

The Berkeley Renaissance:
Its Influence in Context of the "Pacific Nation"
– in Appreciation of Robin Blaser's *The Holy Forest*

Colin James Sanders

For Robin Blaser, and my friends David James Moir and Garth Thomson, in memory

"I believe I heard language through my mother's / belly / both violent and sweet / and wanted / to get to it" [1]

In 1970, I was sixteen years old when in the book department of The Hudson's Bay Company in Winnipeg I discovered *west coast seen*, an anthology of British Columbian poets, published by a young Talonbooks and dedicated to someone named Warren Tallman. I had been reading the poetry of Canadians Al Purdy, Alden Nowlan, Fred Cogswell, Milton Acorn, Irving Layton and Leonard Cohen, and, from the U S , the poetry of Kenneth Rexroth, Gary Snyder, Allen Ginsberg, Philip Whalen and others. Through *west coast seen* I was excited to discover Red Lane, Judith Copithorne, Pat Lowther, Peter Trower, Scott Lawrence and many others whom I continue to read today such as Maxine Gadd, Patrick Lane, Barry McKinnon and especially bill bissett. [2]

Jim Brown, who along with David Phillips edited *west coast seen*, makes the intriguing observation regarding the poets gathered in that volume—an observation I believe still holds regarding Pacific Nation poets, that "the thing that seems important is that every writer that comes out here has a response to the city and to the pacific edge which is unique. The influences are primarily from the sense of immediacy, which is felt here, and throughout the Pacific Nation from Mexico to Alaska. The main influence will be called American [sic] but it is a stupid way of looking at what is more naturally a West Coast community."[3] Brown confirms this intuition in an introduction letter to co-editor David Phillips: "recently I had a talk with Warren [Tallman], Robin Blaser, and Naïm Kattan in which my ideas of the Pacific Nation were much more clarified."[4]

In 1970, I also discovered Donald M. Allen's then ten-year-old anthology, *The New American Poetry*.[5] I found it curious that Robert Duncan was included in the section with the Black Mountain College poets Charles Olson and Robert Creeley, and not with the San Francisco poets, especially Spicer and Blaser, given Duncan's initiation of the Berkeley Renaissance. In particular, the romance, imagination, politics, and attention to the sacred within Duncan's writing captured me, and I began searching for his books, mostly small press, limited edition publications, since he had vowed not to publish commercially until the U.S. departed from Vietnam.

Adding to my autodidactic introduction to the new consciousness then taking form in poetics, I was able to meet Alan Watts at the University of Manitoba's Festival of Life and Learning a year or two before he died in 1973. Watts' *The Joyous Cosmology: Adventures in the chemistry of consciousness* (1962),[6] with a forward by Timothy Leary and Richard Alpert (later, Ram Dass) served as a guide for me as I discovered psychedelics in the late 1960s, while his *Psychotherapy East and West* (1961)[7] was an early influence for me in terms of vocation, along with R.D. Laing's *The Politics of Experience*[8] which my father gave me in 1968. Following his talk, Watts was kind enough to share thoughts with me regarding the contributions of Rexroth and Snyder at that time.

Many of the poets I was reading then, notably Rexroth, Snyder, Joanne Kyger, Philip Whalen, and Allen Ginsberg, were all immersed in Buddhism, and reading Watts' searching works provided me with further inspiration and instruction concerning the relationship between poetry and consciousness. In addition, having read Trappist monk and poet Thomas Merton, I found the contemplative life he wrote about appealed to me, and it remains a practice. Merton's essays regarding the emptiness and violence of materialist culture and his critique of U.S. cold war politics were also of sharp contemporary interest.

Like Watts, Merton was seeking a more ecumenical co-existence between faiths, particularly Catholicism and Buddhism, which I appreciated in light of my own ongoing struggle with Catholicism and an early parochial school experience. Jack Kerouac, too, sought to integrate his Catholicism with Buddhism in *The Scripture of the Golden Eternity* (1960),[9] written at Snyder's encouragement in 1956.

Key further reading encounters have since helped to articulate and clarify the philosophical resonance of the period. As Frank Davey[10] has written:

> What I think is now most visible in the 1960s was a search
> for a new plenitude—for the breath line which not only
> might operate as a super-conductor to transfer the poem, as
> Olson had predicated, without loss from poet to reader, but
> which also promised the poet, in the words of Olson's
> prediction, "secrets objects share"; or a search for the "way"
> of Zen Buddhism offered by Alan Watts and Gary Snyder,
> or for the dictating voices of Jack Spicer, or for the
> enlightenments promised by Timothy Leary, or for all the
> various pop culture plenitudes offered by the Mystic Arts
> Book Club, reprints of the writings of Aleister Crowley,
> musicals like Hair, rock groups like the Beatles and Jefferson
> Airplane.[11]

Veteran Downtown Vancouver poet Gerry Gilbert also offered comment regarding influences upon the artistic and literary communities operating there in the late 1950s:

Zen was there. To look at history not as: did Zen succeed in
changing everything into Peace and Light? No. It was one
of the local tools, and Zen for me was Vancouver's
relationship to Japan ... Zen was where I was learning what
the nature of originality was. The Zen I was learning was
from potters. That was the structure of knowledge they
brought back from the orient.[12]

But more than Zen was in the air. By the early 1970s, a Canadian
nationalist like Milton Acorn could be seen performing his poetry and
song with Perth County Conspiracy, a touring hippie band whose
politics were progressive and left-wing. Several years earlier in 1967,
along with Pierre Coupey, Stan Persky, Dan McLeod, and others,
Acorn founded Vancouver's celebrated "underground" newspaper,
The Georgia Straight. Still published by Dan McLeod as "a news and
entertainment weekly," in the late sixties the paper was politically left-
wing, and outspoken communist city Alderman and lawyer Harry
Rankin was one of its contributing editors. In a similar vein, Acorn's
moving poem, "Where is Che Guevara?" appeared in an early issue
from May 1967. Long interested in Marxism, Acorn had been
involved in a variety of progressive labour activities and poetry
readings, and was vociferous in protesting U.S. involvement in the
war in Vietnam. In *Out Of This World,* Chris Gudgeon's biography of
Acorn,[13] the poet, painter and musician bill bissett recalls meeting
Acorn on Hastings Street at Vanguard Books, a left-oriented
bookstore, adding that the first public poetry readings he himself gave
were organized by Acorn at the Trotskyist Hall behind the bookstore.[14]
Whether by intent or not, when Acorn returned to living in
Toronto he became the flashpoint of a controversy that blew up
between the West Coast's "Pacific Nation" poetry scene,[15] and the
eastern, "nationalist" poetry establishment, when George Bowering,
an original *TISH* poet, was awarded the Governor General's Award in
1969. It may be useful to digress a moment here for the purpose of
understanding the fuller meaning behind the term "Pacific Nation."

In 1967, a year after moving from San Francisco to teach at Simon
Fraser University, poet Robin Blaser produced a journal with the title
"Pacific Nation." Miriam Nichols' commentary in *The Fire*, her edited
collection of Blaser's collected essays, quotes Blaser from the editorial
page of the first edition in which he declares:

> *I wish to put together an imaginary nation. It is my belief*
> *that no other nation is possible, or rather, I believe that*
> *authors who count take responsibility for a map which is*
> *addressed to travelers of the earth, the world, and the spirit.*
> *Each issue is composed as a map of this land, and this glory.*
> *Images of our cities and of our politics must join our poetry.*
> *I want a nation in which discourse is active and scholarship*
> *is understood, as it should be, the mode of our understand-*
> *ing and the ground of our derivations.*[16]

In light of current trans-Pacific cultural ecologies, Blaser's remarks
now seem unusually prescient; however, his journal lasted only two
issues and folded in 1969. A late-sixties-era Vancouver rock group
also performed for a time under the name "Pacific Nation" and gave
the term further period currency.

Returning to the brouhaha regarding Bowering's Governor
General's award, opposition came from Eastern Canadian writers like
Acorn who were concerned at the open admiration of the *TISH* poets
for American writers, and this controversy is summarised
considerately in Gudgeon's biography of Acorn. Ironically, it was
TISH poet Jamie Reid who would later write a compassionate poem
in memory of Milton Acorn: "I can't forget the tears I cried / the day
I read you died. / I dreamt you were indestructible." He describes this
same difficult poet and activist as "a man of infinite arcs and angles,
/ every plane upon your face a new terrain, / the warrant of one single
life / among the many that you led in secret / besides your several
public ones."[17]

In 1977, while studying cultural anthropology in Winnipeg, I
became a subscriber to Gerry Gilbert's journal, *B.C. Monthly*. Gilbert's

appetite was to gather a diverse community of poets, writers, artists and musicians, with an emphasis upon the Pacific Nation. One of the so-called "downtown poets" in Vancouver in the late 1950s and early '60s, Gilbert was associated with this group that also included bill bissett, Maxine Gadd, and the late artist and poet Roy Kiyooka, among others.

While in a recorded seminar conversation with George Bowering and Lionel Kearns addressing "Vancouver Poetry in the Early '60s," Gilbert mentions his recollection from the 1950s of listening to "Jack Spicer and Robert Duncan on CBC from San Francisco...And being a kid with a tape recorder and recording it." Gilbert provided a tremendous service by recording poetry readings for decades and archiving the material, as well as broadcasting it on his Co-op Radio program, *radiofreerainforest*.[19]

In his conversation with Bowering and Kearns regarding the poetry scene in the early sixties, Gilbert comments:

> So I was finding out about the same people [Spicer, Duncan]. Finding out about the poetry that way. And then seeing TISH...I'm saying the sources, the things that we were all talking about, were coming...I got them all with no reference to the university context. There was a living literature. And that was Malcolm Lowry, the guy who lived out on the mudflats...where Dylan Thomas went on drinking parties.[20]

Gilbert's recollections that "There *was* a living literature" bear reflection, suggesting that there were alternative options available as models to Vancouver poets other than those who were associated with the University of British Columbia—although Earle Birney's lengthy teaching role there cannot be ignored. In her biography of Birney, Elspeth Cameron (1994),[21] acknowledges Birney's generosity of spirit and support toward many of the younger poets writing in Vancouver. For example, Birney considered bill bissett's *blew ointment* to be "...the only genuinely experimental / contemporary mag in canada (sic),"[22] and, when bissett was arrested on charges of possession of marijuana for the purpose of trafficking, Birney donated $100 to his defence fund.[23] Cameron notes as well that "Birney's cultural Catholicism was such that he was able to congratulate George Bowering for winning the Governor General's Award in 1969, while at the same time donating money for the counter-celebration of "The People's Poet" award to Milton Acorn (who was also, briefly, his student), and whom many Birney associates thought should have won it."[24] Nevertheless, while he was also responsible for bringing Dylan Thomas, Wystan Auden and Charles Olson to Vancouver,[25] by the early 1960s, Birney's influence upon young Vancouver poets was waning.

II. THE SAN FRANCISCO-VANCOUVER AXIS

Robert Duncan, Jack Spicer and Robin Blaser began their friendship in poetry in Berkeley around 1945. Blaser has written that it was with this meeting "real poetry began."[26] Spicer often gave his birth date as the year he met Blaser and Duncan.[27] Of this meeting of the three, Blaser observes, "In San Francisco, I was tied to two other poets who, it was my superstition, wrote my poems for me." [28]

Duncan and Spicer met following an anarchist meeting in San Francisco. Spicer's father, Blaser wrote, "had an I.W.W. background and some knowledge...of Emma Goldman and Rosa Luxembourg— heroines in Jack's mind." [29] Blaser further situates Spicer as being, "Presbyterian-Methodist-Wobbly"[30] when they first met in 1945, but also writes in his poem, "lake of souls reading notes"[31] that Spicer in 1945 was a "beloved friend, / who was then / somehow both a Presbyterian and a Buddhist." Duncan has indicated that Spicer, too, explored the important grounding of Buddhism:

> By 1945-46 when he came up from Redlands to the
> University of Berkeley, he was seeking in Buddhist readings
> and in universalizing and rationalizing philosophies for a
> belief that would supplant the religion in which he had

known the misery of his soul as it confronted what it could not but see as the impossibility and prohibition of the love it needed...Spicer in the Summer of 1946 when I met him sounded me out with the doctrines of Buddhism in which heavens and hells were but part of the fabric of illusions the mind projected.[32]

David Meltzer has observed how in San Francisco during the 1940s, centred amongst a number of poets including Rexroth, Duncan, Philip Lamantia, Kenneth Patchen, and others, "there was a strong political involvement and very compatible esoteric or mystical involvement as well, along with a sense of the natural community." [33] Duncan's own politics had been informed by anarchist and socialist theory and practice. As Lamantia pointed out, around the San Francisco Libertarian Circle, "Robert Duncan was a participating member...he had a few years back lived in a tiny anarchist rural commune in upstate New York around Holley Cantine and his companion, Dachine Rainer, who were publishers for several years of a high-grade anarchist quarterly, *Retort*." [34]

In those days, Lamantia recalls that San Francisco anarchists and pacifists were reading Wilhelm Reich and Kropotkin, in addition to

...Writings reaching us from [a] British anarchist group, which also supplied us with their newspaper Freedom. *The* Catholic Worker *arrived regularly in bundles from New York. There was even a connection with Albert Camus in Paris around his publication* Combat *and a small group around Paul Goodman in New York and the newspaper* Why? [35]

At various times, Paul Goodman, Jackson Mac Low, and others were part of the San Francisco meetings also.

Contextually, it is significant to observe that the 1940s had been serious times for political progressives who spoke out during World War II. Pacifist conscientious objectors to the war, including San Francisco poet William Everson, were frequently incarcerated. But as Duncan remembers, psychological coercion came just as easily from the Left:

> In '42, Kenneth Rexroth, Kenneth Patchen and almost all of us had great alarm about Stalinists. There were Stalinist murders everywhere. Tresca had just been murdered, and the attack on Trotsky comes in those years. So it's a great period of Stalinist murders. Kenneth Rexroth had spoken out on KPFA, and Kenneth Patchen, just that much older than I, really did think that the Stalinists, they were both beginning open attacks on the Stalinists, writing out there in all directions: both Kenneths thought they were going to be shot down themselves. So meeting Kenneth [Rexroth] you didn't— you wrote a letter, then he wrote a letter back. I didn't phone him. Then he met me in his car and drove me off into—way off to where he was hiding. He was in hiding! (Laughs).[36]

Of this period, Duncan has also stated that, "In the Berkeley period 1946-1950 we dreamed—Jack Spicer, Robin Blaser and I—on the seashores of Bohemia of a Berkeley Renaissance and projected Orphic mysteries and magics in poetry."[37] And, as history has shown, what became known as "The Berkeley Renaissance" was concerned with re-visioning the work of those who Duncan referred to as "Masters," and with evoking and bringing forth spiritual traditions and influences—a renaissance of spirit and imagination:

> That is the story of the romance of forms. It involves for all of us numinous powers, quests and workings of the spirit, apprehensions of our share in history, reverence for our "ancestors" in spirit. Yes, I should name them, the poets that have been my Masters, for they are not everywhere revered. Indeed, in academic circles reverence is thought of as a vice not a virtue. The sources of my virtus lie among those immediately preceding me in Stein, Lawrence, Pound, H.D., William Carlos Williams, Marianne Moore, Stevens, and Edith Sitwell. They are all problematic, arent [sic] they?[38]

Duncan, Spicer, and Blaser were to have a profound influence upon young poets in Vancouver in the early 1960s. That influence has continued into the present, as evidenced by those contemporary poets in Vancouver often associated with the Kootenay School of Writing. In April 2005, the school sponsored the "Robert Duncan Festival: Before the War," and devoted an issue of their journal, *W*, to the conference proceedings, entitled *A Duncan Delirium*.[39]

My own introduction to Duncan occurred in 1976, when he came to Winnipeg to give a reading and to meet with students and professors at the University of Manitoba. My daughter, an infant at the time, was present at the reading and emitted a cry at one point, which Duncan graciously acknowledged, incorporating her into the scene. Following the event, Dennis Cooley, poet and professor of English literature at the University of Manitoba, invited us to a party for Duncan that evening, and we offered Duncan a ride back to where he was staying. My recollections of him are of a generous and patient man who took time to respond to questions he must have been asked on scores of previous similar occasions.

Cooley himself has written succinctly in defence of the *TISH* poets, and of their multiple influences, but especially against the narrow nationalism and xenophobia exhibited by some critics who railed against what they saw as the colonization of Canadian poetry by the American Black Mountain and San Francisco poets mentioned above.

In his book review, *"Three Recent TISH Items,"*[40] Cooley strikes a contrary position to Keith Richardson's *Poetry and the Colonized Mind: TISH* (1976), chiding Richardson for his overall "cynicism," and "blind insistence on 'the Canadian poetry tradition' and its wilful ignorance of Charles Olson's precepts," in pointing out that, "Modern Canadian poetry, like modern American poetry, possesses no one centre; it is richly varied."[41]

I think that poet Fred Wah had a certain sense of this when, responding to a question regarding the East-West poetry tensions and the influence of the Black Mountain poets on Vancouver's evolving scene in the sixties, he responded, "In one sense, I've always been violently anti-nationalist... So I really resist, don't like, that sense of place. I've always been more local, and oppositional to national things."[42] After all, Earle Birney himself had not balked at publishing poems and stories with such diverse, large-circulation U.S. publications as *Harper's* and *Mademoiselle*.[43]

In 1980 I journeyed to San Francisco to interview Robert Duncan and the result was a broad-spectrum conversation with him.[44] We met again a year or two later at the Museum of Modern Art in New York where he read his poetry. In attendance were his long-time friend, fellow anarchist, poet, and surrealist, Philip Lamantia, along with the latter's wife, City Lights editor and poet Nancy Peters. Duncan's friend, the renowned artist R.B. Kitaj, sketched Duncan while he performed his evocative poetry throughout the reading, lending a sense of the historic to the occasion. I have often wondered what became of those drawings.

Regarding the Berkeley Renaissance, Robin Blaser made his views clear concerning Duncan's operative role, remarking, "I think Duncan was the one who thought of it as a kind of renaissance. He thought himself the leader of all this, which annoyed Jack [Spicer]. But it was our renaissance. We were readers, and, joined into that import, had the sense of a movement of some kind." [45] Blaser emphasises the influence of both Duncan and Spicer upon him, and on the creation of poetry in San Francisco, saying, "Poetry in San Francisco was built by Jack and Duncan—they wouldn't have somebody else building it. A lovely thing about San Francisco, that sense of being specially elected." [46] Of Duncan's poetic vision Blaser also proclaims, "Robert Duncan is one of the founders of American art and thought—that is to say, such thought and its newness requires continuous refounding." [47]

Yet the influences between these three were synergistic, and just as Blaser pays homage to Duncan's influence, Duncan makes a strong statement of indebtedness to Spicer, writing that, "...he was throughout an original of such power in my own imagination as a poet that whole areas of my creative consciousness still seem to me to have to do with a matter that was ultimately from him";[48] and writing earlier,

"In the period between 1946 and 1950 when I was living in Berkeley, Jack Spicer (who was six years younger than I was) came to be mentor, censor, and peer."[49] An "original" Spicer certainly was. Further evidence of this was that "he hosted Harry Smith on the first radio show devoted to folk music at KPFA in the late '40s."[50] Alan Watts conducted a weekly radio show on the same community public station from 1953 until his death in 1973, and Spicer, a professional linguist, may have been interested in Smith for his ethnographic fieldwork conducted while "living near Seattle in South Bellingham [where] he began to investigate the rituals, music, and languages of the Nootka, the Kwakiutl, the Lummi."[51] He may also have been curious regarding Smith's own interest in magic, as Smith became known as "the Paracelsus of the Chelsea Hotel" in New York, and was also known as a "fabulist" and "trickster," who sometimes claimed that his father had been "the English Satanist Aleister Crowley..."[52]

An interesting literary genealogical note is that Crowley enjoyed a North Vancouver connection in that the person he referred to as his "Magickal Son," Charles Robert Stansfeld Jones, lived there until his death in 1950. Around 1940, Jones would befriend Deep Cove author Malcolm Lowry and instruct him in meditation and "magickal practice."[53]

A section of the interview that I conducted with Duncan in 1980 has since been published in the British journal *Beat Scene* #48 (Summer, 2005). Meeting with him that August in the San Francisco home he shared with Jess Collins, one could not but be entranced by the extraordinary environment they had created within their home. Jess' collage and other works were on display, as were their sculpture, ornate lamps, distinctive vases, elaborate shades, intricately woven carpets, candelabra, and an abundance of books on mysticism, philosophy, art, history, and poetry. Blaser, too, made note of this influence, writing, "Beginning in 1951, Robert and Jess, as circumstances led them, put together one household after another until they were able to settle in; each time, a visitor would be startled and drawn in by the imaginary conversation among the 'things' of the house...A household of the imagination. The imagination of a household."[54]

Continuing this line of homage, the poet, activist and scholar Stan Persky has also acknowledged that, "Blaser introduced me to the magic of the household":

> As visitors to all of Blaser's domiciles immediately remark, sometimes jokingly referring to them as 'museums,' the house for him is an order of objects, art, furniture, carpets, books, each deliberately chosen and arranged. So that their inter-relations set up a sort of field of activity. The old notion of household gods is treated literally.[55]

Persky notes too the sharp demarcation in Blaser's attitudes toward the public and the personal:

> Finally, beyond the garden, which is the domestic representation of nature and part of the larger entity Blaser calls "the holy forest," there is the city. With its building looming out of the fog of San Francisco, or its downtown towers perched on a peninsula amid the "burning waters" of Vancouver's Burrard Inlet, "the city" is connected to notions of community and the public realm, the political themes of Blaser's poetry.[56]

Ultimately, Blaser would celebrate his poetry and poetics in his many reflections regarding "the holy forest" in his text *The Holy Forest* (2006) where, as Charles Bernstein notes in the Afterword, "...each poem [is] a new way of entering the holiness of the everyday." [57]

Blaser, perhaps, was not so much a poet of place, although many of his poems reflect an intimate connection with Vancouver and with Vancouver poets and others, particularly "Even on Sunday," the piece he was commissioned to write for Vancouver's Gay Games in August 1990.[58] His further contribution was to bring into his poetry reflections upon ethics, as well as on the role of the individual within civic politics, and on his idea of a philosophical community of shared language and discourse. His sense of ethics demanded not only discipline and scholarship, but gaiety, laughter, and elegance.

Blaser and Persky were not the only Berkeley Renaissance alumni to migrate northward to Vancouver. George Stanley, who had also been part of the Duncan-Spicer circle, would join them. Persky himself recalls first meeting George Stanley at a Spicer reading in San Francisco at the Bread and Wine Mission on Grant Avenue in North Beach. As Persky tells the story:

> I can't remember if I understood the poems, but I hung around afterwards and met Jack Spicer, who gave me a copy of his recently published first book, After Lorca...Later, I was invited by one of the younger members of the circle, George Stanley, to attend the weekly Sunday afternoon poetry meetings that were then being held at his apartment on upper Montgomery Street.
>
> It was here that an extraordinary new world opened out before me. What astonished me was not merely its newness, but the recognition that the world—through the intelligence of others—contained depths and dimensions I'd heretofore never imagined to exist, and, further, that the content of that world, unlike the ephemeral phenomena of everyday existence, was the stuff of life and death itself. The poems that we read, criticized, and tried out on each other were crucial to how human beings might understand the world.[59]

Though not as publicly prominent in his adopted new city, Stanley emerged as a fixture within Vancouver's literary community. In an interview with Barry McKinnon, he delineates important distinctions that existed between the poets gathered around Duncan, Spicer, and Blaser, and among Easterners who were migrating to the scene:

> ...Well with the '60s, the group around Spicer and Duncan has sort of been submerged in literary history into the Beat Generation group but we were an actually quite different group, and one of the differences, one difference was that we were more homosexually oriented than heterosexually oriented, although there were gay writers in the group, like

> Ginsberg. And another interesting thing was that we were,
> because of the influence of Blaser and Spicer and Duncan
> and the influence on them of a professor Ernst Kantorowicz
> at Berkeley—we were all very interested in Western history
> and philosophy, whereas the other group were more
> interested in Eastern philosophy and mysticism, and the
> other difference is that we were more oriented towards liquor,
> and the other group was more oriented towards hashish and
> marijuana.[60]

Duncan was open regarding his homosexuality and the place of
sexuality within his writing. He courageously published an essay in
Politics entitled "The Homosexual in Society" in August, 1944.[61]
Writing of Spicer and himself, Duncan declares, "Both of us were
homosexual in orientation; but for me my homosexuality was a
potentiality, a creative promise for love; for Spicer his homosexuality
was a curse, a trick in the name of God who predestined such love of
man for man to damnation."[62]

Persky writes of his own realization around recognizing "homo":

> in the course of writing about, say, Cocteau (later I was
> taken by Spicer and Blaser to see Cocteau's films, Orphee
> and Testament of Orpheus) or Rimbaud, I also inadver-
> tently learned something about homosexual desire,
> including the still-surprising fact that it had existed in the
> past...The irony of all this was that while we poets, even of
> the merely budding variety, could recognize homo simply by
> reading a text or looking at a work of art, in the scholarly
> world such "discoveries" were still a struggle.[63]

Persky and Blaser, partners at the time, moved to Vancouver in
1966, living together in Kitsilano until 1968. Persky was to play a
pivotal role in publishing Vancouver poetry of that time. With Dennis
Wheeler, he also created the *Georgia Straight Writing Supplement* in
1969. The *Supplement* would publish Blaser, Milton Acorn, George

Stanley, Gladys Hindmarch and others, before becoming transformed into what is now New Star Books, publishers of Maxine Gadd and George Stanley, amongst others. Persky was also one of a group of early writers who broke away from *The Georgia Straight* over ideological differences.

Blaser has written with love and compassion of both Spicer and Duncan, especially in his wonderful exegesis upon Spicer's genius in poetry, "The Practice of Outside" (1975), collected in *The Fire*, and in *The Holy Forest*, where Blaser writes of Duncan as one of his "great companions," along with Pindar and Dante. Of Duncan's authority, Blaser writes:

> the first of your poems / I read: *Among my friends love*
> *is a great sorrow*
> (brought to me in typescript by Jack [Spicer], that we
> three should meet) — no
> voice
> like it
> turns, turns
> in the body of thought
> *Among*
> *my friends love is a wage*
> *that one might have for an honest living*
> turns, turns
> in thought's body
> becomes
> O Lovers, I am only one of you!
> We, convivial in what is ours!
> this ringing
> with Dante's voice before the comedy.[64]

David Meltzer has commented upon "the cranky pedagogy of Jack Spicer and Robert Duncan,"[65] which involved principles and poetic ideologies that would at times interject between Duncan and Blaser, famously erupting over Blaser's translations of Nerval's *Les Chimeres*.[66]

Yet Blaser, in situating his "sacred geography," reflects, "The first astonishment...is Jack [Spicer]...Now the next one is Dante— Kantorowicz, Dante—I mean these runs of people. And these people are all in my view angels. I mean, even Robert Duncan, God help me. Angels are not always brightnesses in your life, [to] put it bluntly. But he is angelic."[68] At Duncan's death, Blaser fondly remembers, "I smile / it is the thought of you / a happiness / that could not be / without your having been / there / quarrelling."

Poet Joanne Kyger suggested that "the Berkeley Renaissance was being translated into the San Francisco Renaissance,"[69] and the thread connecting the poets of these renaissances to Vancouver consisted of Ellen and Warren Tallman. The place of Ellen and Warren Tallman in contributing to the creation of an emerging context of Pacific Nation poetry and poetics is pivotal. Significantly for the Pacific Nation community of poets, Blaser and Ellen Tallman, along with their respective partners, shared a home on Trafalgar Street in Kitsilano, from 1977 until Ellen's death in 2008.[70]

Vancouver poet, and one of the young Vancouver writers involved with the inception of *TISH*, Daphne Marlatt suggests Ellen "was really the key figure in the flowering of new poetry in Vancouver at that time [early sixties]," adding, "She had the curiosity of an artist, the sensibility of an artist, but really her gift was working with people. She had an extraordinarily generous spirit."[71] Jamie Reid agrees, saying that her role cannot be overstated: "It was through Ellen's contacts at Berkeley that the young writers and poets were able to meet with the San Francisco poets, first Robert Duncan and then Jack Spicer, not to mention the groundbreaking poetry conference at UBC in 1963."[72]

The initial association of Ellen Tallman with Jack Spicer, Robert Duncan and Robin Blaser, as well as Robert Creeley and others, began in Berkeley:

> In 1946 Ellen was an eighteen-year-old music student at Mills College in Oakland. With her best friend, Marthe Larsen, later to be Marthe Rexroth, she attended the Wednesday meetings where Kenneth Rexroth was a key

*organizer of the Anarcho-Pacifist Libertarian Circle. As
Tallman recalls, "During this period right after World War
II, pacifism remained one of the major issues at our
meetings."*[73]

There was a period during which Marthe Rexroth and Robert
Creeley were involved in a romantic imbroglio,[74] and Marthe would
leave Kenneth, staying first with Ellen in Berkeley, and later in Seattle.
It was in Seattle that Ellen met Warren when they both undertook
graduate studies at the University of Washington (though Warren had
also attended Berkeley as an undergraduate). Ellen and Warren
moved to Vancouver in 1956, to teach at the University of British
Columbia, where they were instrumental in obtaining a sessional
lecturing position for Creeley between 1962-63, and initiating a Black
Mountain College influence upon young poets in Vancouver. Robert
Duncan would fondly recall how "tremendous" it was to have two
poets, Helen Adams and Michael McClure, in 1954 when he gave a
poetry workshop, exclaiming, "Of course, Warren Tallman had more
than that all in one class, a whole generation of Canadian poetry."[75]

The Tallmans, along with Creeley, organized the 1963 Vancouver
Poetry Conference, which included performances and readings by
poets at one time gathered around Black Mountain College, especially
Charles Olson, Duncan, Creeley, as well as Denise Levertov, Margaret
Avison (the sole Canadian presenting), and Allen Ginsberg. This
conference was seminal in its influence upon the Vancouver poetry
scene, especially the crowd that connected around the Tallmans.

In 1965, Spicer visited Vancouver twice. In February he read his
book, *Language*, at the Vancouver Poetry Festival "to a young and
enthusiastic crowd";[76] in June, he gave his "Vancouver Lectures" while
staying with the Tallmans. Stan Persky, a witness to Spicer's reading
and lecturing, suggested that the Vancouver reception was
encouraging, taking place as it did "in a circumstance in which Jack
felt at ease, among young poets in a new Pacific Coast city that, for a
moment, looked hopeful for him personally."[77]

That hope dissipated quickly. In August, 1965, not long after the

Berkeley Poetry Conference, Spicer died at age forty. Persky wrote, "Spicer died of alcoholism—and, one should add, his devotion to language…"[78] George Bowering, in his poem, "Jack Spicer," wrote in remembrance:

> He turned to me in the bar at the bar he turned to me/ &
> said he askt me do they he said take a lot of drugs/ in
> Vancouver or was it do you./ it threw me like they say off
> but did I know who/ he was… That was a month before
> he died, the Giants were still in/ first place & they stayed
> there most of the summer/ but finally finish second. All
> the literary feuding did not stop it was not over./
> Everyone went home to the story of Jack's death.[79]

Spicer's dying words that summer were to Robin Blaser: "My vocabulary did this to me. Your love will let you go on."[80] Considering this final iteration of Spicer's, Duncan commented:

> That "you" is beautiful, for it is not only immediate and
> personal, so that Blaser emerges as the chosen disciple as John
> (Jack's baptismal name) emerges in the gnostic Acts of John;
> but it is also plural—it blesses all who answer to its
> declaration. For the Orpheus-Poet that Spicer came to be
> was not only the Singer of Love but the Hero who entering
> Hell returns and in the rite of passage loses his Beloved to
> sing of unrequited love, of Love of Search: he is the Leader of
> a Circle of those who follow his Song—"impossible
> audiences."[81]

Ellen Tallman, speaking at the book launch for Blaser's *The Holy Forest* and *The Fire*, held at Vancouver's Western Front,[82] recalled first seeing Blaser at an anarchist meeting in Berkeley in 1946, at the Workman's Circle on Steiner Street in San Francisco. In those years, the 1940s, she also came to know Robert Duncan, Jack Spicer, and other poets she and her then-husband, Warren, would subsequently invite to Vancouver.

In Vancouver, through her association and friendship with Richard Weaver, founder of The Cold Mountain Institute on Cortez Island (now the site of Hollyhock Institute), Ellen became a psychotherapist in Vancouver, teaching in the Masters in Counselling program at Antioch College/Cold Mountain Institute, and conducting therapy workshops and leading group therapy workshops for many years. In the mid-1980s, I participated in one of her workshops on poetry and psychotherapy. Blaser, when invited to the institute by Ellen, would perform Tarot card readings.[83]

Upon Ellen's death in 2008, Daphne Marlatt remembered when Ellen had entered into a lesbian relationship, and Ellen and her then partner...

> Decided to live together openly, which was daring at the time. "When she left Warren and came out as a lesbian, that was a very courageous thing to do at that time," Ms. Marlatt said. "A lot of people were shocked and didn't understand why. It was almost a sort of betrayal of the role they wanted her to continue taking in the [literary] community. For me, she was a wonderful feminist and lesbian role model."[84]

The last time I saw Ellen was at a joint reading by Blaser and Robert Creeley at Vancouver's East Cultural Centre, September 11, 2003. Creeley came down from the stage to greet and hug her. Meantime, Marlatt, for her part, continues to be a prolific writer, teacher and editor, and in her own poetry has been "articulating a lesbian erotic."[85] She received the Dorothy Livesay B.C. Book Prize for Poetry in 2009, for which George Stanley's new work, *Vancouver: A Poem*, was also nominated.

Backing the narrative up, Jamie Reid has written, "The first time I ever heard anything about the possibility of a magazine that we might ourselves create was when Fred Wah raised the idea with Warren Tallman at one of the meetings of the group of young writers that met at the home of English professors Warren and Ellen Tallman."[86]

Pauline Butling remembers Ellen Tallman, Daphne Marlatt and herself also were present.[87]

Reid also recalls when Robert Duncan, visiting Vancouver to give lectures to the young poets who gathered at the Tallmans, "offered us enthusiastic encouragement to start the magazine and gave us some decisively important tips about how to begin," Reid recalls.[88] Poet Gladys Hindmarch has also observed how a number of the young poets "...put together money, which I think only cost us five dollars each, to get Robert Duncan to come up and give a series of three lectures. And he came up by bus to do that for us. And from there a number of other names started to fill in that geography or map of the poetics of Vancouver."[89]

Not without surprise, given that the inspiration for the "new" West Coast poetry was deriving from Black Mountain, Beat, and San Francisco-Berkeley Renaissance inspired poetry and poetics, Roy Miki has commented upon the backlash that emanated from Eastern Canada against the *TISH* group:

> There have been many attacks on TISH—critics like Dudek, and I think Purdy mounted an attack, and also others like Milton Acorn. There are lots of critics and writers who didn't like TISH, they wanted TISH to go away. Somehow it was not only an affront to them, but I think it represented a whole different take on poetics in Canada. Things had been going in one direction in the east, and now there was this group of writers doing quite interesting things—powerfully interesting things—on the West Coast, and dealing with the West Coast as a particularized place. In Canada the battle was between nationalism and regionalism. And the TISH poets were bringing in something called localism.[90]

This emphasis upon the local was not incidental, but rather integral and reflective of the writing community of Vancouver and British Columbia. George Bowering has discussed this in suggesting how,

My sense...connects with what Gerry [Gilbert] was saying
because we made the writing of poems out of the materials
learning to live in Vancouver... So the poems actually become
not only the making of poems but the making of history for us,
and a geography for us and a mythology for us, for which we
were absolutely reviled by those people back east.[91]

Within a few years, however, Raymond Souster, who had
collaborated with Louis Dudek and Irving Layton on the journal
Contact, and had also corresponded with Charles Olson, would
acknowledge the "new" poetry emanating from *TISH*, as noted by
David Staines: "In 1966 the *TISH* poets gained recognition as a
national poetic movement when Raymond Souster declared in his
preface to *New Wave Canada* (1966) that the *TISH* group was the
source of new poetical energy. The group was the first Canadian wave
in the postmodern tradition in Canadian poetry." [92]

III. BLASER'S POETICS OF THE SACRED

I believe Duncan was inciting mischief when, in an interview, he
distinguishes between a "truly intellectual" poet (speaking of Kenneth
Rexroth) versus a poet who can learn. Declaring that Kenneth Rexroth
was the first "intellectual" poet he had met, Duncan remarks,

...It was the first time I had met anybody in writing where
the poet was an intellectual. And I think poets are rather—
it's very rare for poets to be intellectual, but that was my
disposition. And there wasn't going to be another one until
Charles [Olson]. Neither Robin [Blaser], nor Jack [Spicer]
are truly intellectual. I'm never asleep. I'm fascinated by
everything. They can learn, but that's very different. There's
a learned tradition that came out of Kantorowicz but that's
different from Kenneth Rexroth's disposition.[93]

In my reading, Blaser has always been intellectual. He pays attention to deep reading and textual erudition; his reading list can be tracked throughout his poetry and especially noted within his essays. Blaser himself notes, "Spicer once said that I was the only person he had ever met who could speak quotation marks." [94]

Blaser's familiarity with languages informs and elucidates his writing. Etymology is crucial in Blaser; the exactness of a word, its origins, shifting meanings, and connotations must be paid attention to. "I go everyday, I have for most of my life, to my dictionary, and it's play, it's not always, sometimes it's 'cause I plain don't know that word, but I'll go and check it. You'll find out how much German you speak, how much French you speak, because our words are made of this conglomeration of languages that has been working and working and working." [95]

Blaser's writing presents an account of being-in-the-world in an engaged and exacting way. He focuses upon the way in which time is in all ways contemporary, thus Dante becomes one of Blaser's great "companions," as does Pindar, as does Robert Duncan. In his poem, "Great Companion: Dante Alighiere," Blaser writes: "I address Dante, who is our contemporary, like us, / speaking out of human violence —who is implicit / in our use of our mother tongues—who is initial / and continuously implicated in the courage of / poetry—whose art records *an attachment to the letter / that lay at the mysterious origin of poetry*—the dazzlement—..."

Blaser remarks, "Poetry and philosophy are hand in hand. Philosophy [is] that language which searches for the syntax of the abstract and so on." [97] Blaser goes on to discuss this notion in relation to Dante's writing, saying, "Dante had no fear of bringing philosophy into his great poem. In fact, the philosophers appear when, near the end of the *Paradiso*, he can't really say what that point of light is so he calls on Saint Thomas Aquinas to help him," [98] and further observes that the thought and writing of philosophers such as "...Agamben, Jean-Luc Nancy, Adorno, and I could name others...are beginning to move philosophy back to where its attention to poetry is noted."

"The sacred," Blaser writes, "in my view, is a central problem of the modern condition."[99] Blaser's attention to the sacred within his writing becomes apparent when juxtaposed to the dominant, secular culture, with its absence of spirit, symbol, ritual, and myth. Blaser has woven an appreciation for the sacred deep within the shimmering lines of his poetry. The final poem in his volume reads, "language is love," recalling Chilean biologist Humberto Maturana's concept of the biology of love, his reflection that language evolved because human creatures had some thing to speak to one another, and that phenomenon was love, is love—*communitas*.

Blaser writes of the *sacred*, and, as with Duncan, of the numinous, fabulous, awesome and imaginative, yet not of *religion*, and he cautions against the "violence" perpetrated by the ideology behind religious doctrines. "This aging Roman Catholic," he reflects in "A Note" appended to his wonderful poem, "Great Companion: Dante Alighiere," "looks across at the three great religions of Abraham— the Christian, the Jewish and the Muslim—and fears they are dying into violence."[100]

Blaser has been clear regarding his position on the Vatican's refusal of homosexuality, yet does not throw out the proverbial baby with the bathwater, continuing to pay attention to what he holds sacred. Blaser writes in his poem, "lake of souls reading notes,"[101] that "I have been taught the sacred in three languages from my / earliest life in words" then proceeds to write in Latin, French and English the beginning lines of the Nicene Creed.

In conversation with *The Vancouver Sun* journalist Douglas Todd, Blaser expressed his perspectives on distinguishing between an organized religion and a cosmology. Todd later makes this observation regarding Blaser's theology: "Blaser seems to have found something close to God, a mystical understanding of love. Love is central to Blaser's cosmology. Love to him has a far-reaching mystical reality to it. Quoting Blaser, 'I don't think intelligence exists without love. Love is intelligence. What kind of intelligence would you have without love?'"[102]

Careful reading of his poetry confirms how Blaser continually brings forth an aesthetic of *presence*. Even in death there remains presence. Again, in his poem for Dante, Blaser writes: "Dante's gift is continuously contemporary in the shape / he gave his poem's discoursing—out of the advent of / language one's life in language, as it life were the / home of it—where the intimacy of sound discloses the / Amors of otherness"—that is, of presence. Blaser's work never forgets those companions who formed and informed a fraternity of belonging and connection, early on—Spicer and Duncan, most notably. Blaser reflects:

> So, I have tried to track The Irreparable—*the destruction of experience, the shattered transcendentals, the current enormity in the recognition of these for what they are—as if by chance to discover an opening into our contemporary task: "to redefine the concept of the transcendental in terms of its relation to language." I call this the* poiesis *of thought—or more simply the honest work of language—never an afterthought, for we are inside* The Irreparable. *We are as we are implications of it. Infants of the task. Infants in the language of it. I have studied and loved the footsteps (yes, you can love footsteps think of your own—these footsteps are news of us)—into the* poiesis *of* The Irreparable—*thus, in Jean Paul, Nerval, Baudelaire, Mallarme, Rimbaud and Jarry—in the currents and cross-currents of modernism and in the mis-said post-modernism—the* poiesis *of these footprints in the poetry since 1945, Jack Spicer pressing the shifting sands of this irreparable aporia—the sundered, risky, refounding language of so many—the astonishment of such honesty that transforms the* poiesis *into beauty out of this walk with ugliness.* [103]

When Blaser describes Dante's "discoursing" he could be describing his own poetic discourse, "where *The Comedy* entangles the amorous / with the discoursing of myth, cosmology, philoso- / phy, theology, history, economics, and current issues...this is the polyphony of The Comedy,"[104] as Blaser's own discoursing encompasses these same realms and disciplines.

In its totality, Blaser's *The Holy Forest* traces a life lived in language—an imaginative life, a life of the mind and of the heart, articulated through poetry, poetics, reading, writing, teaching, and reflecting, within which domain "the other turns out to be art and / writing."[105] As he records, "I have tried for 35 years to / redefine sweetness—it is what / they called being—it is not / behind you or before you / or within you—'the goodness / and sweetness of Dante' is / his composition—the language / composes the good, the sweetness / and. By accident, brightness."[106]

In his poem, "Psychoanalysis: An Elegy," poet Jack Spicer wrote, "I am thinking that a poem / could go on forever."[107] Describing his own practice of poetics, Blaser wrote, "I'm interested in a particular kind of narrative—what Jack Spicer and I agreed to call in our own work the serial poem—this is a narrative which refuses to adopt an imposed story line, and completes itself only in the sequence of poems..."[108]

Blaser adds tellingly, "If you go through Duncan's *Medieval Scenes* for the marvel that that poem is—and it is in spite of the arguments with Duncan—it is a serial poem. It is for Jack and me the first serial poem..." In that context, the poem only comes to an end with the death of the poet. But language survives, and, almost fifty years following Spicer's death his poetry continues to inspire readers in a formative West Coast way, as does Duncan's. In a very real way, these "fictive certainties," as Duncan might put it, form a domain of belief.

Expressions of faith in this domain still percolate. During the writing of this paper, I became aware of a review in the *Globe and Mail* of a new, posthumously published book by Margaret Avison, the only Canadian to have presented at the 1963 Vancouver Poetry Conference.[109] Almost simultaneously, while browsing with my daughter at the Co-op Bookstore in the countercultural neighbourhood of Vancouver's Commercial Drive, I came across and purchased

Daphne Marlatt's new work, *The Given*. Both of these authors, I realized, had been present at that historic literary gathering. Opening Marlatt's book, I immediately encountered a line reading, "The whole thing: just trying to be at home. That's the plot..." It was by Robin Blaser. The reading, writing, reflecting, continues.

Notes:

1. Robin Blaser, *The Holy Forest: Collected Poems of Robin Blaser* (Berkeley: University of California Press, 2006), 326. These lines are from the poem "stop" which Blaser wrote "for Daphne Marlatt."

2. Oddly, regarding bissett, who has published over sixty books, I wondered how Jack Kerouac had heard of him. In Kerouac's *Paris Review* Interview (1968), he asks his interviewers, poets Ted Berrigan, Aram Saroyan and Duncan McNaughton, "You know who's a great poet? I know who the great poets are...Let's see, is it...William Bissett of Vancouver. An Indian boy. Bill Bissett, or Bissonnette." The last time I heard bissett was at the downtown Vancouver Public Library, where he offered his shamanic performance, as always, with verve and enchantment. In that audience were Maxine Gadd and Scott Lawrence.

3. Jim Brown and David Phillips, *west coast seen* (Vancouver: Talonbooks, 1969).

4. Ibid., 5.

5. Donald Allen, *The New American Poetry* (New York: Grove Press, 1960).

6. Alan Watts, *The Joyous Cosmology: Adventures in the Chemistry of Consciousness* (New York: Pantheon Books, 1962).

7. Alan Watts, *Psychotherapy East and West* (New York: Vintage Books, 1961).

8. R.D Laing, *The Politics of Experience* (New York: Ballantine Books, 1967).

9. Jack Kerouac, *The Scripture of the Golden Eternity* (San Francisco: City Lights Books, 1994 [1960]).

10. Davey was one of the founders of *TISH*, the newsletter publishing Vancouver's new poets in the early 1960s. Contributors included George Bowering, Daphne Marlatt, David Dawson, Fred Wah, Jamie Reid, Dan McLeod, David Cull, Sam Perry, Robert Hogg, Peter Auxier, Gladys Hindmarch, Lionel Kearns, and others.

11. Frank Davey, "Al Purdy, Sam Solecki, and the Poetics of the 1960s," http://www.uwo.ca/english/canadian poetry/cpjrn/vol51/davey.htm (accessed 4/14/2009).

12. Gerry Gilbert, ed., "Vancouver Poetry in the Early 60s," The *B.C. Monthly* 3:3 (1976): unpaginated.

13. Chris Gudgeon, *Out of this World: The Natural History of Milton Acorn* (Vancouver: Arsenal Pulp Press, 1996).

14. Ibid., 120.

15. Robin Blaser, *The Fire: Collected Essays*, ed. Miriam Nichols (Berkeley: University of California Press, 2006), 406.

16. Ibid.

17. Jamie Reid, "Milton Acorn," in *I. Another. The Space Between* (Vancouver: Talon-books, 2004), 60.

18. Gilbert, "Vancouver Poetry in the Early 60s," unpaginated.

19. Gilbert's broadcasts on Vancouver's community alternative radio station were legendary. My last encounter with him was seeing him record Blaser's and Robert Creeley's final reading together at the Vancouver Cultural East Centre in 2004.

20. Gilbert, "Vancouver Poetry in the Early 60s," unpaginated.

21. Elspeth Cameron, *Earle Birney: A Life* (New York: Viking, 1994).

22. Ibid., 473.

23. Ibid., 471.

24. Ibid., 562.

25. Ibid., 555.

26. Blaser, *The Holy Forest*.

27. Blaser, *The Fire*.

28. Ibid.

29. Ibid.

30. Ibid.

31. Blaser, *The Holy Forest*.

32. Robert Duncan, preface to *Jack Spicer, One Night Stand and Other Poems*, ed. Donald Allen (San Francisco: Grey Fox Press, 1980).

33. David Meltzer, ed., *San Francisco Beat: Talking with the Poets* (San Francisco: City Lights Books, 2001).

34. Ibid.

35. Ibid.

36. Colin James Sanders, unpublished Robert Duncan Interview, (August 1980), 20-21.

37. Duncan, preface to *Jack Spicer, One Night Stand and Other Poems*.

38. Robert Duncan, "Biographical Notes," *The New American Poetry*, ed. Donald M. Allen (New York: Grove Press, 1960).

39. "A Duncan Delirium" (Spring 2005). Event at Kootenay School of Writing, 201-505 Hamilton Street, Vancouver, BC., V6B 2R1, www.kswnet.org.

40. Dennis Cooley, "Three Recent *TISH* Items," *Canadian Poetry* 3 (1978): 98. In this critique, Cooley reviews *Poetry and the Colonized Mind: TISH*, by Keith Richardson; *TISH* 1-19, edited by Frank Davey; and *The Writing Life: Historical and Cultural Views of the TISH Movement*, edited by C.H. Gervais.

41. Ibid.

42. Fred Wah, in *Poets Talk: Conversations with Robert Kroetsch, Daphne Marlatt, Erin Moure, Dionne Brand, Marie Annharte Baker, Jeff Derksen and Fred Wah*, eds. Pauline Butling and Susan Rudy (Edmonton: University of Alberta Press, 2005), 162-3.

43. Cameron, *Earle Birney: A Life*, 300.

44. Colin James Sanders, "Robert Duncan Interview," *Beat Scene* 48 (2005): 16-22.

45. Ken Bullock, "Blaser to give poetry reading at SF State," *The Berkeley Daily Planet*, September 11, 2007 (accessed 3/17/2009).

46. Ibid.

47. Blaser, *The Holy Forest*.

48. Duncan, preface to *Jack Spicer, One Night Stand and Other Poems*.

49. Duncan, "Biographical Notes."

50. Kevin Killian, ed., "Dialogue of Eastern and Western Poetry," In *Even on Sunday: Essays, Readings, and Archival Materials on the Poetry and Poetics of Robin Blaser*, ed. Miriam Nichols (Orono, ME: National Poetry Foundation, University of Maine, 2002).

51. Greil Marcus, *Invisible Republic: Bob Dylan's Basement Tapes* (New York: Henry Holt & Co., 1997).

52. Ibid., 98.

53. See "CS Jones: A Post-Thelmic Gnostic," in *ecclesia gnostica in nova albion*, blog of Jordan Stratford, http://egina.blogspot.com/2005/02cs-jones-post-thelmic-gnostic. html.

54. Blaser, *The Fire*.

55. Stan Persky, *The Short Version: An ABC Book* (Vancouver: New Star Books, 2005).

56. Ibid.

57. Blaser, *The Holy Forest*.

58. Robin Blaser, "Even on Sunday," in *The Holy Forest* (Berkeley: University of California Press, 2006), 370-74.

59. Stan Persky, "A Note on Robin Blaser and Jack Spicer," *Caterpillar* 12 (1970): 213-216.

60. Barry McKinnon, "Barry McKinnon Interviews George Stanley," *It's Still Winter* 1.2 (1998). http://wither.unbc.ca/winter/number.two/stanley.html (accessed 20/04/2009)..

61. Dwight Macdonald, ed., *Politics* I (1944).

62. Duncan, preface to *Jack Spicer, One Night Stand and Other Poems*.

63. Stan Persky, *Autobiography of a Tattoo* (Vancouver: New Star Books, 1997): 109-110.

64. Blaser, *The Holy Forest*, 336.

65. David Meltzer, *Introduction to Joanne Kyger, As Ever: Selected Poems* (New York: Penguin Books, 2002).

66. Blaser, *The Holy Forest*, 336.

67. Robin Blaser, excerpts from "Astonishments," in *Even on Sunday: Essays, Readings, and Archival Materials on the Poetry and Poetics of Robin Blaser*, ed. Miriam Nichols (Orono, ME: National Poetry Foundation, University of Maine, 2002).

68. Blaser, *The Holy Forest*.

69. David Meltzer, ed., *San Francisco Beat* (San Francisco: City Lights Books, 2001).

70. Blaser, *The Fire*, 407.

71. Noreen Shanahan, "Ellen Tallman, 80: Academic and Therapist," special to the *Globe & Mail*, October 8, 2008 (accessed 3/25/2009).

72. Jamie Reid Interview.

73. Blaser, *The Fire*, 402.

74. Linda Hamalian, *A Life of Kenneth Rexroth* (New York: Norton, 1991).

75. Colin James Sanders, unpublished Robert Duncan Interview, (August 1980).

76. Kevin Killian, ed.,"Dialogue of Eastern and Western Poetry," in *Even on Sunday: Essays, Readings, and Archival Materials on the Poetry and Poetics of Robin Blaser*, ed. Miriam Nichols (Orono, ME: National Poetry Foundation, University of Maine, 2002).

77. Duncan, "Biographical Notes."

78. Persky, *Autobiography of a Tattoo*, 111.

79. George Bowering, "Jack Spicer," *IS* 12, (1973).

80. Blaser, *The Fire*.

81. Duncan, preface to Jack Spicer, *One Night Stand and Other Poems*.

82. December 8, 2006.

83. Blaser, *The Fire*, 407.

84. Noreen Shanahan, "Ellen Tallman, 80: Academic and Therapist," special to the *Globe & Mail*, October 8, 2008 (accessed 3/25/2009).

85. Pauline Butling and Susan Rudy, eds., *Poets Talk: Conversations with Robert Kroetsch, Daphne Marlatt, Erin Moure, Dionne Brand, Marie Annharte Baker, Jeff Derksen and Fred Wah* (Edmonton: University of Alberta Press, 2005), 25.

86. Jamie Reid, Interview. "Jamie and Himself: An Interview with Canada's Jamie Reid." http://www.wordarc.com/SAMAEL/20008/09/25/Jamie_and_Himself:_AN_INTERVIEW_WIIH. (Retrieved 10/13/2009).

87. Ibid.

88. Ibid.

89. Irene Niechoda and Tim Hunter, eds., "A *TISH*story," in *Beyond TISH*, ed. Douglas Barbour (Edmonton: NeWest Press and Vancouver: *West Coast Line*, 1991), 83-98.

90. Susan Rudy and Pauline Butling, eds., *Poets Talk*, 97.

91. Gilbert, "Vancouver Poetry in the Early 60s," unpaginated.

92. David Staines, Chapter 6, "Poetry" in *The Cambridge Companion to Canadian Literature*, ed. Eva-Marie Kröller (Cambridge: Cambridge University Press, 2009), 145.

93. Colin James Sanders, "Robert Duncan Interview," *Beat Scene* 48 (2005): 16-22.

94. Blaser, *The Fire*.

95. John Sakkis, "Interview with Robin Blaser that originally appeared in *The Poker* #5" in Both Both, blog of John Sakkis. (Retrieved 3/17/2009).

96. Blaser, *The Holy Forest*.

97. Sakkis, "Interview with Robin Blaser."

98. Ibid.

99. Blaser, *The Fire*.

100. Ibid.

101. Ibid.

102. Douglas Todd, "The Hippest Guy in the Room: Poet Robin Blaser at 83," Interview with Robin Blaser, *Vancouver Sun*, Sept. 6, 2008.

103. Ibid.

104. Ibid.

105. Blaser, "Desire," in *The Holy Forest*, 273.

106. Blaser, "It springs on you," Ibid., 306.

107. Jack Spicer, "Psychoanalysis: An Elegy," in *My vocabulary did this to me: The Collected Poetry of Jack Spicer*, eds. Peter Gizzi and Kevin Killian (Middletown, CT: Wesleyan University Press, 2008), 31-33.

108. Blaser, *The Fire*.

109. Judith Fitzgerald, review of Margaret Avison, *Listening*, in the *Globe & Mail*, April 10, 2009.

110. Daphne Marlatt, *The Given* (Toronto: McClelland & Stewart, 2008), unpaginated—follows the Dedication page.

That's the Way It Began:
AN INTERVIEW WITH P.K. PAGE AT 92

JOSEPH BLAKE

What is perhaps the most distinctive element is her
wealth of imagery drawn from wide and varied sources,
sharp and startling with the force of the personality they
reveal.

—Alan Crawley on P.K. Page's 1946 debut poetry book,
As Ten As Twenty

JB: *Can we begin by asking you to share your earliest memories of the writing scene in B.C.?*

PKP: I came out here in the 1940s, during the war. But before that I met Anne Marriott, and she was a poet in Victoria who wrote a very fine, long poem, "The Wind Our Enemy," about the drought in Saskatchewan. I met her in Quebec at a conference, and she said there was someone here by the name of Alan Crawley, and that Alan, inspired by Dorothy Livesay, Doris Ferne, Anne Marriott herself, and Floris Clark McLaren were urging Alan to edit a poetry magazine.

Now, you've got to remember in those days there was no Canada Council, no granting bodies for writers, no magazines that published poetry. *Saturday Night* occasionally published a poem as filler, and my husband [Arthur Irwin][1] (who was not my husband then), did commission E.J. Pratt to write a long poem about Dunkirk for *Maclean's*, but normally nobody published poetry. Oh, *Canadian*

Forum published poems, but a poetry magazine simply didn't exist in the country when Alan began this magazine, *Contemporary Verse.* We had no magazines and no funding bodies, and there were a lot of us beginning to write and wanting to publish. So these four women persuaded Alan, (who incidentally was blind) to undertake the editing of a magazine that was called *Contemporary Verse.*

Alan was blind. Everything had to be read to him. He had been a very successful lawyer in Winnipeg who had a very rare germ attack the optic nerve, and he went blind when he was in his forties. He always loved poetry. He always loved theatre and poetry, and he used to go every year to England. He used to go to poetry readings in London, and he was used to poetry through the ear. When he had eyesight, he read a lot.

They persuaded Alan to bring out *Contemporary Verse.* Anne Marriott told me it was coming out, and she said, "Why don't you send him some work?" and I did. In fact, I had two or three or four poems in the first issue of *CV.*

Dorothy Livesay was a great supporter of the magazine and of Alan. Floris McLaren took on the business management of it. She also wrote poetry, published a booked called *Frozen Fire,* I think. To the best of my knowledge, that's the way poetry began on the West Coast in Canada.

Because there wasn't another poetry magazine, Alan drew from all over Canada. First issue was 1941. He stopped finally after more than a decade, thirty-nine issues. He published everyone in Canada— Earle Birney, A.J.M. Smith, F.R. Scott, Jay MacPherson, Anne Wilkinson, Louis Dudek: anybody who ever amounted to anything and a lot of people who didn't.

JB: *What was Alan Crawley like to work with?*

PKP: He was very frank with his criticism if you sent him work that he didn't like...and it was difficult, because he had to use a Braille typewriter. Sometimes the messages you could hardly make heads or tail of—but they were always worth struggling with, because he was so honest with you, and he had a good ear.

Now, a little bit later, in Montreal, *Preview* was started, and I was one of the *Preview* people. My father had died and I brought my mother out to Victoria to settle her down, but where I really was working in Montreal, and there they started a magazine called *Preview.* It has nothing to do with the West Coast, except there was a sort of germination going on. The West Coast began it and Montreal next, not Toronto. It was the West Coast and then Montreal, which is very interesting.

I was working on a stupid job. I wasn't qualified to work. I had no skills at all, but I got some dumb job in an office, a ridiculous job working for H.R. MacMillan. It was during wartime...what was it called? He built ships. He was a dollar-year-man, and he had a big office there, and his secretary, who later I discovered was also his mistress (that didn't come out for years) she got me a job working there. She had pull. I had no skill, but she got me a job. I worked there in a menial job doing bad typing for part of the war.

I was in Victoria on VE Day. I remember going down—I left mother and my aunt on Willows Beach having a picnic. I had taken the car and gone off somewhere, and coming home they were calling "Extra! Extra! Read all about it! The war in Europe has ended!"

I got a copy of the paper of course, and tore back to the beach to tell my mother and aunt, and I passed two old ladies in hats having a nice, little picnic on the beach, and I said "The war is over!" to them, and they said "Were you talking to us?" I thought, [giggling] there's Victoria for you. "Yes I'm talking to you! And everybody else too!" [Now bursting into laughter] I don't think I know much more than that. That's the way it all began.

JB: *When you moved out here in the 1960s, was there much of a writing community in Victoria?*

PKP: Well, [Robin] Skelton owned it, and he wouldn't have anything to do with me. He excluded me. I was not part of anything. He taught at University of Victoria, and he had Susan Musgrave and Marilyn Bowering and all these young writers. He knew a great deal about poetry, Skelton, a very great deal, [icily] *very* informed.

He and another professor at UVic [John Peters] started the *Malahat Review*. The two of them were joint editors, I think. In the beginning he didn't publish any Canadians. I got into a terrible public fight with him about it.

Alan Crawley had letters from all of us. He had an enormous body of correspondence from all the writers in Canada who he had written to. He was broke, Alan, in his old age, terribly broke, and he lived in a terrible little shack on Lee Avenue. Somebody suggested to him that he sell his letters to some university, and he offered them to UVic and Skelton turned them down. He said there was nothing there of any interest. And he was buying letters from European writers. Alan finally sold them to Kingston, to Queens I think. He sold them somewhere, but Alan was absolutely dashed when this trove of letters was rejected. Academia [*grimacing*] is probably one of the *bitchiest* areas in the world.

Today, this very day, there's a Page-Irwin Colloquium Room being opened at Trent. They asked for some paintings, and I gave them some of my paintings, and Zailig Pollock, a professor there is doing my collected works, both on the Web and in print. University of Toronto is going to publish them all. They have been so generous to me. I can't tell you how generous they've been to me. It isn't always that academia is bitchy; I think there's something weird about UVic.

JB: *I've always felt excluded from it as well, and I remember Victoria-based, jazz great Paul Horn telling me he always felt excluded from it too...*

PKP: Me too. I was excluded from it, quite actively. They really had very little interest in me, and I don't care. It doesn't bother me. I get more attention than I deserve already. So it isn't a problem for me, but it is curious.

JB: *How about the writing community or the artistic—the painting community? Were you part of that?*

PKP: Oh, I was excluded from the artistic community too.

JB: *By the painters?*

PKP: Yes, the Limners. They had everybody in town, photographers, anyone you can think of, but not me.

JB: *Did the Limners include writers, poets?*

PKP: Well, they had Skelton. He did little collages of some kind. No, I'm very happy here now. I've got good friends, but the first years here I felt excluded from everything. I was! I didn't merely feel it, I was!

JB: *What about Ivy's Bookshop? Wasn't there a salon-like reading scene there?*

PKP: Ivy [Mickleson] was wonderful, as you know. Oh, Ivy was wonderful! A genius in her own way, knew about books; knew about how to run a bookshop, knew about how to have contact with her customers. She'd quickly glom on to your taste in literature, and if she saw anything she thought was of interest to you she'd phone you up and say, "I don't know if this would be of interest to you, but the next pass-by you might want to look at…" She started doing readings, which were quite interesting, fistfights and all kinds of excitement. I wasn't involved in the fistfights, but I did a lot of readings…

She was a wonder, a remarkable little being. Integrity, the two of them, Aida and Ivy. Aida doing the bookkeeping, and Ivy doing the books. They were a fine team, but Ivy was a character.

JB: *This is a little off-topic but Ivy once took my wife and I under her wing, adopted us really. Friday afternoons we'd spend drinking gin and tonic and discussing politics and books at her beach shack on Gonzales Bay. She didn't know why my wife and I wanted another child, but when our daughter Emma was born, she became the baby's doting grandmother.*

PKP: She didn't understand marriage either. Her mother had told her "Only marry if you're desperate." There was nothing material about Ivy. She didn't want material possessions, on another plane altogether, extraordinary. She was the most loyal friend to me. There was nobody like Ivy.

JB: *Emily Carr is another famous Victoria character. Was Carr or her work an influence on you?*

PKP: No. No. She was alive when I first came to Victoria, but I never met her, and I don't think I'd seen any of her work then. There wasn't an art gallery when I came here first. So there wouldn't be anywhere to hang them even if anyone had the wit to recognize that they were good.

JB: *Were you painting then?*

PKP: I didn't start painting until Brazil. I couldn't write in Brazil, and I started painting. I was studying Portuguese very hard. I had given up smoking, and I associated smoking with writing, and I was not hearing much English, and my language seemed to dry up, and I started drawing. I remember a very famous Israeli painter, Arie Aroch who said to me in Brazil, "Why do you give up an art form that you have mastered to start work in an art form where you don't even know there's more than one [shade of] white in the world? You know nothing." And I said, "I didn't give up writing, it gave me up." He replied, "I think you're making a mistake" So I said, "Arie, come see my work one day, would you, and then talk to me." And he came, and he said, "I take it all back." He said "You begin like a pro."

JB: *You achieved international recognition as a writer from Canada. Wasn't one of your early poems included in* Treasury of Modern Poetry *for Scribner's in New York?*

PKP: I don't know it.

JB: *Oscar Williams included it in the collection...*

PKP: Oh yes, I was in that. I was being published quite early in *Poetry* too, which was the Chicago magazine, *the* poetry magazine really, still exists. I've got a poem coming out in their next issue, I think. I won one of their prizes in the forties. I've had a lot of breaks. That's the only way I can tell it.

JB: *Would you consider the opportunity to travel one of the breaks?*

PKP: That was certainly a break. I've had a lot of breaks. I've had good men in my life. I haven't been subjected to some of the awful things that some women have either through their fathers or their lovers. I haven't had all the travels I would like to have, but I've had very interesting travels.

JB: *Do you think your travel has been much of an influence on your work?*

PKP: I don't know... I don't know. It's very hard to know what influences you. I don't like the word "influence." I think the word "affinity" is much better than influence.

JB: *I'm guessing, because it does seem that your work comes from someplace...*

PKP: ...Else? I've always felt I'm only a vehicle, not necessarily a good vehicle, but a vehicle. You plug in. I've never understood how some people get such swollen heads thinking themselves so big when they didn't...It can't be them, can't be them.

JB: *What about painting and writing? I don't want to say do they influence each other, but do they live in the same realm?*

PKP: Well, I don't know. When I was painting I wasn't writing and when I was writing I wasn't painting. It wasn't deliberate. I just get totally absorbed in the one thing, and it didn't leave me time or room for anything else.

JB: *Were there painters in Victoria who you associated with?*

PKP: Do you mean in the forties?

JB: *No, when you were painting.*

PKP: Pat Bates. She and I, both of us, felt ignored by the local community. Pat was finally accepted, and I suppose I was finally accepted too. Pat was really the only artist I knew.

JB: *We often have a romantic notion of previous eras; times when it seemed that artists, poets, musicians were all part of an artistic community. I always imagined it was better in some of the earlier times, say the 1940s.*

PKP: We were always scrambling around. No, I don't think it was a golden age at all.

JB: *Was there any relationship with musicians like the Adaskins?*

PKP: Harry Adaskin was in Vancouver. Harry loved poetry and used to read poetry at the Vancouver Public Library. I was vaguely in touch with him, because he used to get in touch with me about reading poems of mine. And then Murray, his brother, moved here and I knew Murray very well. I wrote the libretto or whatever you call it for *The Musicians of Bremen,* which the Victoria Symphony had commissioned, and I worked with Murray. I don't remember being part of much of an artistic community here at all. There were individual contacts, not community.

JB: *Did you know Leonard Cohen?*

PKP: Leonard is twenty years younger than I am. But I was in Montreal and knew all the writers in Montreal. Now in Montreal we did have a community. That's when we formed the *Preview* group and there were artists connected with us one way or another. There was a very active creative community there. It was wartime, and we had no money to do anything, but we were a community. A.M. Klein was probably our best poet in my opinion, and F.R. Scott...

JB: *What about Irving Layton?*

PKP: There were two groups, the *Preview* group and the *First Statement* group. Layton was in the *First Statement* group and Louis Dudek was in *First Statement,* but we all knew each other, fought with each other. There were a lot of artists affiliated with the group too... film people. There was a real sense of an artistic community there. I left Montreal and Cohen grew up just after I left and knew all these people. Layton badmouthed Cohen. Layton was a wretched man. He really was. He trashed women. I've never not spoken to anyone in my life, even if I disliked them, except Layton. I finally wouldn't. It was because I despised him so. But he wrote some good poetry. He wrote some very good poetry. I could have forgiven him being a womanizer; lots of men are, but to trash somebody, unforgivable. I saw women absolutely destroyed by Layton. Weird...

JB: *What about Trudeau? A different kind of man, I imagine?*

PKP: He was much more of an intellectual than Layton, I guess. I was a great fan of Trudeau and knew him slightly, very slightly. He read poetry, and he liked my poetry, which was always very flattering. He said it in print somewhere, I don't know where. He was a charmer, an absolute charmer. He gave you his full attention when he was talking to you. He wasn't looking around to see who else was around. It was as if you and he were alone in a room together talking. It was very intimate in a way. I don't mean personally intimate. He created an atmosphere of intimacy. He was fabulous. I can't remember his faults now. He did one or two political things that I didn't approve of, but I think he was wonderful nevertheless.

I wonder if Iggy is going to walk in his footsteps. We're lost if he isn't. We're totally lost if Ignatieff can't come through. I knew his parents slightly. I've known a lot of people in my life, slightly. His mother came from a family that had been Canadian patriots from the beginning. She was adorable. She was a painter, not a great painter but not a bad painter; intelligent, warm and humourous, and if he could have inherited a little of that from her, he'd be perfect. If we love him, he may love us back. That can happen.

JB: *What do you think of Barack Obama?*

PKP: Oh, I love him! That he showed up almost makes you think there is a God after all. What a charmer. Imagine wanting that job. He's something else, that man.

JB: *And Stephen Harper?*

PKP: He's a wretched man. I'd have thought we had more collective sense than that, but we didn't. I've always been NDP, but I'm a little upset with Carole James and her stand on the Carbon Tax. [Premier Gordon] Campbell is a slippery fellow, a clever, clever bugger. Have you met him? I have, and you couldn't meet a more charming man. There are two of him. His social self, who is witty and charming, and his political self, who is...mean-spirited? Seems so to me. I got an Order of B.C. and he was there at the ceremony shaking hands and getting photographed, and he said "I don't imagine any of your friends would want a copy of this photo." [*Laughing*] It disarms you. The private man is quite witty and fast and charming.

Ed. *Seeming to notice the tape recorder for the first time, Page interjects,* "I forgot that I'm being taped..."

JB: *You mentioned Dorothy Livesay earlier.*

PKP: Dorothy was a great one for boosting herself, and she didn't stint in that. We didn't get on, Dorothy and I, but I admired her. She was feisty, liberated a lot of young women. She wrote a passionate piece about the Japanese-Canadians[2] when nobody in Canada was paying any attention to the Japanese. She was an activist. I didn't like her poetry. I found it far too sentimental for my taste, but I admired her for all of that. She was an influence for good, I think. A whole lot of young women were freed by her, which is quite a record to have. Women are much freer today. In the fight to be free of male domination, women have had to face a lot of hard jobs.

JB: *It seems many successful women have still had to choose between career advancement and having children. Do you think so?*

PKP: Maybe we don't need families too much. We're overpopulated already, but we've got to go on having children. It's really a problem for China, India, and countries emulating our lifestyle. They won't be able to do it. There are too many problems. I'm glad I'm not going to have to cope with all of that. I'm getting out of it. I'm getting out of it.

JB: *Have you written poems about these problems?*

PKP: I don't seem to write about issues.

JB: *What about a poem like "Planet Earth" where you conclude with a beautiful short line about "smoothing the holy surfaces"?*

PKP: I wasn't writing about it as an issue. It was an issue of course. I've been going on about global warming since the 1970s. I wrote that short story "Unless the Eye Catch Fire"[3] that was performed as a one-woman show, and this was before the scientists were talking about global warming. I can't say I was prescient. I was just writing a story, that's all I was doing. So, I suppose you could say I do write about issues, but it wasn't deliberately.

Two of my books are being launched today at Trent. One is probably the last serious book I'm going to write. When I say serious, I mean of any substance. It's a book of new poems called *Coal and Roses*, and I doubt I'll write another. I don't know if I have any more writing in me. I've got a kid's book called *The Old Woman and the Hen*,[4] a trilogy of fairy stories coming out in the fall, and Jay Ruzesky is going to do a small book of mine called *Cullen*. He has a small press that's going to put it out this summer. It is five poems about this character, Cullen. *You Are Here* came out recently. It's a quirky little book.[5] I don't know where that book came from. It just spilled out, a series of riffs about identity. Who are we really? That's the sixty-four-dollar question, and that's what the book is all about. It's a funny little book. Anyhow, I've had a lot of books out in the last few years of my life. It's quite remarkable.

Notes:

1. Arthur Irwin, fabled editor, publisher, diplomat and ardent Canadian nationalist, married Page·in 1950 and moved to Victoria with her in 1964, where he was publisher of the *Times Colonist* until 1971. He died in 1999 at 101 years.

2. Dorothy Livesay, "Call My People Home," Original CBC broadcast, Vancouver, March 1949. In *Collected Poems: The Two Seasons* (Toronto: McGraw-Hill Ryerson, 1972) 180-194.

3. P.K. Page, *Unless the Eye Catch Fire* (Toronto: Full Spectrum Press, 1994).

4. P.K. Page, *The Old Woman and the Hen* (Erin, ON: Porcupine's Quill Publishing, 2008).

5. P.K. Page, *You Are Here* (North Saanich, BC: Hedgerow Press, 2008).

Working with
George Woodcock
MIKE DOYLE

George Woodcock first conceived of himself as a poet. This discovery
began around 1925, when he was thirteen. Although born in Winnipeg,
Canada, he then lived and went to school in England, thus naturally
enough he became an *English* poet, influenced by the predominant
thirties group of W. H. Auden and his "McSpaunday" circle.[1]

Woodcock's collection *Notes on Visitations: Poems 1936-1975*, a
readable, modest 100-page collection from forty years' work, has a
salutary introduction of interest by one of Canada's major poets,
Woodcock's friend Al Purdy. Purdy begins by pointing out, as of 1975,
the range and versatility in the general body of Woodcock's work,
which included writing on Bakunin and the anarchists, Gandhi and
India, the Doukhobors, Gabriel Dumont, and much more. "I've
wondered occasionally how he does it," says Purdy. "One big reason
is Inge, his wife. She drives the Volks and he doesn't. She also cooks
and writes, so that they make a pair whose total is more than the
parts."[2] Inge, a professional-level photographer, acted as secretary,
publicist, and general factotum. In other words, Inge Woodcock was
indispensably part of a joint operation.

For George's part in it, Purdy says: "All I understand is that
Woodcock is a great human being, protean and in some understated
way, magnificent. He is largely responsible for the regeneration of a
country's literature."

Another of Woodcock's books, *Taking It to the Letter* (1981),[3] is a

selection of his letters to other writers, mostly from 1972 to the date
of the book's publication. Starting from his long-time friend and book
collaborator, Ivan Avakumovic, correspondents range from P.K. Page
through Margaret Atwood, Hugh MacLennan, Irving Layton,
Roderick Haig-Brown, Earle Birney, Margaret Laurence, and many
others. Mine was a slighter friendship with George than were many
of these people's, but he includes two letters to me and one, to Irving
Layton, about me. I should explain that, through the good offices of
P.K. Page, I began corresponding with George and reviewing for
Canadian Literature in 1970. This happy conjunction continued for
sixteen years, so I have a file of over eighty letters from him.

My first review for *Canadian Literature*, a rather heavy-handed
piece on George Jonas, was followed in 1972 by a substantial essay,
"The Occasions of Irving Layton,"[4] the trigger for Woodcock's letter to
Layton of 17 January 1973.[5] Layton has apparently complained of my
pigeonholing him as an "occasional" poet, which might seem to imply
a lack of seriousness on his part. My actual sense of him and his work
was far from that. As it happens, I saw (and still see) occasional poetry
as an honourable activity, the sort of poetry which arises from its own
occasion, as distinct from Creative Writing department poems which
typically are brought forth as part of a program, contributions to a
"themed" slim volume, etc. George placates Layton:

> *Doyle is indulging in a piece of New Zealand Scottish mist.*
> *I think what he really means is not so much that you are an*
> *occasional poet but that your poems are the occasions of*
> *your poetic personality—presumably something like the*
> *phases of the moon. ...I don't believe he's shaken off the*
> *Victorian miasma of Christchurch, where they're still all*
> *muscular Christians and the schools have beating prefects,*
> *which even the English have abandoned. He's an amiable*
> *honest man, very pleasant to sit with over beer, he still*
> *believes that writing has to be ambiguous to be good, and*
> *that schizophrenia makes the whole world kin. If you care*
> *to write something on his piece, I'll publish it.*[6]

Layton, apparently, did not care to. This benign twaddle of George's is largely a flight of fantasy, but typical of him in its generosity and in the kernel of understanding he offers. Having the greatest respect for the best of Layton's poetry, I emphatically did not mean to suggest that he was a part-timer or hobbyist. I do believe ambiguity is *one* effective writing device: but "Schizophrenia makes the whole world kin"—I'd never have thought of that and don't believe it for a nanosecond.

I have in common with George Woodcock that we each grew up in England, though neither actually belonged there, and we both started out from meagre circumstances. As another poet friend, Peter Bland, put it back then: "I taste the damp recurring thought / of being bred to expect so little." From the age of seventeen, for eleven years, George worked as a Great Western Railways clerk in the well-named city of Slough, west of London. As in my case, George's poetry proved to be his ticket out of a straitened way of life. His work began to be accepted by little magazines and he found a literary environment in the pubs around Victoria Station, an environment that included the solicitor-poet Roy Fuller, the mystery writer and critic Julian Symons, and poet-educationist-art critic Herbert Read. Thus he formed a background in British writing and culture which enabled him to write cogently about a range of figures including George Orwell (in a good book, *The Crystal Spirit*), Aldous Huxley, Oscar Wilde, the political philosopher William Godwin, and the Amazon traveller and botanist Henry Walter Bates.

A major aspect of Woodcock's writing back then derived from his concern with social problems and a political perspective which was to prove key in marking out his identity as a writer, and this takes focus in one of his best known books, *Anarchism: a history of libertarian ideas and movements* (1962).[7] Long before this he had edited *The State* (1943)[8] by Peter Kropotkin, an anarchist figure who crops up many times in Woodcock's oeuvre, including his introduction to an edition of Kropotkin's most famous work, *Mutual Aid* (1989). Other Woodcock titles in this area are *The Basis of Communal Living* (1947),[9] *The Writer and Politics* (1948),[10] a biography of the French anarchist

Pierre Joseph Proudhon (1956),[11] then, jumping over some titles, *Evolution and Environment* (1995).[12] When George Fetherling's biography appeared in 2003, it was titled *The Gentle Anarchist: A Life of George Woodcock.*[13]

Simply put, Woodcock's contribution to Canadian and British Columbia culture rests in the fact that he was a consummate man of letters, with a substantial, wide-ranging body of work, including some pioneering work on Canadian matters. As a good many of us do, he began as a poet and he became an accomplished one, whose *Collected Poems*[14] were published in 1983. But, as often happens, that aspect of his work was subsumed under the "man of letters" category.

The aim in this essay is to look at his direct contribution to British Columbia culture, though as foregoing details have shown, he contributed a great deal indirectly in the sense that his was excellent work coming from a B.C.-based writer: for example, *Walls of India,*[15] with paintings by Toni Onley; a biography of *Mahatma Gandhi;*[16] *Faces of India: A Travel Narrative*, with photos by Ingeborg Woodcock;[17] *The Greeks in India;*[18] *Kerala: A Portrait of the Malabar Coast;*[19] and *Dry Wells of India.*[20]

Toni Onley's readable "as told to" memoir, *Flying Colours,*[21] contains an amusing chapter on the travel adventure that resulted in *Walls of India*. Onley, who developed a lasting friendship with the Woodcocks, portrays his travel partner as a rumpled but buttoned-down sahib. The following little anecdote was preceded some months earlier by a Hotel Vancouver meeting in support of the Canadian Indian Village Aid society:

> *Despite the heat, George sported the same jacket and black tie he had worn to the CIVA dinner months earlier. I shook my head.*
>
> *"I don't think anyone is going to take offence if you take off your jacket and tie, George. You'd be a lot more comfortable."*
>
> *He rested his pencil, then he loosened his tie. "I'll think about it."*[22]

Following this, Onley provides an interesting account of Woodcock's writing methods while "on the road." Equally interesting is the brief story of how *Walls of India* got its name. Onley explains: "I never place people in my pictures," inferring that a good deal of architecture appears in his paintings for this book. Woodcock, for his part, could build on this, observing that: "India is a country full of invisible walls...There are walls of language, walls of caste, walls of religion, and a high wall between the rich and the poor." [23] *Flying Colours* also includes a touching portrayal of the Woodcocks' visits to Onley's ground floor studio, in the years before George's death in 1995 when a frail Woodcock, now crippled by arthritis, was aided by walking stick.

In a piece titled "Fragments from a Tenth-Hour Journal,"(1990)[24] Woodcock says,

> *From the first day of my working life at sixteen...I began to save money, calculating that at forty...I might have a basic income of two pounds a week, on which...I could live in the country and devote myself to writing. Travel then came second. Actually, by heeding the knock of opportunity, by taking calculated risks, I freed myself from nine-to-five servitude by twenty-eight, found the means to travel as well as to dedicate myself to writing...*[25]

Fetherling, in his Introduction to this work, notes that by then Woodcock had published fifty or so books. He also makes a salutary point, that his seemingly eclectic work (Woodcock's oeuvre) in fact has "unity and single mindedness." As Fetherling observes, "The common thread, simply, has been the way man-made institutions pose a threat to human dignity and freedom." [26] Woodcock was among those who believed, first and foremost, in the integrity of the individual.

Among other contributions on what might be called "travel subjects," Woodcock wrote on China, *Caves in the Desert* (1995); on Peru, *Incas and Other Men* (1959); on Asia, *Gods and Cities* (1966); on Tibet, *Into Tibet: the early British explorers* (1971); on Mexico, *To the City of the Dead* (1957) and *South Sea Journey* (1976).

When it comes to direct contributions to Canadian culture, a rough count reveals fifteen titles, including the well-known biography of *Gabriel Dumont: The Métis Chief and His Lost World* (1978)—a work still respected amongst Canada's Métis community—and his 1968 book *The Doukhobors* on which he collaborated with longtime friend Ivan Avakumovic. He also translated a vast work by Marcel Giraud, *The Métis in the Canadian West* (1985). At least ten more Woodcock titles focus on Canadian literature, including *The World of Canadian Writing: Interviews and Recollections* (1980), which appeared not long after his "liberation" from being editor of *Canadian Literature,* and from being a salaried university lecturer (for whom was created the unique retirement status of "lecturer emeritus"). His anthology, *The Anarchist Reader,* published just at "liberation" time (1977) was, he contends, "the last of my books to originate in England." [27]

What followed was *Peoples of the Coast* (1977),[28] an important contribution mingling history and ethnology, a subject which had immediately interested Woodcock from his first arrival in Victoria in 1949 when he "found the chaotic little museum, stuffed with strange and impressive artefacts, which at that time was crammed into a few basement rooms in the Legislative Building." [29] (An interesting sidelight here is that, at the very same moment, in the new and, so to speak, embryonic Art Gallery, worked Assia Wevill, wife of Canadian poet David Wevill, eventually to become a tragic figure in the saga of Sylvia Plath and Ted Hughes.)[30]

Both Peter Hughes and W.H. New write positively about Woodcock's eighteen-year editorship of *Canadian Literature,* which New sees as "instrumental both in encouraging informed critical commentary and in bringing critic and writer together to reflect, and to partake in, the Canadian social milieu." [31] As a small part of this scene in its last eight years or so, I can attest to this. As both critic and writer, I had a positive sense of the combination. My fifteen-year letter friendship with George was entirely beneficial for me; I liked working for him and he gave the opportunity to work on writers and themes that mattered to oneself. In writing full-length essays about

Irving Layton and Al Purdy, and intending to do others, I was attempting to immerse myself in Canadian writing. It was part of my re-education, and George was sympathetic to that. He was enthusiastic about the work I did for him, so I was happy to keep on doing it, the more so as he kept high standards while avoiding turning *Canadian Literature* into an academic journal. I want to elaborate here on one aspect of my collaboration with him, as otherwise his editorship, widely respected as it is, needs no endorsement from me.

Locally, the concept of Pacific Rim writing has come to the forefront recently, as witness the establishment of *Pacific Rim Review of Books*. Back in December 1970, I put to George the idea of making an anthology of Pacific Rim poets. He suggested I send a proposal to a Mr. Blicq at the newly emerging UBC press, but thought I should shift the concept a little sideways and propose an anthology of Commonwealth poets living in Canada. This was a project which came to nothing, but I enjoyed working on it and I think George did, too. On 23 January 1977, he wrote: "I've decided to bow out of *Canadian Literature* after 18 years...I shall be handing over to whoever the university chooses (and they haven't chosen yet) at the end of June...I like your idea of the anthology *The Other Poets in Canada*...Why don't you try it?" This is not the place to go into details, but George said, "I do feel it is an important and timely idea." We soon talked of collaboration and exchanged lists of names of immigrant poets, coming up with thirty or more, with the idea of presenting another "dimension" in Canadian poetry. The project eventually foundered when neither of us could interest a publisher, though in that respect George had a far stronger arm than I did. Both of us took it seriously, George at one point involving Robin Skelton in the discussions; Skelton, however, decided to do an issue of *Malahat Review* on "the West Coast Renaissance" (I suppose he did it; I don't recall.) This interesting correspondence on the anthology went on over two years and demonstrates well George's professionalism, literary energy and commitment.

I am impressed by what sense I have of George Woodcock's overall achievement as a professional man of letters. So far I have not had the pleasure of reading George Fetherling's biography, but I look forward to it. I was very touched when I read Donald Stephens' "Man as Pattern," a joint portrait of George and Inge Woodcock, chiefly in their home, recollected from the times Stephens went there to work on the quarterly paste-ups for *Canadian Literature*. In the fifteen years or so of my closest contact with George, I was engaged in helping to bring up a family of four children in Victoria, so my contact was almost entirely by letter; I was not able to establish closer encounters, such as meeting regularly "over a beer." I regret that. Then, of course, after George achieved his "liberation," and I was therefore no longer one of *his* contributors, we had less to write to each other about. In the mid-1980s I was involved with a group of UVic political scientists in publication of two books on B.C. politics, *The New Reality* (1984) and *After Bennett* (1986). George would have been a distinguished contributor to either of these, though the impulse behind them was essentially Marxist and might not have been a fit. However, he made some moves to contribute to *After Bennett* only to be put off by the project's "house rules."

Rather than dwell on that, I'll take refuge in Stephens' account of their last afternoon at McLeery Street, working on the paste-up, a ritual which had gone on for twenty years. Writing in 1978, Stephens says: "If today we no longer worry about whether we have a Canadian Literature, this is in large part because of George Woodcock, who gave us the pattern we needed to acknowledge our literature as a living presence." From the first, Stephens noticed the details of that working space, among them a largish, primitive terra cotta statue of a South American church.

The last afternoon "was much the same as all the other afternoons had been," Stephens writes. "For the first time in some years," he happened to mention the terra cotta church. "As I was leaving about 5:30...Inge said that Don should have the church, and should have it now, today. As I left the house clutching the church, I was inarticulate." He had his talisman, in an example of Woodcock's "selflessness" he had mentioned earlier. I envy Don Stephens the grace of such an exit. What I have are written recollections of working with and for a remarkable man, of many writing talents, a human amalgam of diffidence and magnanimity, not only an important facilitator at the "naissance" of Canadian literature, but in his own fashion a gift to that literature.

Notes:

1. "McSpaunday" refers to the 1930s Oxford poetry gang of Louis MacNiece, Stephen Spender, W. H. Auden and Cecil Day-Lewis.

2. George Woodcock, *Notes on Visitations: Poems 1936-75* (Toronto: Anansi, 1975).

3. George Woodcock, *Taking It to the Letter* (Dunvegan, ON: Quadrant Editions, 1981).

4. Charles Doyle, "The Occasions of Irving Layton," *Canadian Literature* 54 (Autumn 1972): 70-83.

5. Woodcock, *Taking It to the Letter*, 40-41.

6. Ibid.

7. George Woodcock, *Anarchism: A History of Libertarian Ideas and Movements* (Cleveland: World Publishing, 1962, reprinted 2004).

8. Peter Kropotkin, *The State* (London: Freedom Press, 1943).

9. George Woodcock, *The Basis of Communal Living* (London: Freedom Press, 1947).

10. George Woodcock, *The Writer and Politics* (London: Porcupine Press, 1948).

11. George Woodcock, *Pierre Joseph Proudhon* (London: Routledge & Kegan Paul, 1956).

12. George Woodcock, Introduction to Peter Kropotkin, *Evolution and Environment* (Montreal: Black Rose Books, 1995).

13. George Fetherling, *The Gentle Anarchist: A Life of George Woodcock* (Vancouver: Douglas & McIntyre, 2003).

14. George Woodcock, *Collected Poems* (Victoria: Sono Nis Press, 1983).

15. George Woodcock and Toni Onley, *The Walls of India* (Toronto: Lester & Orpen Dennys, 1985).

16. George Woodcock, *Mohandas Gandhi* (New York: Viking Press, 1971).

17. George Woodcock, *Faces of India: A Travel Narrative*, with photos by Ingeborg Woodcock (London: Faber and Faber, 1964).

18. George Woodcock, *The Greeks in India* (London: Faber and Faber, 1966).

19. George Woodcock, *Kerala: A Portrait of the Malabar Coast* (London: Faber and Faber, 1967).

20. George Woodcock, *Dry Wells of India: An Anthology Against Thirst* (Madeira Park, BC: Harbour Publishing, 1989).

21. Toni Onley, *Flying Colours* (Madeira Park, BC: Harbour Publishing, 2002.)

22. Ibid., 286.

23. Ibid., 295.

24. George Woodcock, "Fragments from a Tenth-Hour Journal," in *A George Woodcock Reader*, ed. Douglas Fetherling (Ottawa: Deneau & Greenberg, 1990).

25. Ibid.

26. Ibid.

27. George Woodcock, *Walking Through the Valley* (Toronto: ECW Press, 1994).

28. George Woodcock, *Peoples of the Coast: The Indians of the Pacific Northwest* (Edmonton: Hurtig, 1977).

29. Ibid.

30. See Yehuda Koren and Eilat Negev, *Lover of Unreason: Assia Wevill* (United Kingdom: Robson Books, 2005). After Plath's suicide, Wevill married Hughes. She later committed suicide in the same manner as Plath.

31. W.H. New, ed., *A Political Art: Essays and Images in Honour of George Woodcock* (Vancouver: University of British Columbia Press, 1978).

32. Ibid.

A Personal and Informal Introduction and Checklist

Regarding Some Larger Poetry Enterprises in Vancouver Primarily in the Earlier Part of the 1960s

Judith Copithorne

Some time ago I began making a list of poetry events that took place in Vancouver in the decade of the 1960s. The list does not purport to be complete; I woke up one morning and wrote some of it as it came to my mind. As an introduction to the chronological list and to try to make my intentions clear, I have included parts of these paragraphs that are entirely personal. They introduce my own emotional substance and explain why I wanted to make the list. The first part of the introduction partially describes some things that happened to me in the years from 1959 to 1963, when I had first come back to Vancouver. The second introductory part, which attempts to be fairly objective, comments on what I am trying to do with the list, and also upon a couple of larger poetry events in which I participated a little later in the sixties.

The third part of this paper, the chronology, attempts to be more objective and to follow tight guidelines but still is incomplete, especially when more consideration is properly given to poetry other than that now available in the English language. Hopefully there will soon be a more extensive and comprehensive study done of what I have begun to present here.

In writing this, my main wish is to indicate the breadth and variety of literary life in Vancouver proper in the 1960s, and I would like to thank all the many people who helped me gather information and edit this work. *Paper, Scissors, Stone,* a catalogue of some Vancouver literary publications written by Robert Bringhurst and published by the inimitable Bill Hoffer, was a useful resource.[1] The Vancouver Public Library was very helpful, as was the *BC Bookworld* Author Bank website.[2] I have used the Internet and have sometimes chosen one of several alternate dates that came from several different sources.

Looking back on that decade, I realize how exciting Vancouver seemed to me. The literary atmosphere was definitely lively. Many things seemed possible. I had come from Regina, Saskatchewan, and the size of the city of Vancouver was overwhelming to me, even though Vancouver was much smaller than it is now. Perhaps there is an optimum size for a city for certain sorts of interactions to occur. In those days, Vancouver was big enough to have a lively artistic scene, yet small enough for there to still be communication throughout many parts of it. There was a variety of bookstores and art galleries; there were art openings and poetry readings, which I had not experienced in Regina, where I had lived until 1958 when I made the move to Vancouver with my family.

One thing that tied my experiences together was the political aspect of my life. I had very little time or energy, but I did manage to go to a variety of political events and marches. When I did, I would also meet my literary friends there, which added another level to our experiences together. There were several intertwined aspects to the political activities that I found myself involved in. Without ranking them, these included the anti-war and peace movements, socialist activities, and feminism, which added a particular aspect to our activities.

Around 1961, I dropped out of university and worked at a number of jobs. A bit earlier than that, thanks to bill bissett's suggestion, I got to hear the unforgettable Kenneth Patchen accompanied by an awe-inspiring Al Neil. Then, I got to meet Fred and Eve Douglas and Curt

Lang, who would soon start the Radiant Bookstore—which would later become MacLeod's Books. A bit before that, I was able to visit the beautiful Kaye's Books on Robson Street; I went several times with bill bissett, who was good friends with the Kayes. There was also the People's Co-op Bookstore, which had moved to Pender Street and was run in those days by Binky Marks.

Roy Kiyooka and his family were from Regina; I had met John Newlove in Weyburn, Saskatchewan, where I had worked as a nurse's aid in the mental hospital. So although I was new to Vancouver, I did already know people here in the arts and literary community. Both Roy and John had moved here not long after I arrived with my family. Artists Brian Fisher (with whom I had gone through high school) and Claude Breeze (whom I had also known in Regina) had moved here not long after Roy did; he had been their professor at the Regina College Art School. I would meet all of them, mostly on Robson Street, at the library or (more often) at the Little Heidelberg Coffee House. I mention these people because their ideas, their friendliness, their quirks, and their activities inspired me.

During that time, I also got to visit San Francisco and spend time in City Lights Bookstore, which, it seems, many of the people mentioned here had also done. City Lights was one of the most exciting places I had visited at that point in my life.

The magazine *TISH* produced its first issue in 1961 and bill bissett produced the first issue of *blew ointment press* in 1963. These two magazines, each in their own way, had a serious impact on the future of Canadian writing. The ideas espoused and the people they published are still active in Canadian writing today.

Then the 1963 Poetry Conference was held at UBC and many famous poets spoke and read there. Sometimes referred to as the '63 Vancouver Poetry Conference, it attracted many people from Vancouver and elsewhere, including Charles Olson, Allen Ginsberg, Robert Creeley, Robert Duncan, Denise Levertov, Margaret Avison, and Philip Whalen. Many other people from Canada and the U.S.A. were there as part-time speakers and full-time participants. The principle organizer was Warren Tallman. Tapes of this, made by Fred Wah, are available online at the Slought Foundation.[3] More infor-mation on this can be found in "Writing in our Time" by P. Butling and S. Rudy.[4]

By this time I had moved to North Vancouver which had a very poor bus service, especially at night. I seldom went out to late events in the city, but luckily I had a chance to go to the amazing Sound Gallery, created by Gregg Simpson, Al Neil, Sam Perry, and others. I performed there one night; soon, more and more people performed there. Helen Goodwin, who had been a mentor to many young women through her dance classes and workshops at UBC, soon joined in the activities. She then went to New York on sabbatical and when she got back, she set up Motion Studio on Seymour Street. Information about these activities can be found through Gregg Simpson's web site.[5] Helen was the guardian angel of interdisciplinary art in Vancouver; she made a huge personal commitment in time, effort, money, and love to Motion Studio, as did the late Sam Perry.

Motion Studio lasted for less than a year, but a huge number of innovative activities took place there. Helen Goodwin, who was truly original, was an organizer along with the Sound Gallery's producers. She had always been interested in an expanded view of the arts and included poetry in her dances. She let poetry lead off into a variety of activities, with help from Sam Perry, Gregg Simpson, Al Neil and other remarkable artists, composers, electronics experts, and amazing innovators. At that time in the art world, the influence of pop art and conceptual art foregrounded the interactions of art and literature, while concrete and sound poetry were becoming better known in the literary world.

The year 1966 was, without doubt, the best and the worst of times. The war in Vietnam permeated everyone's mind; it broke through the usual barriers and filled the space around us with flames. Draft resisters arrived every day from the U.S.A. Meanwhile, there were activities and demonstrations, as well as the "Be-In" organized by Jamie Reid, that also included poetry. After that, the life of poetry in the city appeared to move in several different directions at once. I cannot report on them all, but I have tried to list the best known of the larger events.

One area that I am not able to report on fully enough is equivalent non-English speaking or non-European derived poetry events that might have taken place, or events that mainly involved poets whose primary heritage and interest was not Western European. Hopefully, that lack will be better addressed in the next approach to this material. I have listed the Steveston Haiku Society, which lasted an amazing fifty years considering the small size of the community. When Japanese-Canadians were sent to internment camps during the Second World War, the writing of haiku poetry became a very popular occupation. This is perhaps what the Steveston Haiku Society grew out of in 1952. This is the only group I have listed that did not primarily use the English language in their meetings, so far as I know. The Asian-Canadian Writers Workshop was formed sometime in the 1960s by the brilliant writer and powerful organizer, Jim Wong-Chu.

II.

It might be seen as ironic that in regard to such a subjective discipline as poetry, I have used objective criteria for choosing the events I have listed. For more than one-hundred years, it has been clear that the traditional forms of literary philosophy did not have a wide enough framework, field of possibility, or ideology to support much of what was being attended to in poetry. With this understood, there was then an open field or sphere of possibility available. Some people have chosen to be a part of one school, philosophy, or style, only to remain but part of it. For this list, I have chosen to make note of all speech or writing that called itself (or was called) "poetry," that had a larger, thoughtful audience within the parameters of Vancouver proper in the 1960s. By larger, I mean there was a sufficient number of people interested in it to ensure that the books or magazines publishing it were in demand and that the reading series or shows that featured it were consistently attended.

As for the question of Vancouver as the locale, this determination was as sufficient as any other geographical location and was not chosen in order to naively mythologize the locale for nostalgic or privileging reasons. I contend that if we are willing to look, we will see that "local" and "international" are intrinsically interrelated, with cycling energy and structural activities continuing much the way they do in the human body.

At the local level, the actions of people when aligned can be very productive. There was much of worth coming from the city. Poets, after all, are readers, carriers and forwarders of intellectual, physical and emotional information. The people in the city generated much inspiration, so that the poets of the city helped to produce the gestalt that made Vancouver so interesting. Therefore, this is a list of larger events that happened in the city that helped encourage this gestalt.

There were a number of poetry readings by exceptional and prominent poets each year at UBC, and many exciting poets visited UBC in the 1960s. In the last years of the 1950s and the first few years of the following decade, there were readings by Langston Hughes, Marianne Moore and Kenneth Patchen, as well as others. Leonard Cohen read at UBC at least twice during the 1960s, while M.C. Richards, Eli Mandel and Margaret Avison read there at least once; Margaret Atwood taught there for a year. Earle Birney taught at UBC from 1946 to 1965, and it was primarily through his efforts that the Creative Writing Department at UBC was created. His powerful, innovative and creative poetry and classes and his support and kindness inspired many younger poets and others.

Also, through the efforts and kindnesses of Warren and Ellen Tallman, a number of outstanding and boundary-breaking poets visited and read at UBC or sometimes in the city proper. Poets Allen Ginsberg, Robert Duncan, Michael McClure, Lew Welch, Basil Bunting, and Joanne Kyger visited several times in that decade. Robert Creeley taught at UBC for a year in 1962-63; Robin Blaser moved and took up residence in Vancouver in 1966 and started teaching at SFU. His charisma, erudition, unsurpassed poetry books, classes, and readings inspired and nourished many people in Vancouver and elsewhere. The decade was an exciting time at the universities; I hope that someone will soon be able to make a more comprehensive study of this. I only studied at UBC for two years at the beginning of the sixties, so my personal information of what happened after that is limited. There are others who can do a good job of writing about activities at the universities. Much information about events at the universities is already archived, while events in the city proper do not have that amount of documentation so this list serves this very particular purpose.

There have also been many important and communicative people, poets, teachers, and others in the city who have helped increase the level of our understanding, not all of whom I am able to mention due to constraints of time and space. As I have said, the emphasis here is entirely on city-level events. This may seem contradictory, but to my mind it deals with a level of the poetry community that helped poets interact and grow. Regretfully, there is much I had to leave out but I feel that the most important thing at this point for me is to give a small picture of one part of the life of poetry in this city at a particular point in time, when it felt to me to be inspired as a whole.

It was not easy for women poets in early-1960s Vancouver. Maxine Gadd has always been one of the very best poets around. Her work, her performances, her feminism, and her imagination continue to fascinate me. Pat Lowther was another great and politically dedicated writer who was supportive of women;[6] Beth Jankola and Anne McKay were each superb poets who offered me inspiration and friendship. There were other exceptional women, some of whom were writers and artists, and some who had quite different interests. I met and became familiar with the varied and brilliant work of Phyllis Webb, Dorothy Livesay, Myra MacFarlane, Marya Fiamengo, Gwen Hauser, Daphne Marlatt, Nellie McClung, and Skyrose Bruce. During this time women also came from outside the city: the inimitable Margaret Atwood and Diane di Prima, who read with her company of performers, the Floating Bear; both gave exceptional readings here.

Each of these women's writing had quite different qualities. The work of some has been, for excellent reasons, well remembered; that of others has been undeservedly almost forgotten, but their struggles with the complexities of society formed an important support web in those days—for many people, including me. Each of the women mentioned were strong and talented; they commented on and explored the travails of women in our society, and were usually serious supporters of feminist ideas. As such, they were also involved in the battles being fought to forward the social and economic equality and physical and intellectual freedom of everyone. Feminism has always been an important facet of this movement and is almost inextricably intertwined with it.

This introduction and the following list are impressionistic, personal and perhaps incomplete. I apologize for any mistakes and omissions, but it seemed important to create even a somewhat comprehensive (if not entirely complete) view of the amazing ferment that was happening in Vancouver at that time. The first few events on the list, which were held in the Greater Vancouver area, are mentioned because no comparable events existed in Vancouver proper at that time. All events, with two or three exceptions, were public events. That is, there was easy access to the events by any member of the public and they were, to some degree, publicized.

There are many types of accuracy. I hope this loose compilation will jog some memories and produce further aesthetic and emotional recollections and reconstructions by others. The light in the city on a good day was phenomenal, doubtless due to the presence of water on three sides, the presence of many vacant lots full of undergrowth, and the mountains along the north. The illuminating photographs of Fred Herzog and Fred Douglas would be a good place to start to recreate the gestalt of Vancouver in the sixties.

When I mention the community of writers, this is not to suggest that there were no battles. Writers have been known for their vitriolic speech habits, perhaps since writing began; but in the earlier part of the sixties, differences in style, subject, and ideology seemed to take a place behind cooperation and interest in the range of ideas available. Later in the sixties, this became less apparent to me, but this is very hard to quantify or elucidate. We definitely lived, and still live, in a class-ridden city, rife with sexism, racism, and small and vast crimes being committed in the name of free enterprise; but it is also a city of extraordinary beauty—geographic, artistic, and social.

The writers and artists I met at readings and galleries, I would also meet at demonstrations and meetings. The library was a hub of informal cultural activity. Of course, I was in my early twenties and new to the city, so my impressions are probably much more extreme than if I had been much older or used to the city. But it seemed as if the beauty, the ideas, and feelings around me were woven into an amazing concert, which helped to buoy up the sense of community I felt when I met various people.

Chronological Time-line:

1916-74	Vancouver Poetry Society.
1941-52-	*Contemporary Verse;* Alan Crawley, editor. North Vancouver (later, Victoria).
1951/52– 1999/2000	Steveston Haiku Society
1953-1994	Periwinkle Press; Takao Tanabe, publisher.
1956-1963	The Cellar Jazz Society. Several reading series, one well-known one organized by Barry Cramer.
1958-1973	Klanak Press; W. and A. McConnell, editors.
1959-1962	Poets for Peace. Readings and discussions run by Milton Acorn, Pat Lowther, and Roy Lowther.
1960-CONTINUING THROUGHOUT THE '60S	Vancouver Art Gallery Reading Series. Poetry has been intermittently part of the VAG programs until the present. (1960 series organized by Paul Phillips).
1960-1962	Blackspot Jazz Club poetry readings. Brian Belfont and bill bissett, organizers.

1961-1963   *Up the Tube with One I Open;* Chuck Carlson.

1961-1969   *TISH Magazine* (there are several eras of *TISH*);
             Fred Wah, Jamie Reid, George Bowering, Frank
             Davey, David Dawson, first editors. (To see the later
             groupings of editors see *Beyond TISH*, editor
             Douglas Barbour.) More recently, there are several
             sections related to *TISH* in *Writing in Our Time* by
             Pauline Butling and Susan Rudy.

1963-1965   Vanguard Books. Poetry reading series. Milton
             Acorn, principal organizer.

1963-1966   Vancouver School of Art. Poetry reading series. Roy
             Kiyooka, organizer.

1963-1968   *blew ointment press magazine;* bill bissett, editor. blew
             ointment press published an extensive list of
             contributors of a wide variety of ages, poetic interest,
             and other concerns which made it serve a strong
             communicative purpose in the cultural and other
             life of the city. Various concerts, again, demonstrates
             the interest in poetry during this time.

1964-1968   *Talon Magazine;* First published by committee. In
             1966, Dave Robinson, Jim Brown and Janie
             McElwyne became publishers.

1964-1966   Advance Mattress Reading series. Milton Acorn,
             principal organizer.

1964-1971   *Imago;* George Bowering, editor.

1965-1968   Very Stone (publishing house); Pat Lane, Seymour
             Mayne, bill bissett, and Jim Brown.

1965   Jack Spicer Poetry Lectures. Held at Warren and
             Ellen Tallman's house. For tapes of these lectures,
             go to Pennsound at http:www.writing.upenn.edu/
             pennsound/x/Spicer.html.

1966-Present Returning Press; Judith Copithorne, publisher.

1966-1970   Flye Press; David UU, publisher.

1966   Motion Studio. A large enterprise organized by

Helen Goodwin with much support from Sam Perry, Gregg Simpson, Al Neil, Gerry Walker, and many other people. Helen Goodwin had worked for many years at UBC and during that time, had run a weekly dance workshop each winter. The use of poetry was quite often incorporated into her sessions. There were at least two poetry reading series and several multimedia events including poetry, including many late night readings with the incomparably unique and enlivening bill bissett.

1967-1971 Intermedia. A multimedia organization with a large purview, following and effect. A large poetry contingent was involved from the beginning. Several poetry reading series, multiple multimedia explorations which included poetry, the Pythian Sistrum, the Poetry Band, book production, tours with multimedia performances that included much poetry, outreach workshops and readings, and other activities. For other information on Intermedia poetry events see Gregg Simpson's web site-<http://www.greggsimpson.com/Imedia.65_67 .htm> For further information on Intermedia, also see, among other documentation, the web site of Michael de Courcy <http:www.michaeldecourcey .com/intermedia/> and the thesis written on Intermedia by Gail Tuttle.

1967-Present Talonbooks; Jim Brown and Dave Robinson, first publishers. Now published by Karl Siegler.

1967 Mandan Ghetto Concrete Poetry Show. Brazilia '73 —international in scope. Principal organizer, D. UU, assisted by several others including G. Simpson.

1967-1969 *Pacific Nation Magazine*; Robin Blaser, editor.

1967-Present Alcuin Society Imprints.

1967-Present (in several incarnations) *The Georgia Straight*; 1st editors, Pierre Coupey, Milton Acorn and others. Considerable amount of poetry published in first issues and then intermittently for next several years. In its first couple of years, *The Georgia Straight* helped spread poetry throughout the city. The inclusion of poetry in such events as the "Be-Ins," the first couple of which were organized by Jamie Reid, along with various concerts, again shows the interest in and effects of poetry in the city.

1967-1978 *Iron*; Brian Fawcett, first editor. Brett Enemark, second editor.

1967-1972 Daylight Press; Lionel Kearns, publisher.

1968 -Present Asian Canadian Writers Workshop. Jim Wong-Chu, organizer.

1968-Present Sono Nis Press; J. Michael Yates, first principal editor and publisher.

1968-1971 *Beaver Cosmos Folio*; George Bowering, editor.

1968 *The Western Gate*; Al Birnie, editor. Pierre Coupey, art editor.

1968-70 *radiofreerainforest*; This magazine became a long-running radio show. Gerry Gilbert, editor.

1969-1973/4 Very Stone House in Transit; Pat Lane, editor.

1969-1981 Intermedia Press; Ed Varney and Henry Rappaport, publishers.

1969-1970 *Circular Causation* magazine; Scott Lawrence and George Heyman, editors.

1969-1970 (OR TO THE PRESENT IN SEVERAL INCARNATIONS) *Georgia Straight Writing Supplement* (this became Vancouver Community Press, which in turn became New Star Books in 1974 and is still in existence); Rolf Maurer, New Star Books publisher since 1979.

1970-1974 Vancouver Community Press; Dennis Wheeler,

	Stan Persky, and Scott Watson, first editors and publishers.
1970-1971	See Site Photography Workshop, Poetry Reading Series. Trudy Rubenfeld, organizer.
1970-1978	*Blackfish* magazine and Press; Brian Brett and Alan Safarik, editors.
1970-Present	The Poem Company; Ed Varney, H. Rappaport, J. MacDonald, publishers.
1970-?	Air Press; Bertrand Lachance, publisher.
1970-2002	Press Gang Publishers; Feminist publishing collective.

Notes:

1. Robert Bringhurst, *Ocean/Paper/Stone* (Vancouver: William Hoffer, 1984).

2. http://www.abcbookworld.com/

3. http://slought.org/series/Vancouver+1963+Discussions/

4. Pauline Butling and Susan Rudy, *Writing in Our Time: Canada's Radical Poetries in English* (1957-2003) (Waterloo, ON: Wilfed Laurier University Press, 2005).

5. http://www.greggsimpson.com/

6. In late September 1975, shortly after her breakthrough as a poet in 1974 with *Milk Stone* and the submission of her work *Final Instructions*, Lowther disappeared. Three weeks later, her body was found in a creek near Squamish, British Columbia. Her second husband Roy Lowther, whom she had married in 1963, was convicted of the murder in June 1977. He died in prison in 1985. In 1980 the League of Canadian Poets established the Pat Lowther Award, a prize awarded annually to a book of poetry by a Canadian woman.

The Production of Meaning:
THE RADICAL IMPULSE IN POETRY AND POETICS, VANCOUVER, 1969-1975

MICHAEL BARNHOLDEN

Which explains poetry.   Distances
Impossible to be measured or walked
over. A band of faggots (fasces)
cannot be built into a log-cabin in
which all Western Civilization can
cower.   And look at stars, and books, and
Distance, Einstein said, goes around
in circles. This
Is the opposite of a party or a social gathering.
It does not give much distance to go on.
As
In the beaches of California

It does not give me much to go on.
The tidal swell
Particle and wave
Wave and particle
Distances
                   —Charles Olson ("The Distances" from *The Distances*)

Love knows no distance, no place
     is that far away or heat changes
into signals, and control
                    —Jack Spicer ("Love Poems" from *Language*)

Something was happening in the world of Vancouver poetry. Politics had entered in a big way. In 1970, up on Burnaby Mountain at Simon Fraser University, there were two ever-present ghosts. The low ghost, Jack Spicer, who had died in August of 1965 just after the Berkeley Conference and just before moving to Vancouver to teach Linguistics at Simon Fraser, was present in print and spirit. The big man on campus, however, was Charles Olson who had died in January of that year. In real flesh and blood was Robin Blaser, the connective tissue between the two, who was present at both their deaths. We cannot forget Warren and Ellen Tallman across town at the UBC English department. Poetry was everywhere, not just on the campus but also in the streets, mainly in the *Georgia Straight*. A year's subscription to the underground newspaper was sweetened with a copy of Robert Creeley's *Pieces*. There was journalism by poets as well as articles on poetry supplied by Stan Persky, George Stanley, Maria Hindmarch, Robin Blaser; Allen Ginsberg was everywhere. The Free John Sinclair campaign, replete with Sinclair's latest poetry from jail where he'd been sentenced to twenty-five years for possession of two joints of marijuana, was a highlight of almost every issue. Al Neil's autobiographical novel *Slammer* was serialized that summer. George Bowering wrote a weekly sports column under the name Erich Blackhead, a dig at the *Vancouver Sun*'s Eric Whitehead. Brad Robinson contributed under the name Engledink Birdhumper. Most important, however, was the *Georgia Straight Writing Supplement*, a twenty-or-more-page supplement edited by Stan Persky and Dennis Wheeler. About every three months, 25,000 copies of a literary magazine were sold with the regular weekly issue of the *Georgia Straight* on the streets of Vancouver for twenty-five cents. The *Writing Supplement* published everyone from Jack Spicer to Colin Stuart.

II. BACKSTORY

According to Earle Birney, poetry in Vancouver in the 1950s was pretty much a one-man show and he was it.[1] By 1959, Birney had founded

Canada's first Creative Writing Department at the University of British Columbia. One of the co-founders was Warren Tallman,[2] a professor in the English department with close ties through his wife Ellen (herself a part-time undergraduate English instructor), to the San Francisco and Berkeley poetry scenes. Ellen knew Robert Duncan, Jack Spicer, and Robin Blaser from University of California-Berkeley school days and introduced her new husband to these and other old friends. She and Warren met in Seattle where she went to graduate school and Warren took his doctorate. UBC was his first job and he used his position to introduce the poets and poetics of *The New American Poetry*[3] to a thirsty audience of would-be writers such as George Bowering, Frank Davey, Jamie Reid, David Dawson, Fred Wah, Maxine Gadd, Maria Hindmarch, Daphne Marlatt, Robert Hogg, Dan McLeod, Lionel Kearns and others. Duncan first came to visit in 1959, and by the early 1960s he had suggested the anagram for *TISH*, a poetry newsletter. By 1963 and the Vancouver Poetry Conference, which drew Creeley (Bowering's thesis advisor), Spicer, Olson, Ginsberg, etc., the poets of the New American Poetry were frequent visitors to Vancouver, and their poetics studied and embraced. Of note here is a reading by Spicer, Blaser, and Persky at the New Design Gallery run by Abraham Rogatnik and Alvin Balkind,[4] and the Tallman's living room where Fred Wah recorded Spicer's three Vancouver Lectures.[5]

The effect on Vancouver Poetry was both explosive and reactive, but it is worth following these two streams (Olson and Spicer) even further back in order to rough out the confluence of poetry and politics, then forward to Vancouver in the 1970s. Post-WWII America must have been an exciting place with a whole new class of men attending college and university on the G.I. bill, but there was another darker side to that demobilization. That is the time-controlled release of approximately twelve-thousand Conscientious Objectors (COs) from prison camps throughout the continental U.S.[6] The final few were released in 1952, ostensibly for fear of the bad optics of COs somehow displacing returning war vets. On their return to civilian life, the army could no longer serve as the focal point of the struggle of anarchists, which was one of the political philosophies open to war resistors, against the state. Many COs were writers, and one camp at Waldport, Oregon eventually produced three magazines, *Untide, The Illiterati* and *Compass* as well as Untide Press, which published books by William Everson (Brother Antoninus) and Kenneth Patchen, among others. Many COs were forced to turn from activism to the arts by the tenure of the times as evinced by the post-war phenomenon of McCarthyism and "loyalty oaths." On the West Coast, San Francisco became a centre dedicated to, as Kenneth Rexroth puts it, "re-evaluate and refound the movement,"[7] mainly on anarcho-syndicalist lines as, for example, the Anarchist Circle and the Libertarian Circle, which both sponsored poetry readings. According to Louis Cabri in his essay on Earle Birney, Duncan and Spicer were attending Libertarian Circle meetings in the fifties. Although, as Rexroth points out in his interview in *San Francisco Beat,* with a measure of hindsight the need to organize was dicing out, "It was no longer necessary to educate somebody to make an anarchist poet out of him. He had a milieu in which he could naturally become such a thing."[8]

How any of this materially affected the work of Jack Spicer is fairly easy to see in his relationship to publishing both his own work and *J,* the magazine he edited. In both endeavours Spicer resisted commodification by refusing copyright and restricting distribution mainly to San Francisco. His main contribution however was the "serial poem" and writing by "book." As we shall see, both of these impulses are radical. This same impulse was later made manifest in the magazine *Pacific Nation,* edited by Robin Blaser.

As for Olson, the radicalism in his work was his insistence on projective or open verse. When opposed to closed writing, it could be seen as radical and the insistent equation of projective verse with free speech. There is Ed Sanders' half-serious notion to propose Olson as a candidate for president of the United States, Olson' s outspoken support for Timothy Leary and his LSD experiments, and "Olson is freedom of speech."[9] According to Tom Clark, some of this was Olson's desperate attempt to get with it. The program was "Rock 'n'

Roll, Dope and fucking in the streets"—the motto of the White Panther Party, co-founded by John Sinclair, an attendee at the 1965 Berkeley Conference.

One key issue is that of organization or community, which as we have seen in San Francisco was organized basically on anarcho-syndicalist lines (i.e. non-hierarchical), although some may argue that there were de-facto leaders even if there were no positions or formal titles. This in many respects is the key area in this examination of Vancouver poetics of the late sixties and early seventies. I want to look at the first few years of the *Georgia Straight* and more specifically the *Georgia Straight Writing Supplement* and its morph into first the Vancouver Community Press and then New Star Books.

III. GEORGIA STRAIGHT WRITING SUPPLEMENT & VANCOUVER COMMUNITY PRESS

The first issue, Volume I, Number I, *Georgia Straight*, May 5-18, 1967, was published by a group that included poets Dan McLeod, also an editor of *TISH*, Pierre Coupey, Milton Acorn, Stan Persky, Gerry Gilbert, Peter Hlookoff, Rick Kitaeff and others, in response to a "campaign against youth culture mounted" by Vancouver's two daily newspapers the *Sun* and the *Province*.[10] According to Jamie Reid, one of the original editors of *TISH*, he, Reid, may or may not have given McLeod permission to sell the early *TISH* archives, which may or may not have actually happened, and to use the money to fund the *Georgia Straight*.[11] So in this one paragraph we can connect all three eras of *TISH* with the *Georgia Straight*.

Jamie Reid, Fred Wah, George Bowering, Frank Davey and David Dawson started the poetry newsletter in September of 1961 at UBC after discussions with Robert Duncan in Warren and Ellen Tallman's living room, and worked together from issues 1 through 19. Dan McLeod and Daphne Marlatt were among the editors of issues 20-40. Of note is that Dan McLeod carried on a correspondence with

Charles Olson from shortly after the Vancouver Poetry Conference in 1963 until Olson's death from cancer in January 1970. Olson appointed McLeod environmental editor of the *Niagara Frontier Review*.

If we can believe this quote, Stan Persky moved to Vancouver in 1966 for the express purpose of taking over *TISH* 10: "My secret plot was to capture control of *TISH*." [12] Persky and Dennis Wheeler edited *TISH* 41 to the final double issue of 44-45 in the spring of 1969.

It may be worthwhile to point out that Spicer's last book, *Book of Magazine Verse*, which contained "Seven Poems for the Vancouver Festival," also contained "Three Poems for *TISH*," which were eventually published in *TISH*. The Vancouver Festival poem begins "Start with a baseball diamond high," which just might be the most important poem in Vancouver poetry. [13]

Also worth noting is Persky's mention of an issue of *TISH* that Persky was supposed to publish in San Francisco in 1965 made of poems from young poets that Spicer had found while in Vancouver, and Spicer's three poems for *TISH*. Spicer was supposed to send down the material and Persky was supposed to mimeograph it and return it to Spicer in Vancouver. Persky claims he could only return to being engaged as a writer after his break up with Blaser in May 1968. So the last 4 issues of *TISH* were done in the year between May of '68 and '69. [14]

The *Georgia Straight Writing Supplement #1* came out in the October 29, 1969 issue of the *Georgia Straight*. It featured "Sea Stories" by Maria Hindmarch, Beaver (Indian) tales collected by Robin Ridington, short stories by Dennis Wheeler and Mark Cacchioni, poem/letters on jail deaths by Neap Hoover and Stan Persky, a chapter from *The Way it Spozed to Be* by Jim Herndon, a chunk of an autobiographical thing by George Stanley, a chapter from Fritz Perls' *In and Out of the Garbage Pail*, and poems by Denise Levertov. [15] The GSWS comes from an understanding on Persky's part, driven by Warren Tallman's insistence, that Persky:

> *... Pay attention, and take seriously the writers who are the*

*writers of this place that we are no longer in a bohemian
situation where the only circumstance for the writer is to
have a literary magazine which reaches a small coterie of
readers, consisting of other poets & your aunt in Saskatoon
... Clearly we're living in a political cultural situation that's
changed drastically, & the underground newspaper has a lot
to do with that.*[16]

By issue two (January 28-February 4, 1970) the writer's political
relation to the community is made clear in an editorial signed by
Persky and Wheeler.

What We're Up To

Simply, to publish writing.

*As a literary problem, we think that this form ends the bind
of the "little magazine" with its esoteric coterie of writers
and readers.*

*As a political problem we want to serve a notion like: the
mind of the community, or the imagination of the place,
Vancouver. So instead of a couple of hundred people getting
to see what's being written, it goes directly to a large
audience in the city. It also returns the writer to the people
instead of him being exclusively in a world of private poetic
reputations.*

*Writing and capitalism: rather than $1-$3 litter-chur
mags you get the writing in your regular 25-cent newspaper.
(Not a new idea by the way. Done by reputable 19th century
papers all the time).*

*The general possibility of this idea is that other
underground papers in other cities will do likewise—and
there could be the same kind of national exchange as now
exists for news. So each paper would have the double
advantage of being able to encourage local writing in their
place and yet to print stuff from other places. This idea also*

attacks old ideas of copyright—which are useful as
protection against avaricious businessmen—but all too often
merely serve to remove writing from the public.[17]

The second issue was devoted to work by Jack Spicer, and it
included *A Book of Music; Admonitions;* "After words," a very early, very
partial version of "The Practice of Outside," by Robin Blaser; "Thus
Jack Spicer Refuted Child Psychology" by Jim Herndon; and ends with
"For Downbeat 4," which is a note to Dennis Wheeler ending:

> British Columbia
> Will not become a victim to Western Imperialism
> if you don't let it. All those western
> roads. Few of them
> Northern.[18]

White Rabbit had published both *A Book of Music* and *Book of
Magazine Verse,* but it was the first publication of *Admonitions,* a very
explicit enactment of the editorial policy enjoined by Persky and
Wheeler. It is useful to note that the editorial also mentions *You,* an
autobiographical book by George Stanley "coming out next year." It
was not published until 1974, and then by New Star Books, fore-
shadowing the coming clash with capital.

> *Now that we have a lot of money to run this writing*
> *supplement for a period of about a year, we'll really see if it*
> *becomes daring and immediate, if it really takes up the work*
> *of writers in this place & places that have to do with this*
> *place in an immediate way. Or if it just becomes a*
> *formalized showcase where we end up publishing our real*
> *writing in these mimeographed journals.*[19]

Canada Council Money? Corporate or private donor? *Georgia Straight*
money? No matter, by the end of the first year's six issues the issue of
the private ownership of the *Georgia Straight* came up again. Pierre
Coupey had removed himself from the original group shortly after

publication started,[20] for reasons having to do with concentration of ownership. By the end of 1970, a group variously referred to as a collective or co-operative seized control of the offices of the *Georgia Straight* when editor/publisher/owner Dan McLeod had refused to cede ownership and thus control to the group, arguing that the paper and the community it served was more important than the staff, and that sole proprietorship was the only way the paper and thus a free press could survive. The name of the company that publishes the *Georgia Straight* to this day is The Vancouver Free Press Publishing Corporation. Using the courts to press his case, the dissidents were turfed and not allowed further use of the Georgia Grape sobriquet, thus the short history of the *Grape* and its succession of challengers to the *Straight*.

The collective that ran the *Grape*, which became the *Western Organizer* and finally the *Western Voice*, came out of *The Women's Liberated Georgia Straight* and the VLF-run *Yellow Journal*, later the *Terminal City Express*, were a determinedly antiauthoritarian bunch but hardly hardcore Marxists or Maoists. Something like "Anarcho-Commies" might be the best label.

Sometime after the last *Georgia Straight Writing Supplement* was published in late 1970, Persky and the York Street Commune embarked on an ambitious yet allied publishing venture. The proposal, as Persky outlined it, was to mimeograph books by the twenty to thirty people who fit the definition of "Vancouver Writers." The books were mimeographed 8.5 x 11, stapled, and bound to resemble perfect binding. Members, who included Maria Hindmarch, Stan Persky, Lanny Beckman, and Cliff Andstein, did the work in the basement of the York Street West Commune.[21]

IV. PUBLICATIONS

As reconstructed from records held by New Star Books. None of the books actually contain an ISBN Number; these appear to have been applied at a later date. New Star ISBN Prefix is 0-919888.

8.5 x 11 mimeo format:

1) 19-4 *Should Stick to Carrying Water*. Scott Lawrence [vcp GSWS Vancouver Series #11; any portion of this book may be reproduced without permission in Cuba or China. 400 copies printed May 1971 at York Street Commune.]

2) 17-8 *Money.* Gerry Gilbert [vcp GSWS Vancouver Series #2 400 copies published June 1971 at York Street Commune]

3) 23-2 *The Day*. Stan Persky, 1971 (reviewed by Tallman in *B.C. Monthly*).

4) 16-x *Friends.* Brian Fawcett, 1971. *Georgia Straight Writing Supplement*, Vancouver Series #4. 400 copies printed July 1971 at York Street Commune.

5) 18-6 *Target Practice*. Jorj Heyman, 1971. GSWS, Vancouver Series #5. Reproduce freely if no profit sought. 400 copies printed at York Street Commune.

6) 20-8 *Rings.* Daphne Marlatt 1971 [VPL notation: Toronto, York St Commune].

At this point printing becomes more complicated: although still mimeos, the next two are sent out to be bound. These are 5.5 x 8.5 standard paperback:

7) *Autobiology.* George Bowering, 1972 [vcp: writing series #7]

8) 12-7 *Heart's tide.* Judith Copithorne, 1972 [vcp: writing series #8. 500 copies printed at York Street Commune Spring 1972.]

A Return to 8.5 x 11 mimeo.

9) 52-6 *Tree* Fred Wah 1972 [vcp: writing series No. 9. 400 copies printed at the Root Cellar Press, Argenta, B.C. for the VCP.]

10) 11-9 Scientific Works, etc. fiction pomes dwgs. Chuck Carlson, 1972 [vcp: Vancouver Series #10. 500 copies printed by Kite Press. Title page subtitle: an omnibus of drawings, fictions, pomes & found objects.]

11) 13-5 *The City in Her Eyes* – David Cull, 1972 [vcp: writing series #11]

12) 14-3 *L'An Trentiesme* – Frank Davey, 1972

[*These last two appear to be commercially printed*]

13) 10-0 *Ten Years In The Making* – David Bromige, 1973 [vcp writing series 13] (mentions Vancouver Poetry Commune in dedication).

14) 21-6 *West Coast Lokas* – Al Neil, 1972 [vcp (in cooperation with the Vancouver Art Gallery).] Dennis Wheeler preface, as western liaison, the National Gallery of Canada. Introduction by Christos Dikeakos. Design by D. Wheeler, as catalogue for VAG exhibition West Coast Lokas, March 14-April 30 1972. Co-ordinated by Christos Dikeakos. Unnumbered.

V. Conclusion

Clearly property relations had been overturned. It was not clear who owned what has effectively become Vancouver Community Press. All connections to the *Georgia Straight* had been severed. Meanwhile down the street at York Street East, a series of writers meetings were taking place where a concept called "totalization" was being developed and used. One of the participants, Brian Fawcett, described it as a method for combining "the everyday with what is going on in the world." That is how it was described twenty years later. At the time it was a way of dealing with the personal and the political. The books Fawcett pointed to are *Autobiology*, by George Bowering; *The Day*, by Stan Persky; and *You*, by George Stanley, which was one of the first publications of New Star Books in 1974.

Another and related development was the use of something referred to as the Havana Copyright Convention. This is in no way related to the actual Havana Copyright Convention of 1928. This added nothing to the Berne Copyright Convention, the basis of the Universal Copyright Convention. The UCC governs copyright in the West to the present. The Havana Copyright Convention is based on a quote from Fidel Castro to the effect that useful information is public property. This was used by Fawcett and Persky in *Iron* magazine and NMFG (contemporary, short-run mimeographed limited distribution magazines) to reprint writing they wanted, and to copyright the contents of the magazine.

Property relations are being challenged on three levels:

1. Ownership of the press;

2. Copyright;

3. The writing itself via the serial poem and totalization.

Radical precepts all, embodying radical critiques of capital.

Notes

1. Louis Cabri, "Toward a Trotskyist Poetics?: The Example of Earle Birney," (unpublished essay).

2. Warren Tallman, *In the Midst: Writings 1962-1992* (Vancouver: TalonBooks, 1992).

3. Donald Allen, ed., *The New American Poetry 1945-1946* (New York: Grove Press, 1960).

4. Jack Spicer, *The House that Jack Built: The Collected Lectures of Jack Spicer*, ed. Peter Gizzi (Middelton, CT: Wesleyan/New England, 1998).

5. Ibid.

6. Louis Cabri, "Rebus Effort Remove Government: Jackson Mac Low, Why/Resistance, Anarcho Pacifism," *Crayon* 1, New York: (undated).

7. David Meltzer, *San Francisco Beat: Talking with the Poets* (San Francisco: City Lights Books, 2001).

8. Ibid.

9. Tom Clark, *Charles Olson: the Allegory of a Poet's Life* (Berkeley: North Atlantic Books, 2000).

10. Terry Glavin, ed., *The Georgia Straight: What the Hell Happened* (Vancouver: Douglas & McIntyre, 1997).

11. Jamie Reid, in conversation with the author, April 2001 (the first *TISH* editorial period, 1-19, is generally conceded to be the most important era of the poetry newsletter).

12. Stan Persky, interview with Brad Robinson, "The Oral Literary History of Vancouver," *Beaver Kosmos Folio* #5, edited and published by George Bowering, 1972.

13. Jack Spicer, "The Practice of Outside" in *The Collected Books of Jack Spicer*, ed. Robin Blaser (Los Angeles: Black Sparrow Press, 1975).

14. Stan Persky, interview with Brad Robinson, "The Oral Literary History of Vancouver."

15. *Georgia Straight* Writing Supplement 1, 1970 (circulation approx. 20,000 or 25,000).

16. Tallman, *In the Midst.*

17. *Georgia Straight* Writing Supplement 2, 1970 (circulation approx. 20,000 or 25,000).

18. Jack Spicer, *Book of Magazine Verse* (San Francisco: White Rabbit, 1966.)

19. Stan Persky, interview with Brad Robinson, "The Oral Literary History of Vancouver."

20. Ron Verzuh, *The Underground Times: Canada's flower-child revolutionaries* (Toronto: Deneau, 1989).

21. Stan Persky, interview with Brad Robinson, "The Oral Literary History of Vancouver."

22. Brian Fawcett, "Five Small Presses and How They Started," *Books in Canada*, 1991. [AO: unable to find which issue]

23. E-mail correspondence with the author, 2001. Fawcett attributes the quote to Annie Siegel, right fielder and pitcher for the East End Punks in the Kozmic baseball league, circa 1971-1973.

Facing the Environmental Crisis with Contemplative Attention:

THE ECOPOETICS OF DON MCKAY, TIM LILBURN, AND RUSSELL THORNTON

SUSAN MCCASLIN

Though humans have evolved as creatures of language, filtering the world through a human lens of consciousness based on concepts and words has too often frustrated our desire for union with the other-than-human world. Canadian poet P.K. Page's frequently anthologized poem "Cook's Mountains" explores the Enlightenment's colonization of wilderness and the shadow side of humans' gift of language in a way that foreshadows the concerns of more recent Canadian writers. Page's deft ironies about the human "glazing gaze," which substitutes sign for reality, suggest that words can act as both barricades and conduits to the natural world. Here Page writes of Captain James Cook's naming of the Glass House Mountains:

> By naming them he made them.
> They were there before he came
> but they were not the same.
> It was his gaze
> that glazed each one...

And instantly they altered to become
the sum of shape and name...'

This issue of how our epistemological-linguistic positioning has
made our species what cultural anthropologist Thomas Berry calls
"autistic" in relation to the natural world has been addressed more
recently by three contemporary Canadian poets who have written
profoundly about the human relationship to the land: Don McKay, Tim
Lilburn, and Russell Thornton.² These poets' works offer a means of
rapprochement and reparation to the earth through what Lilburn calls
"contemplative attention" and McKay calls "poetic attention." Held in
the field of the poem, this kind of poetic participation makes possible
the reclamation of language as a means of communion with the earth.
The kind of contemplative attention embodied in the nature poetry
these poets offer has the capacity to transform and amend both the
poet's and their readers' exile from the natural world. If individual
transformation can be a vital tipping point towards collective
transformation, then this kind of poetic attention matters. While
McKay and Lilburn resist what they see as the ills of Romantic
humanism in addressing the breach, Thornton brings forward a new
Romanticism that is not merely anthropomorphic but includes human
consciousness as an expression of the ever-evolving self-awareness of
the earth.

All three of these poets identify "nature" not simply as the
environment or physical world which surrounds us, but as that which
rises up as the central "dream of the earth," to borrow a phrase from
writer-ecologist Thomas Berry, of which humans are finite expressions.
They challenge a merely anthropocentric worldview and move to shift
the exploitive, patriarchal gaze into what McKay calls the non-grasping,
non-controlling "geopoetic" or earth-centred imagination. Rather than
asking how we imagine the earth, geopoetics asks how the earth might
imagine us. Their work needs to be located within a broader
conversation about "deep ecology," a term derived from Norwegian eco-
philosopher Arne Naess in the 1960s to describe the intuition that

every being and life form has intrinsic worth as part of an organic, interconnected whole. They write in the wake of earlier North American nature writers such as John Muir, Thomas Berry, Wendell Berry, Gary Snyder, Aldo Leopold, and Annie Dillard; their work is complemented by the more overtly political writings of fellow Canadians Di Brandt, Dionne Brand, and others who lament and rage against an adversarial human posture responsible to a large extent for our ongoing global environmental crisis.[3]

Contemplative attention for these writers is nothing like the hoarding gaze of colonialism, but its antidote. According to Lilburn, such attention is the essential core of poetry, a self-emptying and "permeability before astonishing otherness."[4] It is a seeing that entails a relinquishment of appropriative knowing and involves instead an ontological "unknowing," or simple being with nature without desire to own, manipulate, or possess. Such a sense of awe before the mystery of nature becomes an initiatory experience compelling interior journeying, a descent, tears, divine drunkenness, and a breaking up of language and the socially constructed self as we have known it.

McKay and Thornton have written extensively about the B.C. landscape, while Lilburn, who moved to the West Coast more recently, has until now focused primarily on the prairies of his native Saskatchewan. His latest volume, *Orphic Politics,* uses disease as a metaphor for an out-of-kilter relation with the body, the body politic, and the body of the world, summoning ancient Hermetic theurgy (magical healing practices) to alchemize destructive modes of seeing and knowing. Though none of these poets is of a single region, all, including Page herself, celebrate the minutiae of place. McKay and Lilburn, along with Robert Bringhurst and Jan Zwicky, form a "school" of sorts, since much of their work has issued from an ongoing conversation about, in Lilburn's words, "How to be here": how to be at home in the earth from which history and culture have alienated us. Thornton's more Romantic and visionary approach serves as a counterbalance and complement to the work of this more rigorously philosophical group with their close academic, interpersonal and literary associations.

Though Thornton is an independent, not having emerged from any particular school, all these poets are philosophical in the deepest sense of the word—"lovers of wisdom." Collectively, their bodies of work access a field of integral being that includes but transcends mere cognitive knowing. Each approaches the natural world through a variety of traditions and perspectives, including the shamanic, mythic, Platonic, Medieval, scientific, Romantic, and postmodernist.

II. McKAY'S GEOPOETICS

Don McKay is a field naturalist with a contemplative loving gaze, a long-looking and longing look that seeks out the sacred in-between of our subjectivity and the arresting reality of what we call the natural world. His poems, deeply respectful of the specificity of things in their individual variations, honour both the interiority of the perceiver and the specificity or unrepeatable "thusness" of nature in process. He brings a field naturalist's exactness of observation to his poems, getting the plumage and movements of the birds right, and not lifting off too quickly into his own emotional responses. For instance, in "Close-up On a Sharp-Skinned Hawk," he urges: "Concentrate upon her attributes: the accipiter's short / rounded wings, streaked breast, talons fine / and slender as the x-ray of a baby's hand."[5]

McKay, moving from this desire to attend to the specificities of the planet in his recent essay "Ediacaran and Anthropocene: poetry as a reader of deep time," borrows the term "geopoetics" from geologist Harry Hess and applies it to the sort of poetry he writes. Hess was a creative scientist who coined the term to describe his imaginative speculations about plate tectonics before his theory became accepted by other scientists in the 1960s.[6] McKay's effort is to reunite science and poetry by placing human presence and language back within the order of wild things, the vastness and immensity of the geological ages:

On the one hand, we lose our special status as Master Species; on the other, we become members of deep time, along with trilobites and Ediacaran period organisms. We gain the gift of de-familiarization, becoming other to ourselves, one expression of the ever-evolving planet. Inhabiting deep time imaginatively, we give up mastery and gain mutuality.[7]

His work challenges the notion that "man is the measure of all things" by setting our humanistic endeavours within the context of "deep time," the memory of the earth. Therefore, he turns to science in its older sense as another kind of "deep knowing" before it was separated from mystical awareness and the felt sense of humans as late-coming expressions of a much larger mystery.

III. An Expanded Definition of Wilderness

McKay's poems and prose not only locate the human within the context of an ages-long process of evolution, but also greatly expand the usual definition of wilderness. In *Vis a Vis: Fieldnotes on Poetry and Wilderness*, he writes: "By wilderness I want to mean, not just a set of endangered spaces, but the capacity of all things to elude the mind's appropriations."[8] Humans, as well as what we normally think of as "inanimate" material things, embody wildness at their core. Therefore, metaphor (language that makes "wild" interconnections between ourselves and the world) can become a way back into the wild. Poetry works, McKay notes, to

Introduce otherness, or wilderness, into consciousness without insisting that it be turned wholly into knowledge, into what we know, what we own. Within poetic attention, we might say, what we behold is always "alien and previous," whether it's an exceptional fossil or an "ordinary" rock or chickadee. In poetry there is no "been there, done that"; everything is wilderness.[9]

So, for McKay, poetic attention makes all things wild and new.

IV. McKay as Apophatic Poet

McKay, along with Lilburn, is what Lilburn calls an "apophatic" poet. Lilburn draws this Greek term from mystical theology of the early Christian centuries that follows the "via negativa," or path of negation of names, or "unknowing," as it complements and forms a base for the "via activa," or way of affirmation of images and ideas for the divine. That is, these poets are intensely aware of the limits of language to contain the divine, and by extension, the numinosity of nature within the ciphers of language. In a recent preface to the anthology *Open Wide a Wilderness: Canadian Nature Poems*, McKay borrows the term "inappellable" from earlier Canadian poet F.R. Scott to talk about how language hovers around the peripheries of the ineffable. To use words without labelling or fixing is, in McKay's words, "a deliberate chastening of poetic hubris," that tendency of language to grow too big for its boots and consume what it signifies... The inappellable "comes on its own and is not to be 'called' to human use..."[10] Contemplative nature poetry for McKay, then, is apophatic because it

> Uses our foremost technological tool, the ur-tool that is language, against itself, against its tendency to be the supreme analytic and organizing instrument. In poetry, language is always a singer as well as a thinker; a lover as well as an engineer. It discovers and delights in its own physical being, as though it were an otter or a raven rather than simply the vice president in charge of making sense."[11]

This recognition forces the human urge to peer into nature back on the poetic resources of metaphor, symbol, oxymoron, and paradox, since these connect, suggest, and point rather than merely describe.

V. Responsive Singing

In light of McKay's sense of the limits of language, what remains for the poet to do, so small, insignificant and temporally bound as she is? One answer that runs as a thread through his work is "praise." His lyrics about "the songs for the songs of" various birds and creatures punctuate his collections with lyricism and provide a contrapuntal music rather than facile analysis or imitation.[12] He writes:

> A mystic who is not a poet can answer the inappellable with silence, but a poet is in the paradoxical, unenviable position of simultaneously recognizing that it can't be said and saying something... [L]anguage is not finally adequate to experience and yet is the medium which we—the linguistic animals—must use. What to do? The poem's own soundplay holds the clue: "we must answer in chime, a term suggesting both rhymed resonance and one that harmonizes compatibly with the appeal."[13]

McKay's answer is to answer music with music in an act of responsive singing. In addition, his ironical flights and wry wit ground the quirky and playful human music within the context of the tumultuous tablature of earth-sound.

VI. McKay as Anti-Romantic?

McKay insists that geopoetry, poetry that places itself within the dizzying spirals of the geological ages of a 4.5-billion-year-old planet, must avoid at all costs "Romantic humanism."[14] He defines Romantic humanism as a tendency to "translate the immediate perception into an emotional condition, which is then admired or fetishized in preference to the original phenomenon—fossil, bird, lichen or landform."[15] Though he does acknowledge a more nuanced Romanticism even in Wordsworth that confronts the darker and more terrifying and unnameable aspects of nature, he more often equates the Romantic poet, especially Wordsworth, with the tourist: "The Romantic poet (or tourist, for that matter) desires to be spoken *to*, inspired by the other, so that perception travels into language (or slide show) without a palpable break." [16] He rejects the Romantic notion of the poet as "Aeolian harp" or "larynx of natural phenomena." [17] Though McKay's work avoids the prettifying of nature or using it as an occasion for human reverie or channelling, his work may be Romantic in a much deeper sense through its questioning of the gains of technology and its erotic longing to participate in nature as in a "geophany" or divine mystery.

VII. Deactivated West 100

McKay's *Deactivated West 100* (Gaspereau Press, 2005) is a series of linked essays where the poet conducts a geopoetic exploration of the coastal bioregion of the Pacific Northwest on Vancouver Island. His experience of following a fault line from end to end on southern Vancouver Island along a line of "geologic scrimmage where earlier landmasses collided" became the inspiration for this book. The essays ponder the record of a mind-shattering "tectonic catastrophe" where the fault line itself becomes a metaphor for the colliding of old and new, human and natural—the "gap" in human comprehension. This evocative collection inverts the question "What am I to the land?" to "What is the land to me?" In the essay "Otherwise than Place," the speaker opines, "What is needed is...a small dose of this eros of oblivion, the capacity to think backward or forward from place to its mothering wilderness." [18]

The wilderness in this volume reveals both its gentler and more cataclysmic aspects, the beginnings and the endings of natural cycles. The title, "Deactivation West," springs from McKay's observations about a deactivated logging road; yet it also echoes an important distinction he makes in the collection between destruction and "decreation." McKay writes that "to 'deactivate' in the sense of to end or destroy is to make something created pass into nothingness, but to decreate is to allow it to pass back into the uncreated from which it came."[19] The logging road had been deactivated because it no longer served the purposes of the human desire to exploit. In contrast, it is the business of the poet both to create as well as "decreate." In many mysticisms, like that of Meister Eckhart, the "uncreated" is the term for the ground of all being and knowing, the unnamable silence beyond all dualities of created/uncreated, time/eternity, matter/spirit etc. So when poetry re-enacts this process of movement from the created back to the uncreated, or "decreated," it (in McKay's words) "calls for attention to release its grip on fixed principles, to risk radical not-knowing without succumbing to the seductive currents which go by the name of nihilism."[20] McKay's brand of apophatic poetry (the poetry of "unnaming") then, affirms that humans, too, are part of a larger process into which our mortality is constantly being gathered. Therefore, McKay's form of natural contemplation, even in the face of the collision of tectonic plates as big as Iceland, does not end in nihilism or despair, where human consciousness comes to seem meaningless, but in an acceptance of our place in the unfolding of mysterious powers within both us and in nature.

VIII. McKay's "Quartz Crystal"

McKay's prose-poem "Quartz Crystal" illustrates the "geopoetic" imagination and is itself an act of contemplative attention. This poem was first published in *Varves* in 2003 and reappeared in *Strike/Slip* in 2006.[21] It contains images of crystalline structures similar to those described in an essay from *Deactivation West 100* entitled "Crystal" where he writes:

> *But when matter—dumb, brute, supposedly soulless rock—reveals that it too has ontological secrets, that it too is subject to such spiritual seizure, we may well be cast into a condition of empty, systematic wonder, as though we had*

discovered that all the walls in our houses were in fact
windows.[22]

In "Quartz Crystal," the speaker is cast into such a condition of "empty, systematic wonder" as he picks up a piece of clear quartz that had been sitting alongside other stones on his desk. This piece of quartz is about to reveal to him some of its "ontological secrets." He describes it with his usual precision, yet soon locates it not just in time, but as a messenger from "another dimension," a living thing "posed to take off and return to its native aether." The solid rock begins to seem a winged thing and a symbol of transcendence (or perhaps "in-scendence"). His allusion to it as a "bit of locked Pythagorean air" associates the crystal with music, mathematics, and philosophy. It is a piece of star music fallen into time hinting at our ideals of perfection: "simple, naked, perilously perfect." Though it embodies sacred qualities it is also mundane, quotidian; the speaker can pick it up and hold it in his finger like a pencil. He then reflects on the ridiculousness of his concept of ownership, the notion that anyone could appropriate a form "reaching back to the Proterozoic." Before the irony of his own grasp, the poet "unnames" the quartz as unimaginable and indescribable, the "Zen before all Zen," emptiness, transparency. In the face of the embarrassment of even the speaker's personified books (symbols of human learning) over his futile efforts to find words commensurate to the integrity of the stone, he is forced to renounce one by one the accoutrements of the human: first his fingers and thumbs whose prehensile grasp has been used to distinguish us as toolmakers from the beasts; then baseball, minuet, cribbage, fugue, dialectic, and finally, last but not least, his poems:

And you,
My little poems, don't imagine I can't hear you
plotting under your covers, hoping to avoid
your imminent depublication.

The quartz crystal's perfection is "perilous" to the speaker because it reminds him of his mortality and even the mortality of the literary legacy he might leave. The stone requires that one return everything we think we own to the source of all temporal things, even our works of art. The crystal "floats like a lotus on my palm, bending the light from a dying star to dance upon my coffee cup this fine bright Cenozoic morning." Through these final lines, the reader is suddenly transported through the exotic eastern lotus of the crystal into deep time through an act of "pure attention." The diminution of self before that which is anterior is ironically also an act of celebration. The ritual renunciations ("I give up, I foreswear'), like Inanna's descent into the underworld, bring us closer home to a state of acceptance in the present on "this fine Cenozoic morning." This is a poem of surrender to the infinite that cups stars and coffee cups in a single consciousness.

IX. Lilburn and Apophasis

Like McKay, Tim Lilburn unites deep thinking with deep feeling in both his poetry and prose. Lilburn is an erudite, eremitic poet who moves back and forth between Hopkinesque verbal explosions to the contemplative reaches of sheer silence. Silence is his home ground for linguistic eruption. Rather than seeking spiritual mentors and practices through non-western spiritual traditions, Lilburn, whose spiritual formation was Jesuit, delves into the desert fathers and mothers of the first two centuries, Medieval mystical theology, Platonism, Neo-Platonism, and Hermeticism, to reconstruct a lost western contemplative tradition to which the contemplative practice of poetry for him is analogous: "Poetry gestures to contemplation and contemplation feeds the poetry, modifying language by letting awe undermine it, pare it back, lending the poems a thinness, compunction."[23] For Lilburn, contemplation and poetry are not identical in purpose, since contemplatives generally open themselves to wordless union with the divine, while poets are creatures of language; yet poets and contemplatives know equally that "all that is" cannot be expressed completely in words: "My hunch...is that contemplation and poetry do not share an identical telos, but that what both want strikes each the same—as quintessentially compelling and as unutterable." [24]

For Lilburn, as for McKay, poetic attention begins in awe. Lilburn defines this state as "what happens to you when you are knocked to the ground by some astonishment: You go very still at some point in yourself and become entirely eye." [25] The "eye," in this case, is not the arrogant, appropriative eye, but the eye of the optic heart, the eye of contemplation, or being beside things as in a sacred space. This eye longs for the integral and seeks to unify disciplines western thought has compartmentalized. Lilburn notes how in the poetry of Homer and the Haida poets Ghandl and Skaay "poetry, philosophy, religion come from and return to the same place in the psyche: contemplative attention." [26] The dense references and allusions that some readers perceive as merely cerebral in Lilburn come out of an integral thinking that is also a singing as suggested by the title of his collection of essays, *Thinking and Singing: Poetry & the Practice of Philosophy* (2002). In other words, the deep lyricism of poetry issues from much more than a concern with "making" or mere poetic technique, but from contemplative longing. Its urge is in Lilburn's words, "autochthonous," that is, desirous of belonging or becoming rooted once more in the earth. [27]

He, like McKay, is apophatic, a poet of unknowing. His reading of Plato interprets the ladder of ascent from becoming to essential being as an erotic of self-transformation through descent, the shamanic journey into a direct experience of that which resists names. He enters the mystery of what one anonymous fourteenth-century mystic called "the cloud of unknowing." His primary project, then, is not transcendence of the world, the earth, but transcendence of our controlling modes of knowing. His poetry and poetics as developed in his various collections of essays form a seamless whole, as both consist of a flinging out and affirming, then cancelling of names for natural things: "The world is its names plus their cancellations." [28] This oxymoronic gesture of what I would call "erotic non-attachment" parallels the way his mystical theologian mentor, Pseudo-Dionysus the Areopagite of the sixth century, names and unnames in a single breath the multiple names for the Godhead or Unnamable One. What Lilburn has done in the body of his work is to transform the ancient language of the contemplative journey or ascent to God into "a dark night of the soul," a descent into absence and loss with reverberations of return, thus forging an earth-erotics for our time. Lilburn uses the term "erotics" and "erotic longing" not to talk simply about sexuality or the appetites of the body (though these are included in his poetic), but to love as a cosmological yearning in all things for the larger unity that eludes cognitive knowing: "Eros has nowhere to go but to become sorrow... It hurts to look at deer, / deer under their name." [29] Penthos or sorrow, "the tearfulness of things," emerges and we sit with our grief for a while.

In his earth-descent, Lilburn is an ascetic, not in the sense of seeking to control the flesh or repress pleasure, but in the older sense of *acesis* (Gk. "askesis") or a pruning back of the false self to afford greater freedom and more holistic way of being. His favourite word, "eros," indicates not simply a celebration of personal erotic love, but, as in Plato, Eros the greater as the cosmological power that holds together and empowers all creation, the manifest world. He writes: "The eros for the world, I believe, unfolds in the same way as dialectic and the eros for God have been understood to unfold." [30] Eros-longing, then, has to be cultivated, for it is our one way back to unity with the earth from which we have separated ourselves, like lovers from an elusive Beloved. And, in this context, poetry becomes a form of wooing: "We are lonely for where we are. Poetry helps us cope. Poetry is where we go when we want to know the world as lover." [31]

Yet approaching the natural world as lover requires mastering the degrees of humility. Humility, in the sense of returning to our origins in the "humus" or soil, the earth itself, along with what Lilburn calls a "slendering" of the self, is the prerequisite to reconnection. Lilburn's asceticism, then, is not a diminution of desire but its intensification: "Humility grows from ravishment, and is the simplification and intensification of desire."[32] Such a kenosis or self-emptying becomes a sharpening of sense and feeling without grasping or holding.

As much as the speaker in Lilburn's meditative poems pants for union with nature, what he settles for more often is a "lying alongside": "But if you come to be innocent, the old desert stories imply, if you set aside confidence in your capacity, if you release your weight into the graceful engine of something other than your will, you may find yourself coming alongside things."[33] He argues that because we are part of a culture that has separated itself from our primordial origins, we have to work our way home slowly, with "compunction" and deference. His poems trace this process of chastening, mourning, and reparation. These stages of courtship constitute a colloquy of erotic postures before a recalcitrant beloved. The process of return is not linear but an intuitive emergence through desire. It is also a discipline modulated through the discipline of poetry.

Lilburn's path homeward to nature is analogous to the path to union with God in the older theologies, like that of John of the Cross or the anonymous author of the *Cloud of Unknowing*. Lilburn is a contemporary nature mystic because his aim is nothing less than ecstatic union. Generally the term "mysticism" has come to be associated in our culture with mystification, angelism (a desire to prematurely transcend the conditions of our earthly existence), or obfuscation, but in Lilburn it is the exact opposite of escape into subjectivity or navel-gazing but has wider ramifications. It requires the hard work of disengaging from exploitive postures and deliberately coming to surrender before the particularities of natural things.

Simply abiding in humility alongside the wilderness our cultures have assaulted can be the ground for sacred activism. Intentional non-engagement and direct engagement can be seen as conjoined polarities. Lilburn writes: "Practice an activism of forgetting the royalty of one's name, of yielding, of stepping aside. This will be like breathing through the whole body, the new, larger body of a place that might take us in."[34] Lilburn's contemplative offerings require a shift in perception that creates momentum toward a global reinventing of what it means to be human. Contemplation, as the major mystical traditions concur, is the complementary side of action, not its opposition—the base in silence for effective action. Lilburn believes contemplative attention is a form of hidden engagement that has political ramifications for both writer and reader: "Poetry, as a transformative, political instrument, cuts two ways, into the author as much as or more than the reader."[35]

For Lilburn, one fruit of apophatic encounter with nature is the public expression of the poem, not a polished artefact but a process in the field of which contemplative attention emerges. The poem is not a record of an experience but an enactment of something like an electromagnetic field. Enter the field of the poem and be changed. In a typical Lilburn poem, the speaker sees that which she calls "deer" or other-than-human life form. The poet tries to capture deer in the net of language and gloriously fails: "Poetry is the rearing in language of a desire whose end lies beyond language."[36] Yet the poet's desire for oneness with the deer never ceases, as names and images are offered and withdrawn. Discursive and even poetic language collides with the otherness or "oddness" of deer. Weeping happens; the tearfulness of things in the larger order pours through the alienated poet. The poem or field of word-woven perception becomes alert with unknowing. The poet finally resigns and agrees to curl into mere humanness alongside "deerness." With luck, the poem falls into deer's otherness. In this process, the poem becomes an act of adoration, a song to the ineluctable essence of the deer. It is possible that longing proceeds from a remembering of "deerness" within ourselves, that part of the deer which has been carried forward into our bodies/consciousness which we've forgotten and therefore grieve.

Lilburn's relatively early volume, *Moosewood Sandhills* (1994), is a good place to go for an illustration of the origins of his practice of contemplative attention. These poems are an astonishing sequence of monk-like meditative lyrics that laid the ground for his later, longer meditations in *To the River* and *Kill-site*.[37] They suggest clearly how each person can be a "lay monk" of the everyday by following our innate longing to lay ourselves open to the beauty and strangeness of nature. Here the speaker's act of digging down into the earth and living in a root cellar becomes a shamanic descent into a chthonic or deep underworld where the interiority of nature has the capacity to touch and heal the interiority of the human: "There is a form of belonging to land that is deeper than having a local address. It would be called chthonic citizenship, earth-Belonging."[38]

X. Lilburn's "Contemplation is Mourning"

"Contemplation Is Mourning" from *Moosewood Sandhills* encapsulates Lilburn's poetics of acesis as a procession of loss, tears, compunction, grief, and lament for the earth.[39] He remains with the grief rather than trying to move beyond it prematurely. The title can be read in two ways: the contemplative path is one where mourning occurs and contemplation herself is always mourning. In the mystical traditions in which Lilburn is steeped, such as the Jewish Song of Songs, separation from the beloved entails grief and the desire for reunion never leaves.

This poem, like many in this collection, uses the second person "you" to include the reader as participant, in this case, one is invited to "lie down in the deer's bed." The poet sleeps in the depressions made in the grass by the deer's bodies as a way of entering their world. The long, loping lines repeat the elongation of the animals' "length of sleep." As in so many Lilburn lyrics, a stanza of sensuous description of aspen leaves, snowberries and fescue finishes with a more philosophical statement: "This is the edge of the known world and the beginning of philosophy."

The opening six-line stanza is followed by a set of four couplets that explore the dynamics of looking from within a world of silence. The first one warns: "Looking takes you so far on a leash of delight, then removes it and says / the price of admission to further is your name." The relinquishing of one's social identity and of the entire business of naming must be suspended as the "price of admission" to paradise. In the fourth couplet, the wisdom voice whispers of the mystery of what the deer is in herself, her pure being or "is-ness": "The deer cannot be known. She is the Atlantic, she is Egypt..." The inability to penetrate her exoticism is to "feel severed, sick, darkened, ashamed." Yet this darkening of human knowing, this sickness, is not unto death, but the beginning of wisdom through terror: "Her body is a border crossing, a wall and a perfume and past this / she is infinite. And it is terrible to enter this." The final seven-line stanza restores us to the deer's bed, "the green martyrion, the place where / language buries itself." The place of poetic martyrdom is a place where language is temporarily sacrificed, the self "shaved and narrowed." The poem finishes with the "smell of last year's melted snow," suggesting spring may lie hidden in a long winter of absence. For now, the waiting is all—the doing, and poetic activity, a non-doing.

XI. THORNTON AS NEO-ROMANTIC

Russell Thornton, in contrast to Lilburn and McKay, is an unabashed neo-Romantic whose work can be located in the tradition of Blake, Keats, John Clare and others. In his work, the Romantic trajectory is corrected and recovered. Though he does not call himself a Blakean, Blakean ideas and images beginning in *The Fifth Window* recur throughout his work.[40] He is also an elegiac poet who celebrates the temporal and fleeting. His poems, often set in North Vancouver nestled beside the Coast Mountains, break down any sense of ultimate division between wilderness and cityscape, and sing their interpenetrations. In "Lonsdale Quay" from *House Built of Rain* (2003), a Blakean child from the world of innocence observing feeding seagulls becomes an emblem of the fusion of the natural and the human:

> Perhaps he [the child] will fall down and down, an exquisite
> morsel for the open mouths of dreams waiting to dream him.

*The seagulls swoop down together, thrust out their wings, all
bright white, awkward-looking manoeuvring angels.*[41]

As we have seen, McKay and Lilburn call the legacy of Romanticism
to account as a form of anthropocentric humanism that uses nature as
an occasion for subjective reverie. Such a false Romanticism prettifies
and tames wilderness so the overriding ego can feel "at home" in an
inauthentic sense. McKay warns against Wordsworthian rhapsodies,
yet also acknowledges a deeper side to Wordsworth in a recent essay
where he cites the famous passage from *The Prelude* where the young
speaker of *The Prelude* is terrified on the lake by looming cliffs
experienced as "unknown modes of being."[42] Lilburn generally
critiques Romanticism and seeks out an older theology and mysticism
as means of return to nature. However, the Romantics, in their
assessment of the impact of the Industrial Revolution and their
exploration of the sublime, a vastness in nature incommensurate with
ideologies and their ability to revision old mythologies, can be seen as
forerunners of deep ecology.[43] For example, my own reading of
Coleridge's "Kubla Khan" is that it displays the cataclysmic powers of
a seemingly chaotic nature shattering the artificial paradise of human
constructs, such as "the dome of pleasure" built by the conqueror
Kubla. The "caverns measureless to man" with "huge fragments
vaulting like rebounding hail" have the same impact on human
consciousness as McKay's colliding tectonic plates.

For Thornton, the best of Romanticism isn't all sentimental
posturing or appropriation of nature for human ends. In fact, he
argues that to view nature through the lens of human consciousness
is inevitable and inescapable. Language may act as a barrier to the
world, but it also has what he calls "magical properties":

> *Language is both a key and a lock when it comes to the poet
> and the natural world. Language came out of the natural
> world (out of the human organism) and although intricate
> systems of words helped produce self-consciousness in
> humans and divided humans from the natural world, words*

also, for my money, have magical properties, one of which is that they can help humans hypnotize themselves back into communion with the natural world. I'd even say that the magical depths of words can open out into the sounds of the natural world; more—that these sounds are the natural world and all of matter itself. The natural world can hypnotize us with our own words. It can "raid" our psychic "inarticulate"-ness, so to speak. Of course, language is also a "crime" in that it walls us off from nature (and the division helps us to think we can commit atrocities against it). I don't see the point in intellectually struggling to escape language-bound-up human consciousness in language. It's like trying to chew off your own teeth. Why not revel in the marvelous contraption of human consciousness and whatever opportunities it offers? You're never going to come into a relationship with nature any other way. It's part and parcel of the terms of human life (the gift of life, period). You're only going to see yourself when you look at nature—of course! (but what worlds that "self" might be or become or "hold" is an interesting question). Of course consciousness is a mirror. The material world, for me, is consciousness, and so nature is a mirror. A mirror that's always looking at us.[44]

Thornton's meditative lyrics illustrate this sense of nature as a living mirror of human consciousness, but a mirror with its own will and intentions. We are therefore not trapped within language but language can become a point of access to communion with an open cosmological order.

"The Ocean at Long Beach," for example, from *The Human Shore*, presents a vaulting, lacerating wave on the Pacific Coast as a natural process that suddenly "turns" to become a human psychodrama containing the image of a mythic man and woman (Orpheus looking back at Eurydice). Here nature simultaneously proffers a non-human and human aspect in a single gesture:

And what is not human turns, and is also human; it
turns [the giant / wave], and as out of the throats of
the presences, lets loose calls; they / echo in the wild
driftwood, the wind-spiralled trees, the sky.[45]

In a commentary on these lines, Thornton explains:

> That single wave turns around...and the speaker "knows"
> suddenly that the unknowable, the "not human" is at every
> instant ushering itself into human consciousness. It's an
> intuition: the universe is human. I mean this to be a radical
> statement of a kind—a radical romanticism. I don't mean to
> say that man is the centre of the universe or that man can
> rationally figure out the secrets of the universe—not at all. I
> do mean to say that the universe will, with infinite subtlety,
> embrace human consciousness and "play" human for us if
> we love it enough (no matter how ugly, terrifying,and non-
> benevolent in terms of the human ego it can be). The
> non-human puts on human masks for us—"presences" such
> as those we might refer to as Orpheus and Eurydice call to us;
> those calls echo through the creation—and are in fact the
> creation.[46]

Lilburn and McKay rightly warn against the dangers of a self-
absorbed humanism. While acknowledging the inscrutability of the
unnameable wild, Thornton affirms its creative and transforming
powers when juxtaposed to those of the human. In an interview he
explains:

> I'd say that nature can be called "pure" in the ruthlessness,
> the grave ruthlessness and relentlessness of its creativity. I
> feel that the only thing that matters to nature is birth. This
> is how nature might be seen to be a healing force. Nature
> may be indifferent to us, but it will work on us...by virtue
> of its being indifferent to us. And if our eyes and ears are
> significant only insofar as they serve as the eyes and ears of

the natural world, then, strangely, all of nature is human.
It may be indifferent to us, yet it's human! For me, this is an
intoxicating paradox.[47]

His paradoxical perspective here is like that of Blake when he envisions the cosmos as a gigantic primordial person (Jerusalem/Albion/Adam Kadmon). This is not the sort of reductive humanism against which the others warn, but a mapping of the liminal spaces between the human and the infinite, an in-between where the universe sometimes, quite surprisingly, stoops to meet our finitude. Since we are local expressions, an emergence of consciousness of this larger whole, nature can mirror back a human countenance, though it might equally mirror a deer face to a deer. While Lilburn and McKay highlight the otherness of wilderness, Thornton emphasizes identity, locating the wildly creative within the human like a microcosm lodged in its corresponding macrocosm. In his poems, consciousness mirrors the natural world and vice versa. It is the universe becoming conscious of itself in and through the human. To write out of this dynamic of joint mirroring, or what Blake calls "Fourfold Vision," is not anthropomorphic but cosmological thinking. As critic Malcolm Woodland puts it,

> *Russell Thornton, like McKay, is a Romantic, but a Romantic of a very different stripe. As the title of his latest collection,* The Human Shore, *suggests, Thornton works at the border between the human and the nonhuman, between knowledge and reality. But if McKay's work makes me feel as though I am staring into the abyss, Thornton's makes me feel as though the abyss is staring back at me."*[48]

In other words, Thornton reopens the possibility of rapturous union with the natural world experienced as personal presence, as is evident in "Fifteenth and Lonsdale" where the ubiquitous Coast Mountains in North Vancouver, Thornton's home, actively play with the human:

I look up again—suddenly I know nothing except that
the mountain sits there secretly transparent as rain.
That it sees us. That it flirts with us. That it is a
person containing all the experience we can ever have.
That it is a pure signal. And whatever the two
alongside me are saying quietly to each other, they
were made to say it.

The mountain sits, dressed in trees, and endlessly
clear—endlessly clear, and endlessly dressed in trees.
It never ceases turning our gazes back to us—it has
no prophecy other than this...[49]

Thornton depicts the mountain as "seeing," "flirting," "dressed in trees" not to reduce it to human tropes but to convey its Protean diversity. The poem reveals how the misty mountain world interpenetrates and cups the human: "The street mist / dribbles out of his [a man's] pockets, becoming numberless names."

XII. THORNTON'S "HERON"

Thornton's "Heron" traces the movements of the "sensitive-still slender, / blue-grey mystery" bird in and out of an urban landscape—exalting in its illusive, unclaimable presence.[50] The bird lives at the meeting place of the human and the natural worlds, the wild and the tame. The observing "I" catches in its peripheral field a beauty it cannot control or fathom.

The poem moves from morning to morning: seeing begins in "the hour before dawn" and comes full circle to "the beginning, morning bird." The first stanza describes the heron as "a grey lopsided bundle / a tent suddenly assembling itself, and in a split-instant / collapsing and assembling itself again in mid-air," creating and "decreating" itself in a single motion. The imagery is as precise as McKay's in depicting the movements of wings, legs and neck:

There it is, opening its near-creek-spanning wings,
trailing its long thin legs, carrying its neck
in an S-shape, head held back....

The second long stanza throws the witnessing I (eye) back into memory, so the tense changes from present to past: "Is it the same heron / I saw once before....?" What the speaker remembers, what is "re-membered," is the inter-flow of heron and creek as a unified piece: "The entire creek unbroken / could be the heron's home..." The third stanza, or musical movement, returns to the present where "The heron / alights somewhere, disappears, and lifts again." By interweaving present and past, the poem enacts the interplay of presence and absence. "The repetition of the phrase, "I see it" works against the sense of constant loss as the heron evades the speaker's eye. The consummation of the action occurs when the heron finds a fish which "swims quick into the poised long bill." Significantly, heron, stream, ravine, and urban environment of "houses, people, streets and cars" cohere in contemplative attention, the heron remaining both itself and "living sign":

The heron lifts, the dark tasting itself, the ravine
flying through the ravine—living sign,
secret heron of the beginning, morning bird.

XIII. CONCLUSION

Out of such earthy mysteries as quartz, deer, or heron, these three contemporary Canadian nature poets resurrect a new-old earth mysticism rooted in poetic-contemplative practice. In Page's "Cook's Mountains" with which this essay began, the speaker beholds "two strangenesses" of "shape and name" in the mountains named by Cook. In the last stanza, the "being-ness" or "is-ness" of the mountains forms "in diamond panes behind the tree ferns of / the dark imagination." As all these poets suggest, when imagination "darkens" to become less assured in its certainties, expected vistas open. These poets assume a posture of "unknowing" in relation to the natural world—an active receptivity or receptive activity. Language as a tool for interrogating, channelling or describing nature is curbed, but as a responsive singing to the universal song, it remains effectual. They respond in distinctive ways to the subject-object split that separated us from our primal origins in the earth. Like the work of elder poet P.K. Page, theirs locates itself within visionary and mystical traditions, moving beyond modernist analytical rationalism. As contributors to Canadian nature poetry, they provide an evolutionary poetics of the earth. Whether through earth-cosmology, mysticism, contemplative tradition, or neo-Romanticism, these poets walk lightly with language, but remain language-tenders. In the mystical theologies of the past, the pilgrim passes through various stages including what Medieval mystics called purgation, illumination, and union. McKay, Lilburn, and Thornton suggest we have to start relinquishing our aggressive hold on the earth before asserting reunion with nature. Yet despite our species' outrages against the planet, the poets hint that what we most deeply desire is mystical union with the earth from which we have estranged ourselves. Poetry is deep listening to the core earth-music as well as responsive song. It offers the possibility of homecoming through erotic longing rather than discursive and linear modes of knowing. However, as Lilburn hints in the context of discussing the *Cloud of Unknowing*: "God is incomprehensible to knowing, but not to loving, where he [she] appears as "sweetness," the feel of the cognition of paradise."[51] The same insight applies to nature: what mere knowledge cannot attain, love may well be able to access, especially through poets who are willing to let their specialization in language serve the larger whole that cups us all.

Notes:

1. P.K. Page, "Cook's Mountains," in *The Hidden Room* (Erin, ON: Porcupine's Quill, 1997).

2. Thomas Berry, *The Dream of the Earth* (San Francisco: Sierra Club Books, 1990), 208. "In relation to the earth, we have been autistic for centuries. Only now have we begun to listen with some attention and with a willingness to respond to the earth's demand that we cease our industrial assault, that we abandon our inner rage against the conditions of our earthly existence, that we renew our human participation in the grand liturgy of the universe."

3. Di Brandt's *Now You Care* (Toronto: Coach House Books, 2003) and Dionne Brand's *Inventory* (Toronto: McClelland & Stewart, 2006) contain more overtly engaged political poems addressing global environmental issues.

4. Tim Lilburn, "Poetry's Practice of Philosophy," from The Anne Szumigalski Memorial Lecture, published in *Prairie Fire* 23:3 (2002).

5. Don McKay, *Camber* (Toronto: McClelland & Stewart, 2004), 4.

6. Don McKay, "Ediacaran and Anthropocene: Poetry as Reader of Deep Time," from the Anne Szumigalski Memorial Lecture, published in *Prairie Fire* 29:4 (Winter 2008-9).

7. McKay, "Ediacaran and Anthropocene," 14.

8. Don McKay, "Baler Twine: Thoughts on Ravens, Home & Nature Poetry," in *Vis a Vis: Fieldnotes on Poetry & Wilderness* (Kentville, NS: Gaspereau Press, 2001).

9. McKay, "Ediacaran and Anthropocene," 11.

10. Don McKay, "Great Flint Singing," in *Open Wide a Wilderness: Canadian Nature Poems*, ed. Nancy Holmes (Waterloo ON: Wilfred Laurier University Press, 2009), 3.

11. McKay, "Ediacaran and Anthropocene," 9-10.

12. Examples of this type of poem are "Song for the Song of the Varied Thrush" in *Apparatus* (Toronto: McClelland & Stewart, 1997) and "Song for the Song of the Common Raven" in *Strike/Slip* (Toronto: McClelland & Stewart, 2006).

13. McKay, "Great Flint Singing," in *Open Wide a Wilderness*, 4.

14. McKay, "Ediacaran and Anthropocene," 13.

15. Ibid., 9.

16. McKay, "Baler Twine," 27.

17. Ibid.

18. Don McKay, *Deactivated West 100* (Kentville, NS: Gaspereau Press, 2005).

19. McKay, "Decreation," in *Deactivated West 100*, 38.

20. McKay, *Deactivated West 100*, 38.

21. Varves are alternating layers of coarse and fine sediment as seen along a fault line.

22. McKay, *Deactivated West 100*, 37.

23. Tim Lilburn, "How to Be Here?" in *Living In The World As If It Were Home* (Toronto: Cormorant, 2002), 11.

24. Tim Lilburn, "Thinking the Rule of Benedict Within Modernity," *Fiddlehead* 228 (Summer 2006): 162.

25. Lilburn, "Poetry's Practice of Philosophy."

26. Ibid.

27. Tim Lilburn, *Going Home* (Toronto: Anansi, 2008), 1.

28. Lilburn, "How to Be Here?" in *Living*, 5.

29. Lilburn, "Learning a Deeper Courtesy of the Eye," from *Moosewood Sandhills* (Toronto: McClelland & Stewart, 1994), 36-37.

30. Lilburn, Preface to *Living*, xv.

31. Lilburn, "How to Be Here?" in *Living*, 17.

32. Lilburn, *Going Home*, 153.

33. Lilburn, "There Is No Presence," in *Living*, 73.

34. Tim Lilburn, "Going Home," in *Thinking and Singing*, ed. Tim Lilburn (Toronto: Cormorant, 2002), 184.

35. Lilburn, "Faith and Land," 59.

36. Lilburn, "How to Be Here?" in *Living*, 9.

37. Lilburn, *To the River* (Toronto: McClelland & Stewart, 1999); *Kill-Site* (Toronto: McClelland & Stewart, 2003).

38. Lilburn, "Faith and Land," in *Prairie Fire*, 56-57.

39. Lilburn, *Moosewood Sandhills*, 15.

40. Russell Thornton, *The Fifth Window* (Saskatoon: Thistledown, 2000).

41. Russell Thornton, *House Built of Rain* (Vancouver: Harbour Publishing, 2003), 37.

42. McKay, "Great Flint Singing," in *Open Wide a Wilderness*, 10.

43. Canadian scholar Kevin Hutchings makes a case for the environmental and eco-logical concerns of the Romantics in *Imagining Nature: Blake's Environmental Poetics* (Kingston: McGill-Queen's University Press, 2002).

44. Thornton, from an unpublished exchange with Susan McCaslin, June 2009.

45. Thornton, *The Human Shore* (Madeira Park, BC: Harbour Publishing, 2007), 12.

46. Thornton, *Lit Futura* (Winter 2004).

47. Russell Thornton, interview with Catherine MacLennan, "Interview with Russell Thornton," in *The Lamp*, a monthly online magazine, 2007. http://www.thelamp.ca/books/index.php?id=21

48. Malcolm Woodland, "Poetry," *University of Toronto Quarterly* 77.1 (Winter 2008), 54-56.

49. Thornton, *The Human Shore*, 11.

50. Thornton, *Open a Wide Wilderness*, 415. An earlier version of this poem appeared in *House Built of Rain*, 38.

51. Lilburn, *Going Home*, 150.

West Coast Literary-Political Clashes:
1960-1985

RON DART

Among the dramatis personae of the West Coast's literary-political feuding of the 1960s were a cluster of central figures. George Woodcock, the editor of *Canadian Literature*, which operated from UBC, lived on the West Coast for decades. One of the most published, active men of letters in Canada, he was also an articulate political and social anarchist. Jerry Zaslove, an English professor at SFU was similarly committed to the European anarchist way, and Warren Tallman—while not as astute a political theorist as Woodcock or Zaslove—through his writings, actions, and affinities leaned toward socially anarchist traditions. If Woodcock and Zaslove shared politically anarchist views—albeit of distinct British and Frankfurt-U.S. orientations—Tallman's close association with the American Black Mountain and Beat poets indicated that although his literary leanings took precedence, they were inherently anarchist in nature also.

Among Canadian literary nationalists, West Coast native Robin Mathews is recognized as an old warhorse who was in the thick of nationalist literary scrimmages from the 1960s onward. East Coast native Milton Acorn, another long time champion of the nationalist vision, headed west to Vancouver for a five-year residence during the 1960s and was a vocal opponent of creeping American cultural influence. A third prominent nationalist, veteran poet and UBC instructor Marya Fiamengo, has enjoyed a long and distinguished career marked by a more moderate, less confrontational style. All three nationalist writers were immersed in the Canadian literary tradition, but interpreted it and wrote in their own respective fashions.

In brief, during the period of 1960-1985, Woodcock, Zaslove, and Tallman emerged variously in their times to embody the "West Coast" literary-anarchist position, as Mathews, Acorn, and Fiamengo would serve as representatives of the country's literary-nationalist stance. Irreconcilable by nature, these positions led to intellectual clashes which took place at both literary and political levels. Their roles are considered in this essay.

II: 1960-67

The publication of *The New American Poetry* (1960), by Donald Allen,[1] made it clear to the interested that a new form of poetry and poetics was in the making, and it was American poetry that was at the forefront of this new poetics. At this pivotal point in twentieth century history, England was rapidly waning as the star from which Canadians would take cultural bearings. This reflected similar shifts in the visual art world at the time, where New York, with its Abstract Expressionists, replaced Paris as the hub of innovation. In poetry, the American tradition in its newest form and guise would now serve as the guide. While other poetic sensibilities in the U.S.A. continued to flourish (particularly in academic environments) Allen's path-breaking anthology captured the attention of many Canadians on the West Coast. When Allen teamed up with Tallman in 1973 to update Allen's earlier book, their new *The Poetics of The New American Poetry* established Tallman's reputation for aesthetic and political inspiration. His Vancouver affiliations stretched almost fifteen years by then and this was not lost upon nationalists.

In the late 1950s, George Woodcock and Warren Tallman were

both active in their working lives at UBC in Vancouver. Each, from different perspectives, personified the anarchist way—Woodcock again from the British model, Tallman from the American. In 1959, Woodcock was chosen to be the first editor of *Canadian Literature,* and remained in the post until 1977. Tallman's essay, "Wolf in the Snow," was published in an early edition of *Canadian Literature;*[2] it is striking that Allen's *The New American Poetry* was published that same year. Tallman's essay applied the American romantic approach to poetry and politics to Canadian literary work. Using five Canadian novels as guide-markers, he argued that Canadian literature was very much about the isolated, alienated, yet passionate artistic wolf, which is surrounded by a cold and unfeeling Canadian culture. The essay's tone suggests that the position of the lone and misunderstood artist speaks truly about the Canadian experience, and this is consonant with the idea of a heroic individual who stands against the oppressive nature of authority and tradition which was at the core of Tallman's thesis. His interpretive position spoke more about Tallman's understanding of the artist than it did about a more comprehensive view of Canadian literature.

Such a reading fit neatly with the new ideology on the West Coast of the artist in Canadian literature. A new generation of young Canadians on the West Coast would be taken by Tallman's reading of literature and by the new American models that embodied his approach.

The small but influential West Coast magazine that reflected more the American anarchist way than that of Woodcock's more scholarly *Canadian Literature* was *TISH*. It began in September 1961 and ended in the summer of 1969, forty-five issues later, going through four editorial periods. *TISH* was consciously indebted to American poetry and anarchist politics; in some of the earliest editions, lines were clearly drawn between the anarchists and the Canadian nationalist perspective.

In December 1961, George Bowering, a student of Tallman at UBC, wrote a critical review of Milton Acorn's *Against a League of*

Liars. By then, Acorn was an important Canadian poet "back east," but Bowering dared to take him to task. Acorn was a good friend of Al Purdy, and Purdy decided to reply to Bowering. Purdy made it abundantly clear in his response that he thought Bowering misunderstood the reason for Acorn's style and content, although he recognized that Acorn's poetic form did need some polishing. To anyone who followed Canadian arts and letters, it was apparent that Bowering and his mentor Tallman were followers of the Black Mountain and American Beat tradition, whereas Acorn and Purdy stood firmly on the Canadian nationalist side of the debate. Thus, within its first year, *TISH* ignited a national debate in Canada about the nature and scope of poetry and politics, nationalism, and anarchism.

Acorn and Purdy had started a small literary broadsheet, *Moment*, in the early 1960s.[3] Acorn and Gwendolyn MacEwen were married February 8, 1962, and within a few weeks of their marriage, they published *Moment #6* in which they turned on the *TISH* tribe. *Moment #7* followed, with an assault on the Black Mountain tradition. Frank Davey, one of the original *TISH* group, replied in forceful voice.[4] At the centre of this debate was a fundamental regional difference of views and understandings concerning the forms and meaning of modern American poetry, appropriate Canadian responses to it, and the nationalist-anarchist political traditions that underlay such a clash.

The fact that the American Black Mountain and Beat traditions were taking literary front stage on the West Coast through the enthusiastic support of Warren Tallman and *TISH* meant a more direct clash was in the making. The historic, well-attended Vancouver Poetry Conference in 1963 made a significant international statement: Vancouver too was now at the cutting edge of avant-garde poetry.

By late 1963, Acorn could not remain in Eastern Canada when the West Coast seemed to be redefining how poetry and politics should be done. In November of that year, escorted to the train station in Toronto by Robert Colombo, he headed to Vancouver. He would remain there until the autumn of 1968.

Acorn soon met some of the downtown poets of the Vancouver streets such as Red Lane and bill bissett. Acorn stayed active, gravitating toward left wing politics and reading poetry at leftist book stores and at the Trotskyist Hall. He published poems in bissett's *blew ointment*,[5] and became a dominant political poet at the Advance Mattress coffeehouse, which had opened in the summer of 1966 at Alma & 10th in the Kitsilano district.

Three useful works that recount the fuller tale of the literary political clashes of these times (and the reasons for them) are Warren Tallman's *In the Midst* (1992), Chris Gudgeon's biography of Acorn entitled *Out of This World: The Natural History of Milton Acorn* (1996), and Richard Lemm's biography, *Milton Acorn: In Love and Anger* (1999), which is more thorough, scholarly, and better researched.

Robin Mathews was also emerging as a vocal Canadian nationalist during this period. A clash between him, Roy Daniells, and George Woodcock in the early 1960s[6] pointed the way to a much larger confrontation on the poetry and politics wars from the 1960s-1980s. The initial tensions began with an article Roy Daniells published in Woodcock's Canadian literature. Daniells was on the committee that hired George Woodcock to be editor of *Canadian Literature*. Daniells had an article published in *Canadian Literature* (No. 12: Spring 1962) called "The Long Enduring Spring." The main thesis of the article was that Canadian literature was stalled in a perpetual spring season, and that no substantive summer fruit was being produced. Mathews sent Woodcock a letter in 1962 that raised serious questions about Daniells' read of Canadian literature. Woodcock refused to publish the article, and in his reply to Mathews, he had this to say:

> I don't agree with your article, any more than I agree with
> the findings of the Royal Commission, nor do I think that in
> general terms Canadian Literature *is the place for the
> political-economic fringes of literary polemics. (12th
> November 1962)*

There are three points to note here: 1) Woodcock and Mathews were obviously heading down different literary-political trails, and Woodcock was in a position of authority (as editor of *Canadian Literature*) that Mathews was not. 2) Woodcock's antipathy to the Royal Commission spoke volumes about his understanding of the relationship between the state and the arts—Mathews was much more committed to the role of the state in supporting the arts, whereas Woodcock, being the anarchist he was, kept the state at bay. 3) Woodcock thought Mathews' perspective was on "the political-economic fringes of literary polemics."

It was more than obvious, therefore, that by the early 1960s on the West Coast a genuine clash was in the making. The publication by Woodcock of Tallman's "Wolf in the Snow" and Daniells' "The Long Enduring Spring" pointed in a certain direction that appealed to a new generation of American and Canadian poets—*TISH* was also a central part of this movement. Such a perspective tended to be suspicious of both the historic authority of the literary and political establishment, of nationhood and previous poetic forms and their content. Acorn and Mathews were, on the other hand, drawing deeply from the distinctive Canadian poetic and political tradition, and, as a consequence, they were suspicious of both the importing of American models of poetry into Canada and anarchist politics that often walked hand and hand with such new poetry. Both thought that Canadian poets on the West Coast were becoming neo-colonials and poetic compradors. Obviously, Daniells, Woodcock, Tallman and *TISH* did not interpret things in quite the same way.

Dan McLeod played a significant editorial role in the final issues of *TISH*. It was McLeod who, with others, founded *Georgia Straight* in May 1967. There was an irony to this. 1967 was the one-hundredth anniversary of Canada as a nation, and Canadians were celebrating a century of national statehood (and all that meant in terms of independence from England and the U.S.A.), but a magazine that flaunted the Canadian tradition had left the publishing tarmac. *Georgia Straight* was viewed as a form of cultural imperialism from one angle (because of its connection with the TISH group), and an assault on a thoughtless and puritan traditionalism from another angle. The nationalists and anarchists were raising different questions about the Canadian soul and society, poetry and politics, and this took them down different paths and trails.

It did not take McLeod long to fold *TISH* into *Georgia Straight*. The final few issues of *TISH* were published as a "Writing Supplement" in *Georgia Straight*. Milton Acorn was a founding member of *Georgia Straight*, but it did not take him long to read the writing on the wall. *TISH-Georgia Straight* was an American anarchist-style publication, and Acorn was a nationalist and socialist. It is impossible to unite such ideological commitments in either thought or action. There is no doubt that Acorn had an explosive temperament, and part of his break from *Georgia Straight* had something to do with this, but Acorn also realized, after writing an article for the *Straight*, and being an insider of sorts at its beginning, that his vision for Canada, poetry, and politics was not that of the protest and anarchist way of McLeod and clan.

Milton Acorn knew the time had come for him to return to Central Canada—his affinities were few on the West Coast. *Georgia Straight* had entered a productive season by 1967-1968, and it would outlive all the other protest and anarchist magazines of the time. *Poetry and the Colonized Mind: TISH* (1976), by Keith Richardson, with a "Preface" by Robin Mathews, is probably the best book in publication that offers a solid and sustained critique of the TISH tradition from a Canadian nationalist perspective. By contrast, "Romantic Offensive: *TISH*," by Peter Quartermain (*Canadian Literature*: #75, Winter 1977) is a spirited and animated defence of the TISH tradition just as Tallman's "A Brief Retro-Introduction to *TISH*" in his *In The Midst* is a must-read from the perspective of a thoughtful and committed insider. It should be noted that Warren Tallman had no patience for Mathews' form of poetry and politics. He called Mathews "an enemy of mine,"[7] and he also lampooned Mathews in "September: A Necessary Politics for Stan Persky in forms of Notes on Robin Mathews Theatre of the New Psychodrama" in the same book. There can be no doubt that there were serious poetry and political disputes on the West Coast from

1960-1967, and Woodcock-Tallman took one direction, and Acorn-Mathews took another direction. It was simply a matter of time before the simmering clashes took on a national focus.

III: 1967-70

The defeat of the Canadian Tory nationalist tradition of Prime Minister John Diefenbaker in 1963 by Lester Pearson and Tommy Douglas moved Canada in a political, economic, and military manner more toward the American orbit and gravitational field. U.S. President John F. Kennedy detested Diefenbaker and welcomed Pearson. George Grant's important publication *Lament for a Nation: The Defeat of Canadian Nationalism* (1965) pondered the 1963 election and lamented the passing away of an older High Tory nationalism, but ignited a new generation of Canadian left-of-centre nationalists. Such a growing nationalism would trigger yet another clash between the anarchist and nationalist visions of Canada.

By 1967 many Canadians were pondering just what it, in fact, meant to be Canadian. Mel Hurtig and Al Purdy worked tirelessly that year to produce a book by Canadians, for Canadians about Canada's relations with the U.S.A. Entitled *The New Romans: Candid Opinions of the U.S.*, this collection of fifty essays and poems, including Mathews' poem, "Centennial Song,"[8] was published in 1968.[9] Most of the West Coast Canadian anarchist activists who were included agreed that the American military-industrial complex and its powerful elite had to be opposed. But what was on the far side of protest and opposition? Most knew what they wanted to be free from, but what did most want to be free for, and how would such a goal be politically achieved? This is where the nationalists and anarchists parted company. Mathews would agree with Bowering, for example, that the price of winning in Vietnam was too costly at a variety of levels. But, under the surface of the anarchist protests against Vietnam was cynicism about the state in bringing about the Imperfect Good. In illustration, many American conscientious objectors fled to Canada because of the war and the role of the American state in continuing it. Often, Canadians were sympathetic to their concerns, but frequently these American dissenters brought with them a distrust of the state. This is where the nationalist Mathews and the anarchists parted political and poetic paths. "Centennial Song" probes how Canadians, like a woman of too easy virtue, will recline for the U.S. Mathews' argument was that Canadians needed a stronger state to oppose the "New Romans" to the south, and to create a more just and peaceable kingdom in the True North. It is fitting that Purdy, as editor, set Mathews' "Centennial Song" beside Woodcock's "Various Americas" in *The New Romans*.

Mathews was back from England and France by 1968. Robin Mathews and James Steele were teaching in the English department at Carleton University at the time. They became aware, after much careful research, that Canadians were often not being hired in Canadian universities. Canadians were being bypassed for teaching positions, and Americans or those from the United Kingdom were offered jobs. This disparity could not be ignored. Their publication of *The Struggle for Canadian Universities* (1969) was to catapult Mathews and Steele to the very centre of the Canadianization movement in the 1970s. The West Coast impact of the Mathews and Steele activism was duly noted in Hugh Johnston's *Radical Campus: Making Simon Fraser University* (2005). The clashes at SFU in the 1960s-1980s between the Canadian nationalists and the American-Canadian anarchists had much to do with Mathews' nationalism, and such a position was further enflamed in 1985 when the English department at SFU refused to hire Mathews. This decision created a national debate on the West Coast, but more of this later.

It was in 1970, though, that these issues reached a new intensity at a national level. The annual Governor General's Award in Canada inevitably has its boosters and critics, but in 1970 the tensions reached a heightened pitch. Most in the literary community assumed that Milton Acorn was going to be crowned for his book of poetry, *I've*

Tasted My Blood (1969). Al Purdy had selected the poems and wrote a convincing "Introduction." George Bowering had written a mildly critical review of *I've Tasted My Blood* in *Canadian Literature* (Autumn, 1969: No. 42). Acorn was portrayed, partially, as part fine poet and part bumbling buffoon that needed Purdy's steady and sure editorial guidance to bring more mature order to the poetic missive. There are kind comments made in the review, but there are also digs. It is significant that the review was published in the autumn of 1969. The storm clouds were gathering, and Tallman-Bowering and Acorn-Mathews would be in the eye of the storm.

The literary community in Canada was shocked when George Bowering and Acorn's former wife, Gwendolyn MacEwen, won the Governor General's Award in 1969. The fact that Warren Tallman, an American and mentor to Bowering, was on the selection committee raised eyebrows and conflict of interest questions among nationalists.

There have been some inaccuracies in who exposed, initially, the Tallman-Bowering twosome, and the work that led to the "People's Poet Award" being given to Acorn. Gudgeon says this: "After the awards were announced in 1970, a group of poets led by Joe Rosenblatt and Eli Mandel launched a concentrated attack on the Governor General's committee." The fact is that it was Robin Mathews who was first out of the gate in opposing the GG Award and the Tallman-Bowering connection. This fact (with a fine cartoon) is amply illustrated in Nathan Cohen's article, "The Canadian Council: Even its best friends are complaining now" (*Toronto Star*: April 25, 1970). Mathews and friends had staged a demonstration outside the Canada Council office in Ottawa, and it was their work that led to the organized opposition, which included Irving Layton. Acorn was given the "People's Poet Award" in Toronto at Grossman's Tavern on Spadina on May 16, 1970. Canadian poetic worthies such as Layton, Al Purdy, Joe Rosenblatt, Eli Mandel and Margaret Atwood were in attendance.

The chasm that opened between the Governor General's Award and the "People's Poet Award" in 1970 can be explained significantly in terms of confrontation between an American-styled approach to new poetry and anarchist politics as embodied in the West Coast traditions of the Black Mountain, Beat, *TISH*, and *Georgia Straight*, and an emerging and committed Canadianization movement as embodied in those like Acorn and Mathews and those who offered Acorn the "People's Poet Award" in the Great Canadian Poetry Wars.

James Deahl lived with Milton Acorn in Toronto from 1979-1981. In an email to me Deahl had this to say about Acorn and the *TISH* tradition:

> *Acorn always had a grudge against the TISH poets. Even in the 1980s he would denounce them. The real target that Acorn, MacEwen, Purdy, Fiamengo took aim at was the notion that literature and the arts should have nothing to do with politics. That is, that the arts were somehow above politics. (That, of course, is itself a political idea).*
>
> *—January 8, 2009*

It might not be totally fair to argue that the *TISH* group were opposed to politics or thought art was above politics. It is true to argue that their notion of politics lacked a certain understanding and commitment to the formal political process and the good that can come from such a process. There are limits, in short, in reducing politics to protest and advocacy activism or merely local and regional concerns. It is at national and provincial levels that policy is thought through, made, and enacted on a variety of issues at the domestic and foreign policy level which cannot be ignored. Anarchist politics, with its excessive cynicism regarding authority, tends to retreat into ever smaller cells and groups as a way and means of doing politics. The nationalist vision thinks much larger about how the common good can be brought into being for one and all.

The bitter clash that took place in Toronto in 1970 had much to do with the Canadian Poetry Wars that emerged on the West Coast in the 1960s between Woodcock-Mathews and Acorn-*TISH*/*Georgia Straight*. The volcano had been smouldering for a decade.

IV: 1970-85

Marya Fiamengo had established herself as a fine and maturing poet throughout the 1960s and into the 1970s. Fiamengo had completed her MA with Earle Birney in the Creative Writing department at UBC in 1965, and she taught as a Senior Instructor at UBC from the 1960s-1990s. Fiamengo formed a solid and lasting relationship with Seymour Mayne and Pat Lane when she was at UBC, and it was Mayne that assisted in the publication of Fiamengo's second book of poetry, *Silt of Iron* (1971). The evocative drawings by Jack Shadbolt in *Silt of Iron* and Fiamengo's poems make this collection worth careful reading, but much more was yet to come from Fiamengo's pen.

It was in the 1970s that the dam broke in Fiamengo's poetry. The themes of poetry and politics and the politics of the Canadianization movement began to take centre stage. *In Praise of Old Women* (1976) was dedicated "To Robin and all those who struggle against the Americanization of Canada." Many of the poems are grounded in the Canadian local, cultural and political experience and ethos. But it is in *North of the Cold Star* (1978) that the Canadian female equivalent of Mathews and Acorn comes to the poetic and political forefront. *North of the Cold Star* is political poetry committed to the personal, public, and national levels of the human journey. There is no slipping away to other times and places. What emerges is the demanding *now*, and there is the future of Canada to be faced. The Canadianization movement is given poetic expression in *North of the Cold Star* in a way that few poets in Canada have attempted.

Fiamengo, in her unpublished memoir, asked and answered this poignant question:

> Now, where in all this was the Canadian, in particular
> British Columbian intelligentsia? Where were the native
> poets, writers, scholars? Earle Birney, like great Achilles,
> sulked in his tent. Dorothy Livesay, a respected senior poet,
> fell in love with U.S. poet Jack Spicer. When I expressed my
> feelings of perplexity and alienation, she replied, "we have

much to learn technically from Jack Spicer." The incompar-
ably brilliant lyric poet, Phyllis Webb, succumbed to the
allure of the Black Mountain versifier Robert Duncan. It
must be admitted that Phyllis Webb had a strong
inclination toward political and philosophical anarchism
before she met Duncan.

The fact that Fiamengo was good friends with Pat Lane, and that Lane was one of Acorn's better West Coast friends when he was in Vancouver, meant that Fiamengo and Acorn met on a variety of occasions. The fact that Acorn had won the "People's Poet Award" in 1970 and the Governor General's Award in 1975 could not have helped but encourage Fiamengo's commitment to the Canadianization movement in political poetry. Fiamengo had, in the 1960s, published a variety of articles and book reviews in *Canadian Literature*, but the more she was drawn to the Canadianization tradition, the fewer the articles/book reviews the leading West Coast literary magazine published.

The main theme of *Canadian Literature* (Spring 1969: No. 40) was "Colonialism and Post-Colonialism." Acorn and Mathews would have been a perfect fit for the publication, but Woodcock chose Roy Daniells to write the lead article, and Purdy-Acorn-Mathews are far from view. In the Winter, 1977 edition, No. 75, the main motif was "Nationalism." William New was the new editor, and he, like Woodcock, ignored some of the leading nationalists in the Canadianization movement. Serious questions need to be asked about this, and the answers will, in some way, tell us something about the West Coast poetry wars.

V: 1985

The initial confrontation in 1962 between Woodcock-Mathews was but the beginning of an intense disagreement between two Canadian intellectuals who interpreted the relationship between culture, literature and politics in opposing ways. The publication of Woodcock's *Strange Bedfellows: The State and the Arts in Canada* (1985) would not go without comment. Woodcock, being the anarchist he was, raised serious questions about the State supporting the Arts in Canada even though he had received largesse from the Canadian government for many years. Mathews responded. His article "Someone Pays the Piper: Robin Mathews replies to John Metcalf and George Woodcock on Patronage and the Canadian Arts" (*Cross-Canada Writer's Magazine*: Volume 10, No. 2, 1988) took both Metcalf and Woodcock to task for their reactionary, anti-Statist and laissez-faire approach to patronage and the arts. The article did not please Woodcock and Metcalf. The core issue was, of course, funding for the arts. Who was responsible for funding the arts and why? Mathews argued that citizens, via the state, should support the arts. Woodcock took the position that society rather than the state should be the primary supporter of the arts. Such positions lead to quite different places regarding who supports the arts and why. The political commitments have substantive practical implications.

The final phase in the drawn-out battle between the nationalist and anarchist tradition began in a rather innocent way, but the law of unintended consequences led to a historic West Coast showdown at Simon Fraser University.

Robin Mathews was teaching in the English department at Carleton University in 1985, and Bruce Nesbitt was teaching in the English department at SFU. Both men decided it might be interesting to switch universities for a year. This happens often, and it is rarely a problem. But, such was not to be the case at SFU. Jerry Zaslove was the chair of the English department there at the time. Additionally, many in the department were aware of Mathews' literary-political nationalism and few wanted him in their midst. Zaslove called a vote, and the department ruled against inviting Mathews. This came as a surprise to Mathews who had played a leadership role in the Canadianization movement from the late-1960s onward. Mathews was in the habit of facing opposition, but, as a Canadian, to be frozen out of a Canadian university was a shock for him. It did not take long for the media to wade into the fray. The *Globe and Mail* took up the issue.

Zaslove has been an articulate, thoughtful and compassionate anarchist for decades on the West Coast. His probes of the anarchist tradition went much deeper than Woodcock, and his contribution to anarchist political theory has been important. But, in the Mathews-Zaslove confrontation, two different ideologies clashed.

The *Globe* editorial makes it obvious that some problems were afoot at SFU between Mathews and the English department. Zaslove is quoted in the article as saying, "We just don't think he would fit into the department... He has attacked members of this university before for being pro-American."[10] By 1985, Mathews was one of Canada's best-known literary-political nationalists, and his reputation could not properly be ignored. There were many Americans in the English department at SFU that knew who Mathews was, and were not keen on having him in their midst. It did not take Mathews long to reply to Zaslove. "Nasty Inside the Wry" (May 28, 1985) took Zaslove to task for the letter he wrote to Carleton that nixed the exchange. Mathews made clear his view that he was not welcomed at SFU because he did not strut the party line. He quoted amply from Zaslove. The latter did not remain silent. "Complex Questions" was published in letters to the editor.[11] Zaslove suggested that Mathews was "fanatical, narrow, fundamentalist and even anti-democratic." Mathews had butted horns with two of the leading anarchists on the West Coast: Woodcock and Tallman. Now he faced Zaslove and clan at SFU.

The incident escalated. The idea that a well known Canadian nationalist could be rejected from a position in a Canadian university was an affront to many Canadians. The Canadian Association of University Teachers (CAUT) had censured SFU twice before for unwise decisions (May 1968-November 1968 & May 1971-May 1977). SFU did not need another censure from CAUT. Margaret Atwood was the Canadian chair of PEN at the time, and she threatened to bring the full weight of PEN against SFU if they rejected Mathews.

Atwood's letters to both Zaslove and President Saywell at SFU are quite poignant, telling documents of this imbroglio. Pauline Jewett, former President of SFU, and Margaret Fulton, President of Mount Saint Vincent, were also active in supporting Mathews—it seemed to be yet another obvious case of the marginalization of a Canadian writer, scholar, and political activist within his country and province. The many letters that are now available from SFU on the Mathews incident make it clear that the situation was more complex than the way it was often framed, but there is no doubt that the clash of literary-political ideologies was a contributing cause.

In the end, a decision was made to welcome Mathews into the Canadian Studies program at SFU rather than the English department.[12] The battle was finally over and Mathews finished his teaching days at the university that had attempted to bar him.

VI. CONCLUSION

Milton Acorn (1923-1986) is no longer with us. Marya Fiamengo continues to publish fine poetry: *Patience After Compline* (1989) and *White Linen Remembered* (1996) are mature poetic works that evoke much within the reader. The back cover of *White Linen Remembered* features a photograph of Fiamengo and painter Joe Plaskett together in a reunion of West Coast cultural elders. In 2006, Fiamengo was honoured by the publication of *Visible Living: Poems Selected and New*. Seymour Mayne, Russell Thornton and Janice Fiamengo wrote the "Preface" to the poetic festschrift. In a letter to me, Fiamengo had this to say: "Robin brought to my attention that the forward made little mention of my entrenched nationalism. I am somewhat disappointed at this."[13] Mathews wrote a blistering, hard-hitting letter to Mayne, Thornton, and Janice Fiamengo that noted this glaring omission.[14]

Mathews has continued to write and publish. Both Fiamengo and Mathews also appear in the important recent anthology *Rocksalt*,[15] the first major collection of B.C. poetry in thirty years.

George Woodcock has been called "Canada's foremost man of letters." In 1994, The City of Vancouver proclaimed Saturday May 7th "George Woodcock Day." Warren Tallman was not honoured nor feted with quite the same public acclaim offered Woodcock. Unaccountably perhaps, Tallman is not even included in William New's *Encyclopedia of Literature in Canada* (2002), even though Woodcock is offered ample space—remembering that it was New who replaced Woodcock as editor of *Canadian Literature*. Mathews and Fiamengo are barely mentioned. Nor is Jerry Zaslove mentioned in the *Encyclopedia*, although many of his faithful students and peers did honour him with a festschrift volume entitled *Anarcho-Modernism: Towards a New Critical Theory*.

The poetry wars on the West Coast were fought at many levels. There is little doubt that both political theory (nationalism and anarchism), contending theories of literature, and the relationship between literature and politics were central to the clashes. Woodcock, Tallman, and Zaslove, for various reasons, took one position, just as Acorn, Fiamengo, and Mathews took an opposite view. The history of Canada's literary-politics would have been much duller without the animated confrontations that took place on the West Coast and, arguably, the positions of those times are in some ways still at play.

Notes:

1. Donald Allen, *The New American Poetry* (New York: Grove Press, 1960).

2. Warren Tallman, *Canadian Literature* 5 (Summer, 1960) and *Canadian Literature* 6 (Autumn, 1960).

3. *Moment* was initially published by Acorn and Purdy in the late 1950s. Purdy had this to say about its early years: "In Montreal we published a little magazine, *Moment*, with a mimeograph machine which I suspect Acorn had purloined without permission from the Communist Party of Canada." Introduction to Acorn's *Whiskey Jack* (Scarborough: HMS Press, 1986).

4. Davey, in *TISH*: July 14, 1962.

5. Some of Acorn's more important works that appeared in blewointment are "Poem," "Poem for Sydney," "In Victory Square," and his classic and well received poem, "The Natural History of the Elephants."

6. The core clash between Mathews and Woodcock/Daniells took place at literary and

political levels. Mathews did not think, like Daniells, that Canadian literature was in a long enduring spring. He was convinced that there was much maturity in Canadian literature before the 1960s, and that only a colonial literary critic would think otherwise. Mathews also thought that Woodcock's ideological anarchism shaped his read of the Canadian literary tradition in a way that distorted such a tradition.

7. Warren Tallman, *In the Midst* (Vancouver: Talonbooks, 1992), 295.

8. Mathews' poem is a shocker that is not easily forgotten, just as Bowering's "Winning" is a frontal assault on the planners and horrors of the Vietnam War.

9. Al Purdy, ed., *The New Romans: Candid Canadian Opinions of the U.S.* (Edmonton: M.G. Hurtig Ltd., 1968).

10. *Globe & Mail*, "Delicate Balance": May 18, 1985.

11. *Globe & Mail*, June 17, 1985.

12. See CAUT Bulletin: November, 1985.

13. See CAUT Bulletin: November, 1985.

14. Fiamengo, letter to the author, October 18, 2006.

15. Mona Fertig & Harold Rhenisch, eds., *Rocksalt: An Anthology of Contemporary Poetry* (Ganges, Saltspring Island: Mother Tongue, 2008.)

Origins & Peregrinations:
CREATIVE WRITING AT UBC

GEORGE MCWHIRTER

Why did Earle Birney split from Creative Writing at UBC after he had forced Creative Writing to split from the English Department and become an independent department? Apart from being exhausted by the process of separation and being fed up with UBC—the English Department approach follows academic method, and Creative Writing, the professional method—the simple answer is that Earle retired. He got a former student and Director of CBC Vancouver, Bob Harlow, to be first Head. Later, in the 1980s when Earle was made a UBC honorary doctor, there was a Creative Writing founders' fight and it was resolved by R.W. Will, the Dean of Arts, who declared Earle the founding force and father, but Bob as the first Head, which he was. It was Jake Zilber who did major committee work on the proposal for a Creative Writing Department through the Faculty of Arts and various governing bodies.

I'll go over some of the ironies about the split, which is endemic to the difference between the Creative Writing process and the English Literature studies approach. The English Department approach follows academic method, and Creative Writing, the professional; hence the Creative Writing degree is a MFA and is terminal, without a Ph.D. dimension at UBC, because at that point it would also get into the study of the writing process as well as the practice. However, other institutions now do offer the Ph.D. in Creative Writing.

The split between the academic *learning about* literature and the creative writing professional's approach to *learning by doing* recurred in the late seventies. I proposed a graduate course in Editing and Managing a Literary Magazine that would turn the production of *PRISM International* with graduate students as editors into a credit course. Surely it could be a learning process even if the student editors were volunteers and not students? Jan de Bruyn, then Chair of the Faculty of Arts Curriculum Committee, said that we could not have a course where grad students were learning by doing, through the business of putting out a literary magazine. His reasoning was that in a course for academic credit, students would have to learn *about* editing a magazine, not actually perform this task themselves.

I accepted this. The process of becoming an editor and editing actually involved two years. Therefore, I proposed that the course cover the first year, where the grad students understudied the actual editors, and learned from what they were doing. The next year, after election to the positions, the students would morph into the editors' roles.

The rationale was to reward editors-to-be with academic credit for the learning in the first year and with research assistantship money for the professional editing and production role. Why were the graduate students given the full responsibility for producing *PRISM* with the Advisory Editor acting in the role of publisher, setting only the financial constraints expenditures on number of pages to be printed, artwork and contributor's fees? The practical rationale was simple: those who manage and raise the money to pay for the content earn the right to select it. In the role of publisher I undertook the mandate of paying contributors the same amount we paid the printer. *PRISM*, in fact, was saved from financial collapse under faculty editorship in the late seventies by the graduate students Hal Gray and his successor as Managing Editor, Sue Stewart.

So, it continues: thirty-three years after *PRISM*'s financial collapse, the magazine is in its fiftieth year of publication. The students provide what was sorely needed in 1977: a renewable source of energy. The limitations of using Creative Writing's small faculty as a source of editorial and production energies were clearly demonstrated by then.

This division of the process into paying with credit for learning and paying with money for doing worked out well for the Canada Council grant. The Canada Council does not fund university course-related arts activities. Therefore, in the first year of coursework, students receive university credits for the learning, and in the second they receive real money as professionals—a kind of work-study or internship program now common in many applied fields.

The relative values of talking about literature and the production of it lay at the heart of the Roy Daniells-Earle Birney academic versus professional feud in Creative Writing's days as it did within the English Department as a series of course offerings, then as a Program in English (1957-65). Roy Daniells had been the Head of English from 1948 until 1965; Earle Birney returned to the UBC English Department, where he had been a student, after the Second World War, on the condition that he have a creative writing course to teach. For two decades this was in dispute: whether the focus should be on the study of English literature, or on the production of writing and the development of new English literature through the writing of writers in the English Department. At issue was the matter of which was the more valuable (books *about* literature or books *of* literature), and which would be recognized for tenure, promotion, and recommendation for salary increases. Within the English Department, publications of poetry, the short story, and readings or performances of original plays were not recognized in the way that scholarly books, articles in journals, and papers delivered at scholarly conferences were. The situation was an ongoing aggravation for a creative writer like Earle in the UBC English Department. Given his prestige and personality, he would have had to argue for every increase in salary recommendation based on his significant and original literary publications. Those increases are rolled into a professor's salary, and the professor becomes richer by that much for the rest of his or her career at UBC. The UBC English Department still says that if one produces literature and wants recognition for it, one should become a part of the Creative Writing faculty instead.

Between 1957 and 1965, this became increasingly contentious when Creative Writing and its courses were recognized as a discipline in the form of a Program within the English Department, while the dissemination of work from that discipline, exemplified by the faculty's publications and productions, was not.

What Frank Davey did through *OPEN LETTER*, an avant-garde journal of literary theory and criticism, was an extension of the English Department Creative Writing Program model that he had been part of while at UBC. He was a member of the *TISH* group, the brilliant barbarians besieging the establishment. They (of the *TISH* era) wisely wrote critical commentary on each other's creative work, and eventually these opinions were accepted into the CanLit canon along with their creative work. This is logical because the only way to get credit, merit, and the money, as well as the prestige, was to publish the commentary as well. A similar cycle is now being repeated in the critical and creative support and promotion given each other between Larissa Lai and Sonnet L'Abbé within UBC's English Department; their authoritative relationship with each other now extends to the work of Rita Wong.

In other universities nowadays (in the University of Alberta, for example) this dichotomy of value is less egregious, and publication of original work in creative writing is acknowledged as not only meritorious, but as what the other half of what literature is all about. The live process and actual production of literature is an equal partner to the study of literature.

However, UBC Creative Writing does acknowledge the value of commentary and critical analysis of process. Those students in UBC Creative Writing who want to study the process and write scholarly commentary on it while producing work in the visual, lively, and literary arts, are encouraged to pursue the Ph.D. in Curriculum Studies at UBC's Faculty of Education. That program encounters criticism, much as the Creative Writing Program did in English, because it uses an individual's artistic creation as the core of its research, for which the studied commentary of the process is the second dimension.

The nature of research into the creative process and production, its institutional place, and funding brings up the other big money-spinner for the university, its faculty, and students: research grants. Until recently, no SSHRC grant for original creative writing research was available. The development of a novel from its initial proposal, however, can involve a time-consuming researching of sources. This has changed somewhat, but it helps if one can argue that the subject matter of one's novel comes close to an socio-economic study, through which a character's life becomes a living chronicle of certain conditions, or perhaps if one has a picaresque novel in which the character, after the fashion of Don Quixote, has read so many picaresque novels and written critical essays—all part of the novel—to the point where his mind pirouettes into picaresque mode, and he becomes a character himself. In the post-modern world of literature, a fictional character's essays can also be actual academic studies, while the behaviour of the scholar—schizoid, ingeniously larcenous, and well prepared—remains fictional.

In short, projects with an extra SSHRC disciplinary dimension that accompany the purely imaginative can help one's success rate enormously. It has also become easier for writers of nonfiction, which is also now taught in UBC's Creative Writing program.

For the creative writer in academia, the Canada Council was pointed out as the source of funding for "creative" artists. However, the Canada Council subtracted any salary, sabbatical or otherwise, from the amount of the grant requested, which always reduced it to zero. The regular poet, novelist, or songwriter on the street will naturally say if the author in question has a sabbatical or a salary, "Why do those creative writer blokes in the university need Canada Council grants for living expenses? Why do they want to take it away from me? They want jam on both sides of their bread."

This is a good point as regards fairness, but the academic critic writing a book *about* that writer on the street can get an extra grant, on top of his or her salary, for the job. Perhaps that adds value to the work of the writer on the street; however, ask the writer how much that is worth and the scholar is likely to hear, "You are making money off of me and my work." Or, as George Payerle put it on behalf of the collective while scolding one of Canada's most prominent literary scholars, "off of *us.*"

The two halves of the arts in the university should be open to the same resentment over the competition for government money, because the Canada Council for the Arts and the Social Sciences & Humanities Research Council fight with wooden and silver spoons around the same pot of shrinking stew. Until research and development money for the arts (including commentary, management, and creation) goes into a single pool, I would argue that the unfairness will persist as sharply as the resentment.

Applied scientists get the same responses from pure scientists that creative artists in the faculty of arts and humanities get from the purely scholarly arts and humanities profs. Pure scientists complain that the applied scientists just invent and produce *things* or modify the design for things. I saw this when I sat on a Governor General's Gold Medal committee for UBC's grad Studies. This medal is awarded to the top graduating student in Science and Arts. I was greatly impressed by a student who had invented a new ceramic that was more heat-resistant and durable than those used for the hull of the space shuttle. Even before he graduated, he was hired by his Department at UBC. Both his "pluses," however, were minuses in the discussion between the two pure scientists on the committee. Doubtless, there was resentment that this applied scientist had reward enough: a job, an invention that could be marketed, a company that might be created from it in the future, and commerce conducted.

If there is a market for scientific inventions, they suffer the same slings and arrows as the artist's work in the market place. As an example, Quadra Logic, Julia Levy's enterprise, can soar, then plunge on the stock market. Those who buy in the surge or are paid in shares can later be stripped and plunged into the cold water of market realities. Only a very few inventors make lasting money, as do very few writers. It is part of the process in every endeavour to reduce the numbers of winners to the few, and the financial winners to fewer still. Excluding and feeling excluded from some reward or prize are conjoined twins.

In this respect, the most adamant and extreme purist I ever heard was one who chaired an English Department doctoral orals examination. Chairs are always invited to give their opinion. The pure scientist in the Chair said that all the research in the arts was bogus because none of the findings in the work could be duplicated and verified by another independent researcher. Someone else pointed out that duplication was called plagiarism in the arts. The need for national councils and university research committees to establish clear criteria for what constitutes a valid experiment in the different areas of the arts and sciences is obvious.

Nonetheless, the scientist Chair insisted that arts and humanities research was all subject to the variables of interpretation and opinion. At the same time, he was ignoring that in the purest theoretical science (as in Einstein's case before the atomic bomb or the nuclear accelerator), a mathematical assumption underpinning the core formula of a theory has to be applied, and disbelief suspended, before the equations will work; and this remains the case until the theory is physically proven as per the Manhattan Project. From Galileo, Copernicus or Kepler onward, a fundamental element of science lies in the correction of mistakes and wrong assumptions that peer groups of scientists have previously accepted as correct.

Being a polymath, Earle Birney created the model for a Department of Creative Writing that offered multiple literary and dramatic forms. Earle used to recommend that after attending UBC, his students go to Iowa—the oldest creative writing program in North America, perhaps anywhere. Its studio/workshop approach provided the base for Creative Writing instruction at UBC. Robert Harlow, who had been one of Earle's students, had also gone to Iowa. Thus, by arriving in 1965 as Director of the CBC Vancouver, he was the perfect person for that stage in the creation of the Creative Writing department.

In the professional world, writers make their living not by poetry, or the short story, or novel alone, but through forms that have a wider, paying audience. Recognizing this, Harlow promoted the idea of introducing film, television and radio-play scriptwriting, as well as his own creative nonfiction course.

When the Creative Writing Department was finally launched with Harlow as navigator, prose study was anchored by Harlow (novel) and Jake Zilber (short story). Douglas Bankson was brought in by Harlow from the University of Montana to teach Drama, and J. Michael Yates was invited in from the University of Alaska to replace Birney and to lead poetry. He would prove as polymathic as his predecessor.

Between 1966 and 1970, Doug Bankson and Jake Zilber would add Writing for Film & TV to Stage Play on the curriculum. J. Michael, who had worked in broadcasting and who wrote radio plays that were internationally produced, introduced the Writing of Radio Play & Radio Documentary. There was an ongoing dispute over whether gathering sound footage and interviews and editing radio documentary was genuinely imaginative and creative, and whether the editing and arrangement of sound recordings, interviews, and commentary was as imaginative or innovative as any other form of composition. This same argument later surfaced when Harlow introduced the Writing of Non-Fiction in the 1970s.

Among J. Michael's many new curricular adventures, he co-taught several early classes with an invited expert in the field. For Radio Documentary, he teamed with the widely-respected Bill Terry of CBC Vancouver, who would later become Head of Radio Drama & Features at CBC, nationally. Similarly, Yates brought in a course in Literary Translation and, with the help of Harlow as Dept. Head, found funds to bring in a renowned expert, Michael Bullock, from England for a term in 1968. Bullock subsequently returned in 1969 to a permanent faculty position.

By the end of the sixties, then, in the wake of the polymath Earle, the UBC Creative Writing curriculum included the short story and novel prose forms, poetry enjoyed a formal singularity of its own, drama had acquired all its literary and dramatic parts (stage play, film & TV, radio play and documentary), and literary translation, covering all forms, was also in place.

To prepare young writers for a professional career, the Department of Creative Writing has always required students in its Majors and Masters programs to write in at least three genres: prose fiction, drama and poetry. Literary Translation (after some argument) may be substituted for one of the three. The three-genre requirement either appeals to prospective students, or repels them. Many want to cleave to their strength in one genre. If that if that were case, however, those students would be doing a BFA or MFA in simply Writing Poetry, or Novel Writing or what have you, not Creative Writing.

Robert Harlow introduced a new genre with the Writing of Non-Fiction in the early seventies. In the mid-eighties, when the Maclean Hunter Chair (now the Rogers Chair) was granted to UBC Creative Writing, the option of working in this one writing discipline would be extended in the Diploma of Applied Creative Non-Fiction. In a similar exploratory vein, during the early seventies, I had begun teaching Introduction to the Writing of Creative Forms for teachers of the newly introduced Writing 11 in the B.C. schools—ironically, same title as the old Creative Writing 201 offered in the English Department.

I explained to the Faculty of Education Curriculum Committee that I was not going to teach teachers how to teach. The problem was that English teachers had been well taught as regards interpretation and addressing of a text through the English Department, and through English Education methods courses how to excite and prepare students for a creative exercise or spree of self-expression where they created the new text and content, but the English teachers were terrified of putting anything of their own original writing on the page. I had to teach them to put in, not take out.

When I taught the new introductory course, I needed to get teachers back to the beginning and the basic relationship between words and things, words and actions (Adam's task of naming things). In the process of getting an idea into a thing, or finding an idea in a thing or meaning in sequence of events, I recommended that they write the action now, and told them to think about what it means later. Letting words follow the things and the action was premonitory of "the act now, think later" dictum practised by professional politicians.

I have sketched the polymathic legacy of UBC's Creative Writing passed on from Earle Birney. Has his highly individualistic personality as a writer been passed down to those who follow in his footsteps at UBC's Creative Writing? Are there still conflicts and clashes to match those between the poets Roy Daniells, the traditionalist, and Earle Birney, the innovator? There is an old saying in academia that "the person is the program." This is true of all studies and professional programs. Teachers teach what they know and have learned and programs lean toward their preferences. Learning by doing has its instructional corollary in that teachers tend to teach young writers what they know and do best. Style being the man or the woman, teachers pass on their style, and learning by imitation is a both a primary and subliminal method. I should add that in those cases where students come into programs because they admire the work of an instructor and wish to be in his or her workshop, the instructor's work and practice cements itself as the model. However, when students and instructor clash, the instructor's work and practice can become the point of departure for the young writer to find his or her own way, in defiance of the instructor's model. Alternatively, instructors look for young writers whose writing they think they can work with.

How do they do this at UBC? By selecting them on the basis of their writing. This brings me to the matter of content for Creative Writing courses. The student's writing constitutes the primary text for study, and unlike in the pure studies courses, it is presented in workshop to see how well it works and is open to editing or suggestions for change and improvement. This idea of the student's writing being a primary text for study can lead to the objection of "how can students learn to write from that level of writing? They can only learn to write better by studying the masters!"

The answer is that in selecting students through their work, instructors are setting a foundational standard for the quality of writing and subject matter interesting enough to warrant further development. In the workshop setting, students will learn how to read and edit each other's and their own work from the instructor's lead. In short, the workshop is a practical, nuts-and-bolts operation.

The cleaning up of a text, the tidying of line action, the removal of bad bits while keeping the good, and the differences in style and approach of its members are what workshop members have to learn from each other's individual talent. In selecting students, I always looked for that extra element of individual talent to develop a way of writing that a student may not have even known was different. Workshops spin in the circle of this conundrum.

Does this individual difference sometimes end in clashes? Did Earle Birney's? More often with UBC's Creative Writers, opposites tend to attract. They cleave together, and each generation of UBC writers sees itself as the one. It may be one led by Dennis Foon and Robert Bringhurst, or a Roo Borson-Daniel David Moses-Ann Ireland-Jane Munro-Morgan Nyberg wave, or a group led by Joan MacLeod and Bill Gaston. At UBC, a generation equals the length of a degree program. Each generation thinks that it is unique and it keeps connected, just like the UBC members of the *TISH* group... Ask Stephanie Bolster, Barbara Nickel, Chris Patten and they will fill in the others with whom they still correspond and meet from their UBC days.

Call it the Creative Writing tie, but a tie which is a major part of their development as a professional writer. That tie isn't found in the curriculum, but in the character of those who come together through it—as different and various in their ways as the very founder of the program in which they took their degrees.

The Breathable, Blue Surface:
OF POIĒSIS AND PLACE

CAROLYN ZONAILO

The emerald sea, the grey-green sea,
the turquoise sea, the final blue Pacific...
pieces of sea glass collect on the beach

(prized most of all, the cobalt blue,
the smoky violet shards);
gather as sea-treasure in a mosaic.
>   —from "Blue and Green"
>   *The Taste of Giving* (1990)

This personal literary essay begins with my birth. There are two items of significance about my birth, in terms of this essay. The first is that I was born in Vancouver. The second is that I was born a poet. They say one is either a born poet or makes themselves into one, or that some will become poets out of emotional necessity whereas others find themselves having become a poet by accident. These are all viable ways that one can come to be a poet. In my case, I did not have a lot of choice in the matter. I was born this way. If the poems stopped coming, the lines ended, the images disappeared, the rhythms dried up, I would never write another poem. But for me, the poems arrive. They hammer at me and bother me and keep me awake until I give in to them. I write poetry by listening. I know when a poem is finished, because it leaves me alone. Sometimes a poem will keep on pestering me over and over again, at times for something so small as a misplaced comma. Like it or not, I've spent my life since age fifteen being a poet. Prior to that, looking back, I can see that I was in apprenticeship, my poetic sensibility shaped by early life experiences.

Then there is the issue of being born in Vancouver. As places go, Vancouver is one of those geographies that indelibly shape those who are born there. Lots of people are born in a place, move during their formative years or when they are grown, and never much look back. They become attuned to wherever they live their adult lives. They leave the old hometown behind. They move on—to other places, other cities, new locales, different continents, interesting countries. Not so with most Vancouverites. Sure, we can live in other places—but the sea, the mountains, the lush forests, the rain, the coastal essence is like one of Odysseus' sirens, calling us back to where we started. The saltchuck is in our veins. The mountains are part of our identity. The rain is native to us, part of our natural habitat. Vancouver largely shaped the kind of poetry I have written; it imprinted itself on the DNA of my psyche. I can pull myself away from the beaches of the West Coast, but I can't quite shake the sand out of my hair, or keep the seashells from hiding in my jacket pockets.

I was greatly influenced by three books in my early years: my copy of *Mother Goose,* given to me on August 25, 1952, when I had my tonsils operation; my illustrated Lewis Carroll's *Alice in Wonderland* and my Grade Four textbook, *Poems Worth Knowing.*

There were three men who had a profound influence on the development of my early thinking. The first was my father, Matter Zonailo, who was born in the small community of Castlegar, British Columbia, from Doukhobor and Russian parents. My father's name—had the birth registrar been able to record it—would have been somewhat like Matvey Zhyalov. Although he was my parent, I have always considered this unique and intelligent individual to be one of my life teachers.

The second man who influenced my thinking was my first father-in-law, Dr. John Weir Perry, psychiatrist, Jungian psychoanalyst, and author, who studied with Carl Jung in Zurich, Switzerland. Dr. Perry, upon his return to the United States, founded one of the first Jung Institutes in North America. I was just eighteen when I met Dr. John Perry, who introduced me to the writings of Carl Jung. I have been a lifelong student of Jungian psychology.

The third influential man, whom I met before I was barely twenty, was the classicist scholar, university professor, and famous author, Norman O. Brown. Two of Brown's books, *Love's Body* and *Life Against Death* were intellectual best sellers at the time when I studied with him. It was an incredible experience, as an undergraduate, to have Nobby Brown (the name he was affectionately known by with his students) as one of my professors when I attended the University of Rochester, New York.

There were three women poets whose work I read early in life who influenced my poetic sensibility. The first was Sappho. I read the existing fragments of her poetry in translation when I was still in high school. The next was H.D., imagist poet, youthful friend of Ezra Pound, and later on a patient of Freud. The third was Anna Akhmatova, the great Russian poet, whose work and life stands as a testimony to the perseverance necessary to be a truly fine poet and woman, giving witness to her own turbulent, historical times. When forbidden to write her poems because they were considered too subversive, several of her friends memorized them, keeping the work alive until such time as Akhmatova's poetry could be written and published again.

In addition to the books, teachers, and poets mentioned above, there were three experiential factors in my life which formed who I was to become as a poet. The first was spiritual. As a child I had mystical experiences, moments of the numinous, which I can still remember to this day. These events, which I call mystical for want of another term, created the basis for the spirituality that continues to influence my poetic sensibility.

My Russian Doukhobor (*spirit-wrestler*) heritage is a lifelong influence on both who I am and in my writing. The Doukhobors are not Christian *per se*, but rather a Christian-based sect. Theirs is a spiritual philosophy of non-violence, gender equality, and a way of life, more than a religion. The Doukhobors are committed pacifists. They effectively held the world's first peace rally in 1895, when they burned their firearms and refused to serve in the Czar's army, in Russia.

The Doukhobor Burning of Guns predates Gandhi and twentieth century acts of non-violent protest and peace activism. The Doukhobors were comprised mainly of peasants who originated from many different regions of Russia. They faced persecution, and by the time of the Burning of Guns, most of the Doukhobors from different areas of Russia had been gathered up and forced to live in the mountainous Caucasus region. In 1899 the Doukhobors sought political asylum. They immigrated to Canada, the largest single *en masse* immigration in Canadian history. The great Russian writer, Leo Tolstoy, was instrumental in negotiating and financing their passage from Russia to Canada.

I consider myself extremely blessed to have grown up knowing the amazing Doukhobor family members on my father's side.

I also spent the years of my growing up attending first Sunday school, then C.G.I.T. (Canadian Girls In Training) and church at St. Giles United Church near Cambie and 41st Avenue in Vancouver. As well, I attended masses at a Catholic church when staying with my American cousins every summer. Compared to the simple services of the United Church, I was awed by the beauty and ritual of the Catholic mass, held in those days in Latin.

As a teenager I was involved with a born-again Christian group called Young Life. Their exuberant approach to religion added another positive dimension to my early spiritual experiences. Thus, by the time I left Vancouver to attend university I had been exposed to different kinds of religious expression. This gave me a broad base for understanding ways to the Divine, which I continued to explore by taking comparative religion courses while an undergraduate. The mystical experiences of childhood; together with being of Doukhobor heritage; along with experiencing Protestant, Catholic, and born-again Christianity, gave me a profound grounding in the spiritual possibilities of life.

The second major experiential factor in who I am as a poet was my involvement with nature and the outdoors. Born in Vancouver, British Columbia, the beauty of the natural world was all around me. From birth on, I was taken on journey after journey on boats, up and down the West Coast. My father was an avid fisherman, hunter, and outdoorsman. Throughout my growing up, my father often brought our whole family along in his explorations of the coastal and mountainous territories of British Columbia, as well as along the U.S. West Coast, all the way to Mexico. We camped, we fished, we hunted, we explored.

We travelled by boat on the West Coast, by station wagon up-country—into the Interior, to the Okanagan, the Cariboo, and the Kootenay regions of B.C. We also fished and boated on the many inland lakes, rivers, and streams. I had my own fly-fishing rod; I owned a .22 calibre rifle that I knew how to shoot and earned badges doing target practice competitions; I caught many varieties of fish, including the elusive Tyee salmon. The largest salmon I played and landed myself weighed in at thirty-four pounds. I was also on deep sea fishing trips off the coast of Mexico. I knew how to jig for cod, shuck an oyster, pluck a game bird, and tie fishing flies. My father's passion as a sportsman, and my mother's willingness to be a good sport at bringing along her children—no matter what the terrain, marine conditions or weather—made for an incredible growing up experience. The wilderness of the West Coast, as well as of the rest of British Columbia, was not just theoretical but was lived first-hand.

So it is from the three books I treasured in childhood, the influence of three men I knew before age twenty, as well as my early reading of three major women poets that I derived my early influences. Added to this was my deeply ingrained spiritual sensibility, my intense love of the West Coast and its rich natural beauty and my childhood discoveries of literature. And there you have the basis for a lifetime of writing and publishing poetry. I began writing in my teens; the first poems I published were in my high school yearbook and the school's literary magazine *Gambit*. That name was the one I came up with; it was chosen from other submissions. I was the valedictorian of my high school graduating class of over four hundred and fifty students. My speech began with a quotation from the American poet, Vachel Lindsay.

I suppose I could say that I've never deviated from the writing process that began so early on in my life. To be a poet, and to be able to present my work in public, continues to be my lifelong mission, a gift for which I am tremendously grateful. It is also an ongoing challenge—because poetry does not in actual fact come easily, rather it demands dedication, commitment, trial and error, a lot of hard work and discipline, as well as an ability to pay attention to the world, listen to language in all its nuances, and observe life at the same time as we are plunged into the midst of living.

I had American cousins, and I spent part of each summer living with them in the Seattle area. Early on I had a feeling for the differences between the States and Canada. As soon as I graduated from high school, I moved to southern California to attend a private university for women, Scripps College.

I chose Scripps because it offered a special humanities core curriculum. As a student there, I studied classical Greek history and literature, in translation, as well as classical Greek language. At Scripps, I began my studies in comparative religion, and continued my lifelong interest in mythology, begun while still at school in Vancouver. I also took other literature classes. Scripps College was part of the Pomona and Claremont Colleges, located in Claremont, California (east of Los Angeles nearby the foothills of Mount Baldy where Leonard Cohen famously took up residence as a Buddhist monk). While a student at Scripps, I met an astrophysics student at Pomona College, John Perry, who I later married. One night, John and I accompanied his father and stepmother on an evening outing into San Francisco to see a premier screening of Stanley Kubrick's *2001: A Space Odyssey*. On our way into the city, we stopped to pick up Alan Watts from his houseboat located on the coast, not far from the Perry's inland home. Watts was the popular author of such books as *The Way of Zen* (1957) and one of the important spokespeople for the 1960s' social revolution. He helped to introduce Zen Buddhism to the western world.

The years in California, New York, and New England certainly involved a widening of my literary sensibilities, from the West Coast poets whose work I already knew, such as Robert Duncan, Gary Snyder, Jack Spicer (to mention only a few) and from the excellent grounding in poetry I had in high school in Vancouver. My high school studies consisted of pre-modernist English poets, although I had already read American and British modernist poets, in the small-sized anthologies edited by Oscar Williams and in any books or magazines I could find while still in school in Vancouver.

While a student at the University of Rochester, I marched in New York City in one of the first high-profile anti-Vietnam peace demonstrations on May 2, 1964. I read the work of American poets such as Hart Crane, Wallace Stevens, W.C. Williams, Sylvia Plath, T.S. Eliot, H.D., and Ezra Pound, and more Pound. As well, I read poets as diverse as Denise Levertov, Charles Olson, Theodore Roethke, and Louise Bogan, among others. I heard John Cage play his daring, atonal music and heard poets like a young W.S. Merwin read. I saw the Gurdjieff whirling dervish dancers, since the original Gurdjieff farm in New York was just outside of Rochester.

From 1970 to 1990, I fully immersed myself in the literary life of Vancouver, but with some caveats. First, I had spent several years living in the United States, mostly the eastern U.S., and I had experienced a different culture than where I had grown up. I had read American poets who were not associated with San Francisco or the West Coast. Therefore I looked at the Vancouver poetry scene—although born and raised there—with somewhat of an outsider's eye.

Another caveat about living in Vancouver when I moved back at the beginning of the 1970s was that of being a woman. When I jumped into the milieu of the poetry scene, women's voices were just beginning to be heard, especially here in Vancouver—although Canadian literature has long featured outstanding women writers, from Susanna Moodie to Margaret Laurence and Margaret Atwood to Gwendolyn MacEwen. But it seemed that when I first began to publish and give readings in Vancouver, male writers and poets mostly dominated the city's literary landscape. There were however, a few truly extraordinary women poets, such as Daphne Marlatt, Maxine Gadd, Gladys Hindmarch, and Pat Lowther, who was so brutally murdered, and who I regret never having a chance to meet.

These women writers were a groundbreaking generation ahead of me, as were the *TISH* poets, who gathered around professor Warren Tallman and his wife Ellen at the University of British Columbia. As well, there were poets who were members of The League of Canadian Poets, who lived on the West Coast but had a national outlook on Canadian poetry. These poets, also, were a generation or two older than me. My final caveat was that because I was younger than the majority of the Vancouver poets I was meeting, I (at first) lacked for contemporaries; of course, this would soon change.

Despite my caveats, I was fortunate to be living in Vancouver during what turned out to be a very rich, diverse, and creative time. It was a time when Canadian literature was still in a growth spurt, especially West Coast writing, and when local organizations were coming into being. As a young poet, I was able to mix with and meet most of the older, established, and senior poets, both in B.C. and across Canada. The literary communities here in Vancouver and nationally were open, fluid, and—although there were the inevitable cliques—it seemed that we all came together as a community; we were "the tribe of writers" as Margaret Laurence once said.

During those foundational times, I was one of the original six writers on the founding executive of The Federation of B.C. Writers, which included journalist Daniel Wood, the late James Barber (who was famous for his cookbooks and television shows) writer David Watmough, poet k.o. Kanne, and writer Jan Drabek. Drabek, a childhood friend of Václav Havel, later became an ambassador for the newly formed Czech Republic. I had the pleasure of editing Drabek's memoir, *Thirteen*, for Caitlin Press (1992). This book told the story of his childhood in Prague and his family's escape from the Communist regime. The Federation of B.C. Writers was a humble organization at the beginning stages, although it was created with great enthusiasm. For the first three years, the founding executive met in one another's homes. I carried a cardboard file box—essentially the Federation—from place to place. Toward the end of this period, the entire executive seemed to have dwindled to k.o. Kanne, me, and the box. But luckily the Federation, despite some major ups and downs in its history, is still going strong.

I was also on the founding executive for the B.C. Book Prizes, along with Alan Twigg, now known as both a writer and the founder of *BC BookWorld*.

In 1977, I founded Caitlin Press, the first literary small press in B.C. founded and run by women. Cathy Ford, a young poet and creative writing student I met at UBC, and Ingrid Klassen, an editor, soon joined me. Together we ran Caitlin Press until 1983, when I took over management of the press by myself. Around this time poet Mona Fertig founded and ran The Literary Storefront in the Gastown section of Vancouver. She went on to establish a private letterpress, Mothertongue Press, on Salt Spring Island. In 2007, Fertig published a beautiful limited edition hand-set chapbook recounting the history of The Literary Storefront. Press Gang Printers Ltd, a printing business owned and operated by women, was established in Vancouver in the 1970s. Several of Caitlin's titles were printed by

Press Gang. The feminist journal, *A Room of One's Own*, was founded by a collective of women. The downtown writing and publishing centre of SFU was established, under the guidance of Ann Cowan, who was the wife of Peter Buitenhuis; he had moved from Montreal to Vancouver to be the head of SFU's English department.

Poet and artist Ed Varney joined with Henry Rappaport to found and run the successful printing and publishing house Intermedia. Some of the poetry anthologies, published by Intermedia from those times include: *Pomegranate: A Selected Anthology of Vancouver Poetry;*[1] *New West Coast: 72 contemporary British Columbia poets;*[2] and *D'Sonoqua: An Anthology of Women Poets of British Columbia, Volumes I & 2.*[3] Intermedia also published the two-volume Canadian Short Fiction Anthology.[4]

It was not only a fervent, interesting, and active stage in the growth of Vancouver and B.C. literature, it was also a time when there was much work to be done—when many of the institutions and organizations and publications and literary presses that writers on the West Coast now take for granted had to be created. There was an emphasis on making a contribution. Since writers, literary press publishers, and others were actively in the process of putting B.C. writing on the map, it seemed there was a genuine spirit of community. And, because I had spent the time described above away from the West Coast, I was not stuck in any one specific group or clique of writers. This gave me a wonderful freedom to know many different poets and writers of various bents.

I took three creative writing courses in the 1970s, prior to founding Caitlin Press. None of these courses were taken for credit, as both my B.A. and M.A. are degrees in literature, not creative writing. My first creative writing course was an audit of a year-long poetry seminar in the creative writing department at UBC in 1973-74. Poet, novelist, and professor George McWhirter taught this workshop. Although I often didn't understand exactly what George was saying, due to the speed at which he talked and his Belfast accent, he was a wonderfully supportive and encouraging creative writing teacher. One of my fellow students who took that class went on to do a creative writing degree with George, and he, too, admitted to me later that he never understood all that George was saying, for the whole duration of doing his degree. Nevertheless, McWhirter became a celebrated B.C. novelist and poet and is beloved by many former U.B.C. creative writing students.

McWhirter's seminar allowed me to meet several writers who were my contemporaries, some of whom became close friends, such as poet and editor Cathy Ford. Tim Stephens, who became the well-known astrologer who writes weekly columns for *The Vancouver Courier*, was also part of the poetry seminar. Other students included West Coast poet and teacher David West, maritime poet Don Domanski, and esteemed B.C. poet Robert Bringhurst.

Cathy Ford was undoubtedly one of my very first poetry friends in Vancouver. Five years younger than me, Cathy is a talented poet and editor. She and I shared several passions: a love of poetry, an ongoing interest in the politics of administrative and committee work, and the distinct gift of being able to edit poetry—an ability not every editor has. We also desired to contribute to the literary community as a whole. Cathy served as President of The League of Canadian Poets in 1985-86; she was a member of a national task force, Woman and Words, where she worked to create a draft constitution for the national association of PanCanadian Women and Words. Ford has also been an important editor for the Living Archives of the Feminist Caucus and League of Canadian Poets, and she currently serves as the League's representative for the Public Lending Right (PLR) Commission.

We began working together with Caitlin Press in 1979. In addition to her poetic and editorial skills, Cathy was also able to do typesetting, paste-up, and layout. When we first started, she was living in Vancouver. She then moved to Mayne Island and our work sessions always had to be done with the ferry schedule in mind, especially since Cathy did not drive in those days. We became adept at doing paste-up on the run, sometimes resorting to using a window of my house as our light table. When my husband built us a beautiful, proper table it was like manna from heaven. This light table was moved to an office I rented for writing and as the headquarters of Caitlin Press, in the Alm Building, on a corner of West Broadway. Cathy, like myself, had a love of book design and we devised many ways to create appealing covers at minimum cost. Not only were we always pressed for time, but Caitlin operated on the proverbial shoestring.

Cathy and I travelled together in 1978 to attend what was our first League of Canadian Poets meeting in Montreal. We were each toting bottles of codeine cough medicine prescribed for us at the last minute by my physician father-in-law, because we didn't want to cancel the trip. In spite of this, our first national-level meeting was an incredible experience for us both. Cathy Ford's books include: *Tall Trees* (1977), *The Womb Rattles Its Pod* (1981), *The Desiring Heart* (1985), and *Cunnilingus, or How I Learned to Love Figure Skating* (1997).

The second creative writing course I took was a poetry workshop taught by the late Charles "Red" Lillard, who wrote so lovingly and in detail about the West Coast. It was the summer of 1974, and there I met poet and painter Nellie McClung, author of several books of poetry including *My Sex is Ice Cream: The Marilyn Monroe Poems* (1996) and *I Hate Wives!* (2003), as well as the wonderfully humorous autobiographical book of short stories *Tea With the Queen* (1979).

Nellie became a great personal friend from the time we met until her recent death on February 13, 2009, concurrent with my writing the final section of this essay. Nellie is the granddaughter of the renowned Canadian suffragette, first woman Member of Parliament, and author of seventeen books, Nellie L. McClung, her namesake. My Nellie was always very proud of being named after her famous grandmother. She wrote a story about this that is online at Coracle Press, entitled "Charles Tupper and Me" (2004). My friendship with Nellie included poetry, books, readings, openings, parties, a trip I took with her to give poetry readings in her native city of Edmonton, and years of laughter together. Nellie McClung possessed enormous wit and a brilliant sense of humour, evident both in person and on paper.

At poetry readings, it was always a delight for me to hear her read "Downing Daquiris with Fidel & Discussing Moncada" from her book *Baraka* (1978). Nellie loved her adopted city, Vancouver, and always said she "took her inspiration from the mountains and the sea."

The third creative writing course I took was in 1976, when I attended a special writer's school at the University of Toronto organized by Gerald and Arlene Lampert. There I had the rare opportunity to take a poetry workshop with P.K. Page. I write about this experience, plus that of knowing Dorothy Livesay, Marya Fiamengo, and Anne Marriott in an essay entitled "Foremothers: Four Modernist Women Poets from the West Coast" published in *Re: Generations, Canadian Women Poets in Conversation.*[5] This essay was first written for presentation to the conference/festival, "Wider Boundaries of Daring: The Modernist Impulse in Canadian Women's Poetry," held at the University of Windsor, Ontario, in 2001.

The years that I was involved with Caitlin Press were from 1977, when I founded the press in Vancouver, until 1991, when I sold it to Howard White's sister, Cynthia Wilson and her partner Ken Carling, who relocated it to Prince George. Both Ken and Cynthia are now deceased, and after her death, Caitlin Press was in limbo until March 2008, when Vici Johnstone purchased the press. In my fourteen years with Caitlin the press published over twenty-one writers; some of the West Coast poets include Elizabeth Gourlay, David West, Cathy Ford, Beth Jankola, Carole Itter, Norm Sibum, David Conn, Ajmer Rode, and Mona Fertig.

Prior to 1977, I became friends with poet Patrick Lane, who encouraged me to begin a literary small press. I am grateful to Pat Lane for four contributions to my literary life. As an older and more established poet—now one of Canada's best-known writers—he was generous to me when I was young. Besides encouraging me to begin a small press, which led to the founding of Caitlin, it was his idea that I join The League of Canadian Poets. Patrick was one of my sponsors. He took me to West Vancouver to meet a woman he told me I would like very much. Thus began a wonderful friendship with poet, reviewer, and UBC lecturer Marya Fiamengo, who is twenty years my senior. Patrick also told me to write poems about my Doukhobor heritage, something I've continued to do throughout my literary career.

When Pat Lane proposed that I should become a member of the League, he lined up Lantzville poet and writer Kevin Roberts to be my second sponsor. I had first met Kevin in the initial seminar I attended while beginning my M.A. at SFU. This graduate class in Canadian Literature was taught by Lionel Kearns. Poet and professor Kearns was an original member of the *TISH* poets. The seminar was held at Lionel's home in North Vancouver. I remember going up the hill to find his house for the first class; it was early September and the weather was warm and gardens were colourful with flowers. I passed house after house with neatly manicured lawns and front yards, until I came to a house where the lawn was completely overgrown, with little evidence of any yard work having recently been done. I had found the right address for Lionel Kearns. I have kept this image of what a poet's yard looks like ever since.

Kearns' poetry books from that time include *Practicing Up to be Human* (1978) and *Ignoring THE BOMB: New and Selected Poems* (1982). Later on, I became known to Lionel as his matchmaker, since I introduced him to a high school friend of mine, Gerri Sinclair, whom he later married. Gerri, at that time a Shakespearean scholar, went on to found one of the early high-tech companies. She later became CEO of Microsoft Canada and is now known as one of the leaders of Canadian business and technology.

In 1978, I attended my first annual general meeting of The League of Canadian Poets, held in Montreal. Cathy Ford, U.S.-born Vehicule poet Ken Norris, Ontario poet Laurence Hutchman, Montreal poet Sharon Nelson, and myself were the youngest members of the League at that time. I have written about this first visit to Montreal in a short article entitled "Journals & Journeys," published in *QWrite*, winter 1998.[6] Thus began many years of travel to attend League meetings in different parts of the country, which allowed me to meet both older and contemporary poets from all over Canada.

In the 1980s I served on the national council of the League as Vice-President of Membership, as well as in the position of B.C. Representative. Those years on national council gave me an opportunity to meet and often work with poets that, as a West Coast writer, I would never have come in contact with otherwise. Established writers, from poets such as Dorothy Livesay to poet and novelist Michael Ondaatje and everyone in between, were always generous to me as a younger poet. I loved getting to know all the different regions of Canada, along with their poets and writers. I gave poetry readings all across the country as well as taking part in executive meetings. I got to feel at home in Canada and gained a huge appreciation for the contribution writers make to this country.

I feel privileged to have had this experience, made possible in large part by the Canada Council. Unfortunately, these face-to-face meetings with writers are no longer so prevalent in these days of conference calls, email, and the subsequent scarcity of public funding. During the 1970s and 80s, poets from all over the country, from F.R. Scott, Louis Dudek, and Margaret Atwood on down, made an effort to attend annual meetings. The League ones were not sedate gatherings; rather, they were very much the opposite. They were filled with drama, drinking, politics, partying, and the occasional brawl. I remember one meeting in particular where—before the first evening was over—someone had punched Patrick Lane, and sometime later a woman poet fell down, cut her head open, and had to be taken to emergency. And this was just the opening night!

The Writers' Union had its own meetings, but TWUC always seemed to be less rambunctious than the League's annual gathering of poets. At one League meeting, when mild-mannered and soft-spoken Francis Sparshott was President, Miriam Waddington interrupted the proceedings so many times that Francis ended up breaking down in tears and imploring Miriam to shut up. There was another meeting where a rough-hewn Milton Acorn yelled and screamed throughout the business sections. This provided some comic relief, if nothing else, since the sessions when the League's business was being conducted were often either dull or tension-filled political events.

In those years of the 1970s and 80s in Vancouver, the late poet Gerry Gilbert was producing his handmade literary journal, *B.C. Monthly*, from his large loft-like space at the New Era Social Club near Oppenheimer Park in what is now known as Vancouver's Downtown Eastside. I used to visit Gerry there; his dedication and discipline as a writer became an ongoing inspiration to me. His *B.C. Monthly* and later on, his radiofreerainforest broadcast allowed him to give voice in print and on the radio to many West Coast writers. There were three of Gerry's books from that time that I particularly liked: *Grounds*,[7] *From Next Spring*,[8] and his selected poems *Moby Jane: sounding*.[9]

bill bissett was also publishing poetry titles with his blewointment-press in Vancouver at this time. He published three of my early books between 1977 and 1983. A prolific poet and painter, bill bissett is a Canadian institution. He was at the forefront of performance poetry both in Canada and internationally. Bill is one of the bravest people I have ever known. After a serious fall as a young man, he almost died from neurological complications. He had to relearn all speech and motor functions. Not only did bill write and publish his many collections of poetry, and was he an accomplished painter, but he also gave his time and energy to other writers through his literary small press activities with blewointmentpress. He was always a great inspiration to me in my efforts to keep Caitlin Press alive. To put it quite simply, I adored bill as a poet and a friend.

Another literary small press publisher who was a big help to Caitlin Press was Stephen Osborne, founder of Vancouver's Pulp Press, as well as of *Geist* magazine, which has become a national favourite. In the early days of Caitlin, when we were publishing with limited funds, Steve generously let us use the typesetting equipment at Pulp Press to set our books. Without this, Caitlin would probably not have survived.

Through my friendship with Saturna Island painter Anne Popperwell, I met the young poet Richard Olafson when he attended a poetry reading I was giving on Saturna. Richard went on to found Ekstasis Editions, based in Victoria, B.C. More than twenty years later, Richard told me that hearing me read and talk about Caitlin Press, that day on Saturna Island, was in fact a direct inspiration for him to establish Ekstasis. The poet, professor, filmmaker, and one of the founders of the Kootenay School of Writing, Colin Browne, was another poet my age who spent time on Saturna Island. He was also a friend and fellow M.A. student at SFU when I did my graduate degree. He became the life partner of another high school friend of mine, photographer and Emily Carr art school teacher Marian Penner Bancroft, but in their case I did not introduce them.

Up the coast, Howard and Mary White were running Harbour Publishing in the coastal area of Madeira Park near Pender Harbour. I remember visiting them back when Harbour Publishing was relatively unknown. From their fairly remote coastal location, they built one of B.C.'s foremost literary publishing endeavours. Howard also became a prominent West Coast writer. As well, he ran for provincial political office. From the 1980s on, I also taught creative writing courses in various locations including Sechelt, one of which both Mary White and Howard's congenial father participated in.

These are years in which I also got to know the Sunshine Coast's celebrated poet Peter Trower. When I first met Pete he was living with his elderly mother in Gibsons, the coastal village made famous by the television series *The Beachcombers*. Since I was travelling up and down the coast frequently, I often visited with Pete, and we also gave poetry readings together in Vancouver. He became a valued friend.

When I was an emerging poet in Vancouver, I corresponded with a young John Pass, who once wrote to tell me that both myself and a woman in Toronto were sending him our poems about Emily Dickinson, and why didn't we just write to each other and leave him out of it? That is how my friendship with Vancouver-born poet and lawyer Susan Zimmerman began. Poet John Pass later became the prominent author of *The Hour's Acropolis* (1991) and *Radical Innocence* (1994) from his home base near Pender Harbour that he shares with poet and novelist, Theresa Kishkan, and family. One of John's early chapbooks had a title, *There Go The Cars* (1979), which has somehow stayed with me, even though it is seemingly not that memorable. It always amazed me that such an intricately cerebral writer as John could take that same attention to detail and apply it to building a house himself, which he did. Together, John and Theresa also run the letterpress High Ground Press.

As a graduate student at SFU I was able to take a course on Henry James with the wonderful scholar Peter Buitenhuis; I took another seminar on the Romantic poets with the late Robert Dunham as well as a seminar on American fiction with George Bowering. George is one of Canada's most pre-eminent poets and writers, having won the Governor General's award for both poetry and fiction. He was also Canada's first poet laureate. Bowering was a lively and informative teacher and became an important influence and literary inspiration. I learned a lot from him, both as a professor and as a poet. His late wife, the beautiful Angela Bowering, was a fellow student of mine in Robert Dunham's seminar. It was a significant experience for me to get to know both George and Angela over the SFU years.

My time at SFU brought me into contact with Dr. Ralph Maud, internationally recognized scholar on Dylan Thomas, Charles Olson, and other subjects. I benefited greatly from his interest in subjects that we had in common, and he was tremendously supportive of me when he became my thesis supervisor, even though my interests in Keats and Henry James were not academic specialties of his. From our professional relationship we developed a close personal one. Ralph and I travelled together to the Queen Charlotte Islands, a place we both considered to be one of sacred geography. Together we saw the Haida landscape and art, an experience that engendered another of my long vision-quest poems entitled "Ceremonial Dance."

I met Charles Watts when I was finishing my extended papers. Charles had already written his important M.A. thesis on Ezra Pound when I hired him to help me get my thesis papers into the format required by the university library before they could be accepted and bound. Not only did Charles come to my aid in preparing my papers, he did such a good job of it that he also managed to create for himself an ongoing paid position doing formatting for the library. He held this job for many years afterwards. Thus began my knowing Charles, and to know him was to love him. Charles was a poet, scholar, political theorist, and a very gentle man. He was special. Charles Watts loved poetry. Originally from Southern California, he embraced his adopted home of Vancouver. Charles went on to write a Ph.D. dissertation on the poetry of Wallace Stevens.

We travelled together to Toronto to attend one of Greg Gatenby's infamous Harbourfront International Literary Festivals. Among others, we heard Denise Levertov read her poetry, and the truly dramatic Robertson Davies read from his *Deptford Trilogy*. During the week of the festival, Charles and I spent quite a bit of time with Denise Levertov. She was an unpretentious and lovely woman, interesting to talk with, and friendly. She had an endearing gap-toothed smile, reminding me of Chaucer's famous Wife of Bath. That smile made her less intimidating and all the more approachable. Charles wrote a poetry chapbook based on this time we spent together in Toronto. I've always remembered that Charles and I were together at the time of John Lennon's murder on December 8th, 1980. Charles was taken far too young, a victim of cancer, but his life still managed to touch the hearts of many, including mine.

I can't begin here to cover all the students and professors that I met, learned from, and was enriched by during the years I spent at SFU. I will, however, single out a few, beginning with Professor Sandra Djwa, who wrote an outstanding biography of Canadian poet, lawyer, McGill professor, and political activist F. R. Scott, *The Politics of the Imagination: A Life of F.R. Scott* (1987). (Scott was a major figure in helping to found the CCF, which later became the New Democratic Party of Canada.) One of Canada's top literary biographers, Sandra is currently working on the life of poet P. K. Page. Fred Candelaria was a professor and poet who I knew while at the university, and as fellow poets we did several readings together.

A young Roy Miki served on the examining committee for my M.A. thesis defence.

During the mid-1970s and 1980s, I was fortunate to become close friends with several women poets, writers, editors, and artists. In September 1975, during the first week of my M.A. studies, I met scholar and writer Jean Mallinson, who was then just beginning her Ph.D. in Canadian literature. Jean is twenty years my senior but we started talking and have been in a literary and personal conversation ever since. Besides publishing many scholarly articles and contributing to books on writers such as Margaret Atwood, Jean has also published a book of short stories, *I Will Bring You Berries* (1987), two books of poetry, and recently, the non-fiction work *Terra Infirma: A Life Unbalanced* (2007), a book about the destruction of her balance function caused by taking the antibiotic gentamicin. At times Mallinson and I were a part of a women's literary group and over the years we've known many of the same women writers from Vancouver and across the country. Other poets I have already mentioned include Cathy Ford and the poetry foremothers P.K. Page, Marya Fiamengo, Dorothy Livesay, and Anne Marriott. There were so many other women poets who helped make those times in Vancouver rich and meaningful. To name a few: Leona Gom, Judith Copithorne, the late Dorothy Manning, artist and poet Elizabeth Gourlay, Dona Sturmanis, Helene Rosenthal, Rosemary Hollingshead, Florence McNeil, Lorraine Vernon, and poet and artist Beth Jankola.

I first met Beth Jankola in 1975, when we were both participating in a poetry reading along with other poets. When she got up to read, she shook so hard all over her body that the papers in her hands rattled. It was painful to watch someone as nervous as Jankola perform. We gave a second reading together in a bookstore out in Langley. She shook a little less that time, and less so in every subsequent reading. Beth is ten years older than me and we shared a close friendship and literary relationship for many years. I published four of her books, including one of the early Caitlin Press titles, *Mirror/Mirror.*[10] Beth's husband, Joe Jankola, also grew up in Castlegar along with my father and aunts. Joe was of Italian heritage, and I have always marvelled that so many different ethnic groups lived together during the Depression in this tiny town in the interior of British Columbia. Beth and I travelled together to Toronto, San Francisco, and Los Angeles to give readings, and we organized a poetry series entitled "Studio B" at Beth's art studio in Burnaby.

For many years, Beth and I enjoyed a tradition of meeting on Vancouver's Main Street for monthly dinners at inexpensive East Indian, Italian, and other small restaurants. We would talk about poetry, poets, creative work, and domestic life. We were generally a help to each other in our individual juggling acts of poetry, family life, and maintaining our creativity. Beth published poems in the two literary magazines run by Montreal Vehicle poet Stephen Morrissey. She also corresponded with him. Sometimes she brought his letters to our dinners to read to me. One time she even brought a photograph of him in which he looked quite ascetic. We began to refer to him as "Monk Morrissey" (In 1989 I edited and published Morrissey's book, *Family Album*, but I had not met him, and we did not share a literary or personal friendship). Jankola was an excellent source of literary gossip and introductions. She now lives on the Sunshine Coast, where she devotes her time to her artwork, operating the Field Road Studio.

Mona Fertig, poet and publisher, came from a family that lived next door to the Jankolas in Burnaby, B.C. Mona's father, George Fertig, was an accomplished painter who was devoted to Jungian ideas. Unfortunately, his paintings were ahead of their time in the suburban city of Burnaby and he was not a commercial success, but his work can be seen on the cover of Mona's *Invoking the Moon: Selected Poems 1975-1989* (2006) and at her websites.

Regarding characters, I worked with Vancouver's legendary jazz pianist, composer, and author Al Neil. On the back cover of Al's book of stories *Slammer* (1981), it talks about Neil's international reputation as a major jazz innovator, hipster, veteran, and multi-disciplinary artist. At the time that Al and I connected, he was working with percussionist Howard Broomfield, whose percussion instruments were comprised mainly of bottles of booze that had been consumed by self-confessed former heroin user Al Neil. Somehow Broomfield managed to create—by filling an assortment of used bottles with different quantities of water and suspending them from a homemade frame—a beautiful and unique sound instrument.

Al Neil liked my long vision-quest poems, and he invited me to perform live with him and Howard. We performed my poem "The Dreamkeeper" with Al on piano and Howard on percussion, both musicians creating original jazz to accompany my reading. We gave this performance for the first time on November 18, 1978 at the Pumps Gallery in Gastown, Vancouver. We then performed and taped this work at Psichord Studios on December 20, 1979 in Vancouver. Tapes exist of both these performances.

Both the legendary Al Neil and the innovative Howard Broomfield were highly charged creatively, and a handful to work with. Nevertheless, working with them became an act that we took on the road. We presented my long vision-quest poem "Journey to the Sibyl" with vocal reading by myself, Al Neil on piano, and Howard Broomfield on percussion. From Montreal, we then visited Toronto, where Al and Howard produced an album of Neil's work entitled *boot & fog*. This 33 1/3 vinyl long-play album was produced by The Music Gallery, Toronto, Ontario (1981). Included with the record, made over the same few days in Toronto, was an extended-play 45 entitled "Journey to the Sibyl," which consisted of my performance of the poem with Neil and Broomfield's jazz accompaniment.

Working with these two in rehearsals, in studio, and in live performance was exhilarating, exciting, off-the-wall, and unforgettable. One of the important reasons this show hung together was Howard's calming influence and pragmatism. Only a few years after this collaboration, the artistic community was stunned and saddened by the news that Howard Broomfield had committed suicide. Al Neil is still alive, an incomparable fixture on the Vancouver music and literary scenes. He has lived for many years in a wooden house on the mudflats of North Vancouver, near where the famous novelist and author of *Under the Volcano* Malcolm Lowry once lived. Neil has long been the romantic partner of Vancouver artist and writer Carole Itter. Al Neil is both a survivor and one of the last true bohemians.

In 1983, I took on the job of producing all Caitlin Press titles by myself. However, Canada Council funding was a big help by this point. At this time I served for several years on the national executive of The League of Canadian Poets, which included extensive travelling throughout Canada. From 1981 to 1991, I lived and raised my children in a renovated home in Kerrisdale, up the hill and not far from where I had lived during the 1970s. There was George Bowering, Elizabeth Gourlay, George Woodcock, Ed Varney, and myself who were fellow poets and writers living in the neighbourhood at this time. Bowering's book-long poem, *Kerrisdale Elegies* (1984), based on the work of Rilke, still resonates with me from those twenty years spent living in the Kerrisdale and Dunbar areas of southwestern Vancouver.

In those days, we went to each other's readings, read fellow poet's books, and gathered frequently to drink beer together and talk shop. The pub at the Cecil Hotel (which is now a place where strippers perform) was where George Bowering and other poets would gather on Friday nights to generally argue, carry on, and have fun together. After poetry readings we usually went out to whatever was the nearest pub.

These poets included David Phillips, Pierre Coupey, and the argumentative Brian Fawcett, who at that time was publishing his lit magazine *NMFG*, as well as any poet who was in Vancouver from out of town. A personal gift George Bowering had was to be able to mix with other poets in an informal way. He was witty, fun to be with, and dedicated to literature. George was a catalyst for gathering other poets around him. Not only that, but he had (and still has) a great radio voice. Part of his gift is an ability to joke around with poets of different ages and accomplishments, putting everyone around him at ease.

Brian Fawcett was a fixture on the poetry scene in Vancouver during these years. He published his magazine *No Money From the Government*, partly as a sounding board for his leftist political ideology. A talented poet, Fawcett announced in the 1980s that he was officially quitting poetry. His last poetry book was *Aggressive Transport* (1982). From then on, he wrote fiction and non-fiction social critiques. Brian also married a friend of mine from high school; he divorced her and then remarried her. Luckily, I had not introduced them.

Montreal Vehicle poet Tom Konyves, whom I originally met in Montreal in 1978, moved to the Vancouver area in 1983. Konyves is an experimental poet who coined the term "videopoems" to describe his multimedia work. His videopoetry and performance works make him one of the original pioneers of the form. Tom also ran a video production company, AM Productions, for many years in Vancouver. One of Konyves' books published in Montreal was entitled *No Parking* (1978). In 1998, I published Konyves' book of poetry *Ex Perimeter*. Konyves and I at one point shared the position of B.C. rep for the League of Canadian Poets, and in Vancouver we organized the first of what has now become the League's national W(rites) of Spring annual fundraising event. I've continued to see Tom over the past eighteen years at various readings and poetry-related events. Its always seemed odd to both Tom and myself that he ended up living out West, when Montreal was much more his natural milieu and I, a born and bred West Coaster, have made my home in Quebec for many years.

When the 1980s ended and the 1990s began, sweeping changes came into my life. My book, *The Taste of Giving: New & Selected Poems*, was published in the fall of 1990. This book was comprised of a selection of my poems written between 1975 and 1990. It includes a lucid and intelligent introduction by Jean Mallinson. Around the same time, I co-founded The Poem Factory with Ed Varney. When Varney and I began working together, we were both living within close walking distance of each other in Kerrisdale.

In April of 1991, I sold Caitlin Press. Moving from Kerrisdale to the new house had involved a great deal of downsizing. By selling the Kerrisdale home, publishing my selected poems, and selling Caitlin Press, I was unconsciously clearing the decks for what turned out to be an entirely surprising new phase of my life.

At the end of May 1991, I attended a Writers' Union national meeting at John Abbott College in Ste.-Anne-de-Bellevue, Quebec, an hour west of Montreal. Having published Stephen Morrissey's poetry book in 1989, I wrote to let him know that I was planning to visit Quebec for the weekend. He wrote back, saying, "The least I can do is pick you up at the airport." And, as they say, the rest is history. My mother said I took one professional trip too many.

Ed Varney and I continued collaborating with the renamed small press The Poem Factory/Usine de Poeme, from 1992 until 1999. This cross-country literary endeavour was a creative and unique contribution to Canadian small-press publishing. We concentrated on producing broadsides, limited edition books and chapbooks, and anthologies. The philosophy behind the press was to keep costs to a minimum, thus leading to many ingenious approaches to production. Our publications were often hand-folded and sometimes hand-sewn, or otherwise bound by hand by Ed Varney, the enormously talented graphic artist and poet. Varney's books include *What the Wind Said* (1992) and *Solar Eclipse* (1994).

Among the many authors we published were Glen Sorestad, Robin Skelton, Victor Coleman, Gerry Gilbert, Cathy Ford, Barry Dempster, Ken Norris, and David McFadden. This productive partnership between Varney and myself was possible because we used his Kerrisdale home as our base of production, and I commuted on a regular basis to Vancouver, to visit my family and to work with Varney. There was no formal decision to end work with the press; rather, it became more difficult for Ed and I to meet once he moved to Vancouver Island and I stopped regularly commuting to the West Coast. Ed Varney still publishes occasionally as The Poem Factory.

As a poet and writer, I've always listened to and followed the writing, rather than imposing my own designs on it. I always consider that every piece of writing I do—be it poem, essay, story, or book—has a life of its own, separate from me. This essay is only the mere tip of the iceberg regarding the many poets, writers, editors, publishers, scholars, readers, and others who I met during the 1970s and 1980s in Vancouver and across Canada.

I would like to thank my assistant, freelance editor Marie Thone, for keyboarding and for her keen editorial expertise. I thank Stephen Morrissey for research, fact checking, and his overall unfailing support.

I dedicate this essay to the lives and writing of three deceased Vancouver poets. I felt their presence with me during this work of reaching back through memory to hear the voices of Vancouver's poets. This essay is dedicated to Eric Ivan Berg, Nellie McClung, and Jon Furberg.

think like a poet,
use your wits like Odysseus,
enjoy the story
of your own life
and watch for me, Coyote,
I may cross the road
in front of you
or visit you in your dreams.

from "Coyote"
Carolyn Zonailo
(Montreal - Vancouver 2008-09)

Notes:

1. Nellie McClung, ed., *Pomegranate: A Selected Anthology of Vancouver Poetry* (Vancouver: Intermedia, 1975).

2. Frederick H Candelaria, ed., *New West Coast: 72 contemporary British Columbia poets* (Vancouver: Intermedia, 1977).

3. Ingrid Klassen, ed., *D'Sonoqua: An Anthology of Women Poets of British Columbia Volumes 1 + 2* (Vancouver: Intermedia, 1979).

4. Paul Belserene, ed., *Canadian Short Fiction Anthology* (Vancouver: Intermedia, 1982).

5. Di Brandt and Barbara Godard, eds., *Re: Generations, Canadian Women Poets in Conversation* (Windsor, Ontario: Black Moss Press, 2005).

6. The article can also be found on Carolyn Zonailo's personal website, http://www.carolynzonailo.com/poetics/11.php.

7. Gerry Gilbert, *Grounds* (Vancouver: Talonbooks, 1976).

8. Gerry Gilbert, From *Next Spring* (Toronto: Coach House, 1977).

9. Gerry Gilbert, *Moby Jane: sounding* (Toronto: Coach House, 1987).

10. Beth Jankola, *Mirror/Mirror* (Vancouver: Caitlin Press, 1978).

The Great Story of British Columbia:
ROBERT BRINGHURST AND HAIDA ORAL LITERATURE

PAUL FALARDEAU

The hardest part of anything is the beginning. Every story needs one. Sometimes they are hard to find, but without a beginning we have nothing to build on. And so with Canadian literature (often portrayed as a new breed, the product of a transplanted European art form onto North American soil), only part of a great story that is anything but new is being told. In reality, the story of Canada, or the area of land that has been drawn within its borders on maps, is as old as any other in the world. For a long time the Eurocentric gaze simply left out the beginning.

Colonial and post-colonial literature in Canada has been strongly based on European written forms and has rigorously reflected the story of our country since adventurers like Jacques Cartier washed up on these shores. These literatures, however, have told a story that is out of context and impossible to properly understand. To understand a story as long and complex as the epic of Canada, what is needed are roots.

They can be found in aboriginal literature. In the foreword to Gary Snyder's revolutionary work *He Who Hunted Birds in His Father's Village*,' which demonstrates a full breakdown of Haida myth, discussing it in the same way other European classical works are discussed, Robert Bringhurst writes, "Any healthy and sustainable human culture in North America has to rest region by region and watershed by watershed, on indigenous foundations."[2] Further, in his essay "The Polyhistorical Mind" he observes, "Canadian writers and critics...have been saying for many years, with almost perfect unanimity, that Canadian literature speaks from the land, that its allegiance is to *place*. If we believe any of that, doesn't it follow that our literature, and our literary history, has to begin with the voices that spoke from this place first and have spoken from it longest and appear to know its deepest layers best?"[3] Logic argues that the literatures that should form the base of our national or provincial literatures are those that are tied closest to the land, which is where all stories inevitably come from. It follows that the stories which form the base of British Columbian literature must undoubtedly shape the container which can then be filled by stories from aboriginal cultures as well as European and Asian immigrants from colonial and post-colonial times. Bringhurst says of this, "If we do want to learn how to live in the world, I think the study of Native American Literature is one of the best and most efficient ways to do just that. It is, after all, a literature of ideas. The ideas are expressed in images, not abstract language, yet the thought is often dense and profound. And the fundamental subject of this thought, this intellectual tradition, is the relationship between humans and the rest of the world."[4] Speaking of the unique form and symbolism in the literatures of Native Americans, Bringhurst contends that when properly regarded, they enable a suitable integration of literature and place.

British Columbia accounts for approximately sixty percent of Canada's First Nations languages. The larger diversity of languages indigenous to Canada is found on the West Coast;[5] because of this, Native literature in B.C. is an important area of study. In British Columbia, our literary foundations must come from the traditions and stories that are a part of the Salish and Tsimshian language families, as well as many others from the 203 First Nations communities native to the province. In "The Polyhistorical Mind," Bringhurst explains how "a literary map of [Canada] would be first of all a map of languages, several layers deep. On the base layers there would be no signs at all of English and French. At least sixty-five, perhaps as many as eighty, different languages, of at least ten different major families, were spoken in this country when Jacques Cartier arrived."[6]

Haida culture, in particular, has been a focal point for much scholarly discussion, including Bringhurst's, due in part to its powerfully symbolic, immediately identifiable artwork that has been made famous by artists like Charles Edenshaw and Bill Reid. More significantly, Haida language and storytelling have received widespread international attention through a number of beautiful translations, which have recognized the brilliance of some of its iconic figures.[7]

The tradition of translating First Nation stories into forms accessible to people outside of these cultures was started by thoughtful Europeans who listened to Canada's indigenous people, to the elders, mythtellers, and poets who were patient and kind enough to share their stories. Émile Petitot listened to Ekunelyel, a blind elder who taught him Chipewyan and told him stories, which he later transcribed. Petitot also recorded the words of Big Rabbit Woman, possibly the first Native Canadian woman recorded in her own language. Later, Franz Boas worked with Q'elti for three summers in 1890, 1891, and 1894 on the Northwest Coast around Haida Gwaii[8] and produced *Chinook Texts* and *Kathlamet Texts*. His work with Q'elti would inspire him to suggest his student John Swanton pursue the Native literatures of the Northwest Coast.[9]

Swanton arrived at the Haida town of Skidegate and began working with the Haida poet Skaay. Along with the poet Ghandl, who also worked with Swanton, Skaay became recognized as one of the great masters of Haida literature. However, this was only later when younger men such as Gary Snyder, and subsequently Robert Bringhurst, revisited Swanton's translations years after Swanton's work *Haida Texts and Myths: Skidegate Dialect* was published in 1905.[10]

As he recounts, Bringhurst was driven to discover the literatures of Native Americans upon his realization that "I knew nothing of the literary heritage of the land in which I lived, nor the mountains I'd grown up in, nor any other part of North America."[11] Through his research he acquired reading and oral fluency in Haida, worked with Bill Reid on several historic projects, and has since published three large books of classic Haida myths as told by Skaay and Ghandl.[12] These books lay groundwork for the foundations upon which all future studies the literature of B.C. must be built on.

In three magisterial volumes prepared under the series title of *Masterworks of the Classical Haida Mythtellers*, Bringhurst offers immediate insight into the storytelling style of the Haida people. These volumes are entitled *A Story As Sharp As a Knife: The Classical Haida Mythtellers and Their World* (1999),[13] *Nine Visits to the Mythworld* (a reinterpretation of the stories of Mythteller Ghandl of the Qayahl Llaanas, as collected in 1900 by John Reed Swanton) (2000),[14] and *Being in Being: The Collected Works of a Master Haida Mythteller—Skaay of the Qquuna Qiighawaay*(2002).[15]

The stories these books contain are arguably some of the most important pieces of writing to come out of British Columbia. Indeed, as Margaret Atwood declared in *The London Times*, Bringhurst's work is "is an American Iliad."[16] Her pronouncement came as a severe rebuke to academic voices in Canada who had cavalierly accused Bringhurst of "cultural appropriation," and began an effective rollback in Canadian intellectual life of academic political correctness. An exciting firsthand look at the lives of people indigenous to the province, these volumes illustrate such daily activities as hunting, gathering, and craft-making. They also reflect for us such typical cultural activities as carving, painting, playing with gambling sticks, and sports.

Frequently humorous, the stories have moral underpinnings, such as in the story "Spirit Being Living in the Little Finger" from *Nine Visits to the Mythworld*. In this tale "they say they [the local villagers] turned against a mother and her child." The boy who has been spurned by the villagers nonetheless shows sympathy for a Heron, who rewards him with a way to exact his revenge by putting a curse on the child of a "good family." The morals here are not so black and white, although there are simple ones such as the what-goes-around nature of the curse; the protagonist eventually lifts the curse, promoting forgiveness and a realization that evil will only beget evil.[17]

The nature of Haida storytelling Bringhurst exhibits for us is poetic, entertaining, and above all, human. Repeated phrases such as "they say," which is often tagged on to the end of lines, adds coherence between sections, as well as an echo of history and authenticity. Themes re-occur, as in "How the Weather Chose to Be Born" from *Nine Visits to the Mythworld*. When one day a young lord goes hunting for birds, "The next day he brought in a Stellar's Jay / and he skinned it / and dried it." Shortly thereafter, we hear "Next, they say, he went out in the skin of the Stellar's Jay. / And he said to his mother, / "Come look at me." / She followed him outside. / Above the sea, her son was spread out wide and blue."[18]

Along with sophisticated use of reoccurring themes, Bringhurst's source mythtellers incorporated an elaborate symbolism. The Stellar's Jay, we learn, is meant to represent clear weather, a time when the creature is active. Similarly, the nominal protagonist of this story concerning the birth of weather dons many bird skins in order to produce different types of weather. Symbols compound when the bird he chooses pair not only with the weather they are often associated with, but also the colours of those seasons and weather-types.

As dazzling as Bringhurst's interpretations are—an outcome of the pioneering hard work of Swanton—they still lack a key component, which is the storyteller. These, let us remember, are oral poems and entertainments; the extra dimension of understanding is lost without a proper telling. Instances such as "One day the child said / 'Mother like this' / he was gesturing with his hands" feel incomplete without proper enunciation and visual gestures.

Still, even in the written version of these stories we find a tone and a set of morals that permeate the works. Although our knowledge of all pre-colonial British Columbian works is minimal, we can begin to trace certain foundational ideas.

First Nations literature aside, all of the world's enduring literature is based on oral traditions and the litany of humanity's beloved and influential stories based on oral traditions includes such perennial favourites as *The Iliad* and *The Odyssey, Beowulf, The Nibelungenlied, El Poema de Mio Cid,* Ireland's *Táin Bó Cúailnge,* the *Ramayana* in India, the *Hōjōki* in Japan, and *Journey to the West* from China. All find beginnings within oral tradition, and, like Haida myths, owe much of their style, tone, subject matter and ideals to the storyteller. It is through the voice and tone of the teller of the tale that we experience deeper levels of interactions with the literature.

In light of this, Bringhurst devotes much of his interest to preserving the oral element of these invaluable cultural artefacts, lecturing internationally on the importance of oral traditions. In an interview in *The Pacific Rim Review of Books* with Sergio Cohn, Bringhurst says, "Oral literature is different from written literature. There is no fixed text. If you reread a printed book, you will find things you didn't see before, because you, the reader, have changed, though the book has probably not. In oral culture, the teller changes as well as the listener, so the story itself is being constantly revised."

Conventionally, oral literatures have posed the academic problem of being difficult to classify as "literature," which traditionally has been defined by a canon of written works from a specific culture. Through his published translations, Bringhurst demonstrates convincingly that this represents only one, narrow version of the evidence. Oral literatures are not merely acceptable, he argues, but in some cases superior, for they provide the literature with flexibility that written literatures cannot. The distinction boils down to differences between tellers of the same story, whereas written works only change with the reader-listener. Naturally, written literatures offer permanence. Unless recorded, oral literatures vanish when their languages die.

"Language is different from writing," Bringhurst argues. "Both must be learned, but every human society shelters and nurtures a language which all full-fledged members are expected to acquire. Writing is an optional technology which most human beings and most human cultures have done happily without."[20] In this sense, seeing writing as a technology, we can separate what is simply written from that which constitutes literature. The same holds true with First Nations literature. Even if kept orally as cultural artefacts, important story traditions retain as much merit as any written literature. Bringhurst says of this that "The subject of classical Native American literature is nothing more or less than the nature of the world. It is a literature concerned with fundamental questions. At its best, it is as nourishing and beautiful and wise as any poetry that exists."[21]

As an obvious, foundational component for the conservation and study of the larger corpus of B.C. literature, especially its multi-dimensional form, the distinct oral literatures of First Nation cultures such as the Haida and others require preservation; not only in being written and re-told by elders who know them and speak the original languages, but by new ears who will listen and learn them in order to pass them down again. As the celebrated travails of Bringhurst in his translations have shown, the etiquette involved in these cultural transmissions and re-transmissions can be problematic and need refinement: even so, these are projects that must be undertaken, for all stories, Haida, European, or otherwise.

As Bringhurst explains of the process, "Culture is exogenetic heredity, nothing less and nothing more. It is everything we transmit from generation to generation by non-genetic means. Ethnological identity has to be learned, where biological identity does not, but it has to be learned from those who possess it."[22] In addition to tradition, ritual culture is transmitted through language; unfortunately many of the languages that are critical for passing on the key pieces of our B.C. literature, its indigenous foundation, have been lost or are quickly slipping away. Bringhurst expands upon the existential urgency of this in contending, "A language is a life form, like a species of plant or animal. Once it is extinct, it is gone forever. And as each one dies the intellectual gene pool of the human species shrinks,"[23] and that "in a state of environmental health, when languages die, other languages—neighbours and children of those that are dying— are growing up to replace them. When you kill a language off and replace it with an import, you kill part of the truth."[24]

What defines British Columbia's literature? It may be that every person who creates a story or poem, or whenever water creates a wave or a tree produces a cone, it has created something that is a part of B.C. literature. In his essay "The Tree of Meaning," Bringhurst says, "If you embody oral culture, you are a working part of a place, a part of the soil in which stories live their lives."[25] Only by looking organically at the fuller picture, one that includes Native literatures, the influence of European and Asian literature, and the very literature the land has inspired, can we come to a genuinely meaningful sense of a true B.C. literature. A beginning, middle, and end are all part of the story of what we call British Columbia, and they are not given to take any sensible order; each facet demands our attention at once. What literature this grand story creates cannot ever properly be written down in full. Instead, the story speaks to us every day, from every face, every tree, every rock. The true story of British Columbia's literature is spoken by many tongues.

Notes:

1. Gary Snyder, *He Who Hunted Birds in His Father's Village: The Dimensions of Haida Myth* (Bolinas, CA: Shoemaker & Horde, 1979).

2. Robert Bringhurst, "Foreword" in *The Tree of Meaning: Thirteen Talks* (Kentville, NS: Gaspereau Press, 2006).

3. Robert Bringhurst, "The Polyhistorical Mind," in *The Tree of Meaning*.

4. Ibid.

5. See "First People's Language Map of British Columbia"; First People's Heritage, Language and Culture Council. http://maps.fphlcc.ca/

6. Robert Bringhurst, "The Polyhistorical Mind," 24.

7. These include works by Bringhurst: *A Story as Sharp as a Knife*, *Nine Journeys into the Mythworld*, and *Being in Being*.

8. The traditional Haida name for The Queen Charlotte Islands.

9. The accounts of the studies of these men are further detailed by Bringhurst in *The Tree of Meaning* as well as in Vernon J. Williams Jr., *Rethinking Race: Franz Boas and His Contemporaries* (Lexington: University Press of Kentucky, 1996).

10. Much of Swanton's work had been left stashed in government offices and was almost forgotten.

11. Robert Bringhurst, "Foreword."

12. Other works on Haida myth and culture include *The Raven Steals the Light* with Bill Reid (1984) and *The Black Canoe* with photographs by Ulli Steltzer (1991), as well as numerous essays, many of which are collected in *The Tree of Meaning*.

13. Robert Bringhurst, trans., *A Story as Sharp as a Knife: The Haida Mythtellers and Their World* (Vancouver: Douglas & McIntyre, 1999).

14. Robert Bringhurst, trans., *Ghandl of the Qayahl Llaanas: Nine Visits to the Mythworld* (Vancouver: Douglas & McIntyre, 2000).

15. Robert Bringhurst, trans., *Skaay of the Qquuna Qiighawaay: Being in Being* (Vancouver: Douglas & McIntyre, 2001).

16. Stephen Henighan, "Vancouver Vistas," *The London Times*, September 19, 2003.

17. Bringhurst, trans., "Spirit Being Living in Little Finger," in *Ghandl of the Qayahl Llaanas*.

18. Bringhurst, trans., "The Way the Weather Chose to be Born," in *Ghandl of the Qayahl Llaanas*, 45.

19. Trevor Carolan and Richard Olafson, *Against the Shore: The Best of the Pacific Rim Review of Books* (Victoria: Ekstasis Editions, 2008).

20. Bringhurst, *The Tree of Meaning*, 128.

21. Ibid., 78.

22. Ibid., 88.

23. Ibid., 30.

24. Ibid., 163.

25. Ibid., 175.

The Mountain in the Lake:
REFLECTIONS ON THE INNER AND OUTER LANDSCAPE IN THE WRITING OF NORTHERN BRITISH COLUMBIA

CHELSEA THORNTON

Life in Northern British Columbia is inextricably linked with the land. We build islands of civilization, towns clinging to the coast or huddling at the bottom of steep mountain valleys, light them with streetlights, fill them with grocery stores, link them with highways, but still, the landscape invariably reminds us that we exist here only because it grudgingly allows us to. Always it sends reminders of its power, sometimes subtle, sometimes sweeping and unmistakable. Carefully landscaped gardens are grazed by deer that casually roam the city streets, and wolf packs trail the deer, their paw prints marking the gardens' freshly turned earth. Streetlights go out with the power in winter storms, plunging towns into the gloom of long winter nights. The storms also attack the highways, cutting off the tenuous link of asphalt from town to town, and the bright, shiny shelves of grocery stores slowly empty, the trucks destined to stock them trapped further south on friendlier roads. A town is still largely defined by the natural resource it exploits: a fishing town, a logging town, a mining town. The people who live in Northern B.C. are constantly forced to be aware of the landscape that they live in.

Barry Lopez, an American writer and environmentalist, suggests that there are two landscapes, the landscape *outside* of the body, and the landscape *inside*. Lopez sees these two landscapes as closely linked. The first landscape he describes is "the one we see—not only the line and colour of the land and its shading at different times of the day, but also its plants and animals in season, its weather, its geology, the record of its climate and evolution."[1] The landscape of Northern British Columbia is powerful. Mountains tumble into the sea and sweep upwards to claw at turbulent storm clouds in the winter, or to caress the Northern Lights in the summer. The coast is a series of flooded mountain ranges. The animals and plants are diverse and resilient, capable of capturing the imagination. For Lopez, the second landscape is "an interior one, a kind of projection within a person of a part of the exterior landscape."[2] A person adopts the characteristics of the outer landscape they inhabit, integrating it into their interior landscape. We can apply this model to the people of Northern British Columbia. In a region where the outer landscape is so dramatic and such an integral part of daily life, the projection is extremely strong. The inner landscape of Northern people is marbled with the characteristics of the region they live in.

For writers, interior landscape is in turn integrated into writing, so that ultimately, their writing is a reflection of the landscape. This integration can be conscious or unconscious, and range from the smallest quirk in the writing that mirrors some aspect of the landscape to the near complete translation of the landscape that is apparent in Northern British Columbian writing. Jacqueline Baldwin is a poet who has lived outside of Prince George since 1969. Like all things in Northern B.C., my information from Baldwin travelled a long distance. I contacted her after reading some of her poetry while I was living in Prince Rupert, 718 kilometres to the west of Prince George. So began a series of letters and emails, during which she shared her thoughts about the influence that the landscape of Northern B.C. had on the area's writing. She said that for herself "it is a deep influence; in fact I would say it was and remains the guiding influence on my writing. Everything in my mind comes back to the land, eventually."[3] The influence of the outer landscape on the inner is evident in the writing of other Northern B.C. authors as well, thanks to the intimate relationship that the people share with the region. The writing of Northern B.C. captures pieces of both the outer and inner landscapes. It is characterized by simplicity and honesty of language and diction, a detailed knowledge of the land, and a deep respect for it.

Northern B.C. is rough. The landscape offers up infinite reminders of nature's realities, even for city dwellers, since they are at best precariously perched on the edge of wilderness. It is impossible not to be aware of the ecological relationships and environmental pressures of the area. Jacqueline explained that her "life on the land has been full of experiences of deep intimate connections with the stark realities of living close to nature and the wilderness."[4] The bluntness of a landscape that does not hide its harsh realities engenders a similar directness in its writing. This directness is sometimes shown through the simplicity of the language used to portray dark events. Northern writers often avoid metaphors and euphemisms, relating events simply and bluntly. Eden Robinson's writing is especially tough. Robinson pulls no punches when describing an attack on a chicken coop by a hawk: "A chicken ran through the yard with its guts trailing behind it, flapping its one wing, shrieking. A hawk plunged...squashed the screeching chicken...and pecked its eyes."[5] She does not shy away from the brutality of the situation, and makes no effort to cushion it with language. Robinson's depiction of the hawk is as direct as the animal's attack, mirroring the hawk. The Lower-Mainland-raised poet and novelist Tim Bowling's treatment of death is by contrast much more stylized: "Guilty men skulk along the dyke carrying burlap sacks / of mewling kittens...The tossed sacks throb like hearts as they sink."[6] Bowling's use of metaphor lends a dreamlike quality to his description of death that is absent in Robinson's depiction.

Robinson is not the only Northern author who makes use of simple language to starkly and effectively depict subject matter that other authors might tip-toe around. Jacqueline Baldwin even quotes the voice of a dying deer: "with the coyote in hot pursuit / she left blood on the snow / a message that read / I am destined to die / I will never leave this valley."[7] This simplicity is not limited to representations of the animal world either. Human life is often described with the same blunt pen. Death is a reality for people as surely as it is for animals. For Northern writers, humans return to the earth the same as everything else, and there is nothing to be squeamish about. Robinson tells us to: "Pick wild blueberries when you're hungry... Realize that the plumpest berries are over the graves."[8] The juxtaposition of simple language with complex subject matter serves to ensure that the reader's full attention is dedicated to the subject. Like the landscape, Northern British Columbian authors often force an awareness of life's realities, using language as natural, and sometimes as rough, as the landscape itself.

Life in Northern B.C. often provides writers with a collection of technical and instinctual knowledge of the landscape. Living closely with the land engenders a deep understanding of it. Technical knowledge arises from needing to understand the life and land you live so closely with, while instinctual knowledge comes from *wanting* to understand it. This technical knowledge has always been evident in First Nations stories. Even children's stories read like an ecologist's observations, assessing the complex links between the seasons, the land, and the animals. Children's author Christie Harris writes in *Mouse Woman and the Muddleheads*, "The sun was shining on ice rimming the river; eagles were circling overhead; and far downriver there was the bellowing of the sea lions who—like the seals and the seagulls and the people—were following the crowded tribes of tiny oolichans into the river."[9] Northern writing continues to be typified by an understanding of the history, geography and ecology of the landscape. From the Romantic period of Byron onward, writers elsewhere have had too predictably an undifferentiated, stylized view of nature, as in Byron's description of wilderness: "There is a pleasure in the pathless woods, / There is a rapture on the lonely shore, / There is society, where none intrudes, / By the deep sea, and music in its roar."[10] A forest is a forest, the shore is the shore. For Northern writers like Eden Robinson and Baldwin a forest is a collection of "spruce and cedar groves," [11] and the shore is where "you [can] watch crabs skittering sideways over discarded clam and cockleshells, and shiners flicking back and forth. Kelp the colour of brown beer bottles [rises] from the bottom, tall and thin with bulbs on top." [12] Susan Musgrave's writing epitomizes the mixing of concrete knowledge with a yearning for still greater understanding typical of the region's writing: "After the great earthquake in Alaska, fishermen began catching halibut that were full of stones. The fish had...ingested the stones to ballast themselves against the shocks...What did the stones feel as they were gulped down into darkness?" [13] Perhaps writers in the North include detailed descriptions and explanations about the region and all its life because they are motivated to share the influence of the landscape with those who cannot live in it. In response, Baldwin says: "For example if I am writing a story about children playing in a schoolyard in the city, I feel sad when I notice that there is a disconnect between the children's feet and the land because they are playing on pavement ...They do not have the luxury of looking up through leafy branches of trees to the beautiful Northern sky." [14] The urge to share the landscape they live in is compelling for Northern writers.

Many North Americans have a tendency to deify wilderness, an untouched nature, completely separate from human influence. This habit, passed down to us from the Romantics and American essayists like Henry David Thoreau and Ralph Waldo Emerson, is evident in the popularity of eco-tourism and the pervasiveness of our search for the ultimate "wilderness experience." However, a lack of under-standing of actual landscapes often leads us to superficially worship an imaginary nature, untouched, remote, and distant. We are awed by the Amazon, but we ignore the forests just outside of our cities. Or we only admire our forests until they suffer the smallest human impingement. The moment we fell the first tree, the forest loses its fairytale quality, its majesty, and our awe; as well our desire to protect the forest falls along with that first tree. This is the problem with the deification of pristine nature: it removes our ability to respect nature in all its forms, which makes us complicit in the degradation of all but a few last great strongholds of what we imagine to be wilderness. For American author Wendell Berry, this is a terrible failure on our part. He says that "There is simply nothing in Creation that does not matter ...We cannot be improved—in fact, we cannot help but be damaged—by useless or greedy or merely ignorant destruction of anything."[15] Northern writers agree with him. This is evident in Musgrave's writing: "A single grain of sand is as worthy of our praise as the open white flowers of the shining summer plum; we should beware when too much light falls on everything because if we are blinded by darkness we are also blinded by light."[16] She encourages us to appreciate and respect the small, obscure and often ignored aspects of nature and landscape, as well as the more obviously beautiful parts that we already respect. If we fail to do so, we are more likely to accept its destruction. As Native-American and Irish writer Louis Owens explains, unless "all human beings can learn to imagine themselves as intimately and inextricably linked to *every* aspect of the world they inhabit...the earth simply will not survive."[17] This view is echoed in the stories of the Haida people. In one story, the cruel killing of a simple frog brings pitiless retribution: "Like burning oil, fire flamed even on the water. And there was no escape for the people who had forgotten their respect for the world around them, the world of creatures and spirit beings."[18] In Northern British Columbia, respect for the real landscape, the landscape you learn "not by knowing the name or identity of everything in it, but by perceiving the relationships in it,"[19] infuses local writing. Northern writers' respect stems from an understanding that "the land doesn't belong to us / we belong to it."[20]

This respect often manifests itself as a link between Northern speakers and the land. The link is a mix of awe and reverence that the writers have for every piece of the land, a sense of stewardship towards it, and a comfort that the inner landscape draws from the outer landscape. Northern writing often reverberates with wonder about the landscape, great and small. Musgrave writes: "A beach pebble unadorned, a river rock licked into an egg—the wild, tumbling-free stones—are the ones most precious to me. Stones pulled by the tides, polished by the moon." [21] The writers are capable of evoking in the reader a childlike awe for details of the landscape that most readers have long forgotten, encouraging us, like Baldwin does, to "*gently* touch the hard-curled edges of the lichen on / surrounding rocks and stones or *admire* the / sponginess and *intricate* patterns of the moss / *exclaiming* over the colours and shapes of / tiny flowers that peek through it / like *hidden jewels* suddenly revealed," [22] [*author's emphasis*] and in doing so also encourage us to rediscover our reverence for these details. This reverence is then translated into an awareness of our responsibility to the landscapes we inhabit.

In Northern B.C., there is a struggle to strike a balance between resource extraction and conservation, between economics and emotion. The writing of the region captures this struggle. In Baldwin's *A Northern Woman*, two poems are placed consecutively. First, she tells us the story of a logger, who "tired, triumphant / would put his pay-cheque on the table / say to [a] mother: / for you my darling." [23] In juxtaposition with this poem, the next describes a man's reaction to logging activity outside his childhood home: "he cried when he saw the clearcuts / saw the forest was gone from the hillsides / he made wailing sounds / howled at the sky / shaking his fists in despair." [24] In her letters, Baldwin explained the effect she feels the alteration of the outer landscape in this way affects the inner landscape: "I have observed how the landscape of a clearcut is destructive to those who have the sad experience of seeing it, or living within these areas, or worse, actually working to make their living from destroying the forest in this way." [25] Where does the right compromise lie for the two men in Baldwin's poems, representative of so many others? For the Haida, the balance rests on respect. They have a long history of meeting all their needs by hunting and harvesting the land and the sea. They balance these practices by offering the landscape their respect in return: Christie Harris notes in her story about Mouse Woman that "They would always be ready with gifts of berries and mountain goat fat; they would always be ready to waft eagle down reverently over troubled waters; they would never, never spit in the sea."[26] This respect is evident in the work of Northern B.C. writers.

Respect for the landscape also stems from an appreciation for the calm it sometimes provides us. For writers in Northern B.C, living in a region where the landscape is woven through the experiences of every day, chances to gain calm through the land are endless. The writers often refer to the sense of quiet and rightness that the region affords them. Musgrave tells us that: "In this timeless place, where the ravens speak in tongues as the tides rise and fall, my own life and times begins to make sense to me."[27] It is often when exploring this power of the region that writers most effectively demonstrate the link between the outer and inner landscape. Lopez suggests that "the shape of the individual mind is affected by land."[28] Nowhere is this so clear as in the writing of Robinson: "As I was drifting off to sleep...I felt light, free, as if a warm wind blew through me...I was filled with a sense of calm, peace, and I saw Kitlope Lake, flat and grey in the early-morning light, mirroring the mountains."[29] The similarities between the inner and outer landscape are striking. First, the speaker feels light and free, like the breeze she imagines blowing through her. Then, the description she provides of the lake, so quiet that it mirrors the mountains, is obviously a description of a lake completely calm and at peace, just like the speaker at that moment. The lake not only mirrors the mountain, it mirrors the speaker's inner landscape exactly. Northern writers' recognition of the influence the landscape has over their feelings deepens their respect for it.

The links between the inhabitants of Northern British Columbia and its landscape are complex. They are linked by proximity and by the landscape's tendency to interlace itself with the lives of the people. More importantly, they are linked by a reflection. The outer landscape, the region itself, is reflected in the inner landscape of the people. The influence of the outer landscape over the inner landscape is particularly strong in Northern B.C. because of the many ways the population is tied to the landscape. Through writing, the shape of the inner landscape is revealed as Eden Robinson writes: "A bear—a hazy, dark brown figure in the distance down the shore—paws at seaweed. It raises its head, stands on its hind legs, and for one moment, as it swivels around and does a rambling walk into the woods, it looks human."[30] The inner landscape in Northern British Columbia is one that has completely taken on the shape of the outer landscape, so that the divide between the two, between the human and the non-human, between the self and the landscape, has all but melted away.

Notes:

1. Barry Lopez, "Landscape and Narrative," in *Saving Place*, ed. Sidney Dobrin (Toronto: McGraw-Hill, 2004), 39-45.

2. Ibid.

3. Jacqueline Baldwin, in email correspondence with author, April 13, 2009.

4. Ibid.

5. Eden Robinson, *Monkey Beach* (Boston: Houghton Mifflin Company, 2000).

6. Tim Bowling, "On the Disappearance of Two Million Sockeye Salmon," in *Open Wide a Wilderness*, ed. Nancy Holmes (Waterloo: Wilfred Laurier University Press, 2009), 429.

7. Jacqueline Baldwin, *A Northern Woman* (Prince George: Caitlin Press, 2003), 116.

8. Robinson, *Monkey Beach*, 82.

9. Christie Harris, *Mouse Woman and the Muddleheads* (Vancouver: Raincoast Books, 1979), 35.

10. Lord George Gordon Byron, "Apostrophe to the Ocean," in *Adventures in English Literature*, ed. Katie Vignery (Austin: Holt, Rinehart and Winston, 1996), 531-533, lines 1-4.

11. Baldwin, *A Northern Woman*, 113.

12. Robinson, *Monkey Beach*, 13.

13. Susan Musgrave, *You're in Canada Now...* (Saskatoon: Thistledown Press, 2005), 59.

14. Jacqueline Baldwin, in email correspondence with author, April 13, 2009.

15. Wendell Berry, quoted in "Hundreds of Little Jonahs," in *Northern Wild*, ed. David Boyd (Vancouver: Greystone Books, 2001), 190.

16. Musgrave, *You're in Canada Now*, 55.

17. Louis Owens, "The American Indian Wilderness," in *Saving Place*, ed. Sidney Dobrin (Toronto: McGraw-Hill, 2004), 68-71.

18. Harris, *Mouse Woman*, 128.

19. Lopez, "Landscape and Narrative."

20. Baldwin, *A Northern Woman*, 111.

21. Musgrave, *You're in Canada Now*, 54.

22. Baldwin, *A Northern Woman*, 132.

23. Ibid., 121.

24. Ibid., 123.

25. Jacqueline Baldwin, in email correspondence with author, April 13, 2009.

26. Harris, *Mouse Woman*, 50.

27. Musgrave, *You're in Canada Now*, 50.

28. Lopez, "Landscape and Narrative."

29. Robinson, *Monkey Beach*, 176.

30. Ibid., 136.

Jumping the Helix:

GENOMICS AND THE NEXT GENERATION OF CHINESE-CANADIAN LITERATURE ON THE WEST COAST

FRANCES CABAHUG

The interest Chinese-Canadian literature has in genetics does not necessarily spring from scientific findings, but in preoccupations with bloodlines, lineage, miscegenation, fertility, and hybridity. Moving into the future, Chinese-Canadian literature has explored the identity of the multicultural families living in the country. Unsurprisingly, several works discussing this emerging field of literature have been written by writers from Canada's West Coast, long known for its diversity. Through these works of prose and poetry we are able to examine not only a unique style of writing, but the unique cultures which it grew from and the genetics that pull the strings behind it all.

These works include SKY Lee's *Disappearing Moon Café*, which uses genetic interests as a way to locate and fix identities based on family history. Lineage is useful, not only in tracing roots, but also in claiming a legitimate space within the community. Despite attempts to carve out an ethnic space for minorities to speak from, genetics can also make such singular racial identifications obscure. While genes can be used to locate racial identities and affiliations, there are many genetic interactions and contact spaces that escape categorization, such as those described in Fred Wah's *Diamond Grill*. These hybrid poems speak of the confusion of resisting classification because genetic mixtures and interraciality cannot be contained within the corresponding and often inflexible current social structure. More recent Chinese-Canadian texts, like Larissa Lai's *Salt Fish Girl*, focus less on the confusion generated by genetic mixtures and instead address the subversive but potent possibilities of these new hybrid formations. *Salt Fish Girl* focuses on channelling the potential to question established boundaries and rise against systemic oppression.

Last February,[1] at UBC's Cecil Green College, Dr. Michael G. Kenney conducted a lecture called "Ethnopolitical Identity in the Post-Genomic Age." While the processes involved in mapping genes are highly technical and scientific, Kenney suggests that developments in gene-mapping have taken a personal, commercial, and political turn, especially since a few genomics companies now extend their services to the public. Genomics companies such as 23andMe[2] offer not only health traits, but also ancestral and racial information from the analysis of their customers' saliva samples. Given this information, customers can turn to the companies' websites, which link them to blogs and community groups where people can interact with others who share similar genetic data.

Genetic codes contain molecular stories of historical connections, migrations, kinships, famines, diets, and deaths. Kenney's lecture raises questions about the possibilities of the largely unseen application of genomics in human interaction. Kenney anecdotally shares how he paid for a genomic kit, and received information that his ancestry stems from an Anglo-Saxon background, just as he had expected. The results also indicate a surprising Asiatic strain, though faint and minute, is nonetheless present. The genomic ability to provide such information challenges perceptions of identity, and affiliations change when people discover that their mitochondrial DNA contains a previously unknown record of their ancestry. In a world where the census still categorically separates humanity in distinct racial boxes, genomics can then potentially destabilize the myth of the immutability and certainty of race.

According to Tara Lee, Chinese-Canadian literature has occasionally questioned "the myth of stable identity reproduction," even while trying to speak from the position of racial difference.[3] SKY Lee's *Disappearing Moon Café* shows how genetics can be used to locate and place identities, and at the same time highlights how this approach can be problematic. The dilemma from a racial standpoint lies in trying to recover an authentically pure past: a place and time beyond recovery because it denies the occurrence of interracial contact. In *Disappearing Moon Café*, genetic concerns manifest themselves in the text's examination of the Wong family's genealogy. Before the novel begins, the text offers readers a genealogical chart that seemingly summarizes the Chinatown clan in a glance. However, not only does the novel flesh out the story of the family tree, it also highlights a genealogical crisis. Much of the Wong clan's story has been left out of the tree, because of genetic twists and problems that cannot be adequately addressed in such neat charting. In a linear charting, there is no room for the ambiguities of race, the fear of miscegenation, and the incest that occurs throughout the generations of Wongs.

Many of the characters in *Disappearing Moon Café* concern themselves with the preservation of the family bloodline, primarily as a reaction to the racist state policies which restricted the number of Chinese workers and brides allowed to immigrate to Canada. Donald Goellnicht points out the significance of setting *Disappearing Moon Café* after the 1923 Immigration Act[4] that called for all Chinese in Canada to be registered, which "excluded virtually all Chinese from entering in the future," driving the need for second-generation families to expand to fill that population gap.[5] Within Chinese communities, the drive to preserve their numbers and culture explains how fertility becomes a huge issue. Propagating genes is a Darwinian move for community survival, and reproduction becomes the tool for perpetuating not only population but culture as well. A growing community legitimizes its presence in Canadian soil by its numbers so that the community cannot be so easily dismissed and pushed aside.

While maintaining the bloodline is necessary to promote the growth of the Chinese communities, according to Goellnicht, "an obsession with racial and cultural authenticity becomes pathological."[6] While reproduction can be used as a weapon, women are not necessarily empowered by their biological capabilities. Solely championing reproduction creates conflicts for women who are required to bear the burden of replicating culture through childbearing and rearing. In *Disappearing Moon Café* the Wong family initially orders Fong Mei from China as a bride for the Wong son, Choy Fuk. While Fong Mei is a good wife and a tireless worker in the Chinatown café, her acceptance within the family solely depends on whether or not she gets pregnant. When the couple fail to produce children, the Wongs are unable to procure another bride because "there's a new Chinese Exclusion Act. [...] The government is saying no more Chinese immigrants!"[7] In the eyes of Fong Mei's mother-in-law Mui Lan, Fong Mei's empty womb makes her a bad investment, and this barrenness warrants ill treatment. When women's worth and contribution to society rests on their childbearing capabilities, women who are not actively contributing to population growth are easy targets for oppression.

Even though guarding and perpetuating genetic lines fosters a sense of cultural authenticity for community survival, a staunch insistence on authenticity suppresses the possibilities of diversity and equality, which are also necessary in the community's growth. Other characters in *Disappearing Moon Café* are also treated oppressively when they transgress established racial and cultural boundaries. For instance, the novel begins and ends with the appearance of Kelora Chen, who is born of a Chinese father and First Nations mother. Kelora Chen is the first wife of the Wong patriarch Gwei Chang. Even though Kelora's Chinese father and First Nations mother prove that an interracial union can be fruitful and compatible, Gwei Chang believes that he owes filial loyalty to his Chinese kin, and abandons Kelora for a wife from the Chinese mainland. Gwei Chang's betrayal of his union with Kelora denies not only diversity but also personal happiness over the fear of miscegenation and for the sake of maintaining a rigid concept of what constitutes acceptable affiliations within a culture. His choice and regret resonate throughout the novel, yet he repeats the same mistake with Ting An, his son with Kelora. When Ting An has an affair with a French woman, Gwei Chang dismisses his romantic ties by insisting that he will procure Ting An an "authentic Chinese wife."[8] Gwei Chang's second dismissal of an interracial union leads to Ting An's realization that his mixed-race mother had been treated as "a dirty half-breed," and Ting An separates himself from the Wong family.[9] Gwei Chang is not the only one who loses family over his rigid ideas of genetic racial purity. As the Wong family extends the same exclusionary approaches towards Ting An's descendants, more secrets create ignorance of bloodlines, leading to disastrous results. The rejection of interracial unions leads to the dismissal of many branches of the genealogical tree in order to uphold the honour of the family. Because interraciality is seen as a taint to the purity of the bloodline, shame and embarrassment result in the dismissal of the illegitimized descendants. The silence that accompanies the shame and denial cause the descendants of the Wong family to be ignorant of their true lineage. The Wong descendants' tragic suicides, incest, and stillbirths results from their ignorance of the genetic contacts that have occurred in previous generations.

Returning to Kenney's lecture, the propensity to interact with people who have similar genetic and racial profiles still exists, but there is a growing need to find a space that allows the discussion of multiple racial identities. Understandably, difficulties abound when it comes to speaking of interracial experiences, but providing a voice and a vocabulary becomes central to the hybrid subject, especially since new ways of interaction—whether genetic or cultural— inevitably happen. Fred Wah's *Diamond Grill* speaks of the difficulties in negotiating multiple racial affiliations in a place and time where genetic purity and singular racial identifications were considered the norm. *Diamond Grill* covers how young Fred grows up making sense of his "half-Swede, quarter-Chinese, and quarter-Ontario-Wasp" background.[10] Wah's particular genetic soup was often met with confusion and occasionally the fear of miscegenation by his fellow residents of Nelson, B.C. in the 1950s. In one telling incident, Wah reports that every year in elementary school, he fills out a form that asks him for a singular racial identity. In his confusion over what to write under "Racial Origin," young Fred concludes that he will write down "Canadian," only to have his teacher insists that his racial origin is Chinese. This incident repeats when Wah goes to China, and this time, the Chinese tour guide, "with racial purity so characteristic of mainland Chinese," dismisses Wah and insists that he is "Canadian ... white, Euro. But not Chinese."[11] Wah notes that his lack of racial purity on all sides is received as a transgression of many cultural boundaries. The insistence of a singular racial identity casts the interracial subject as lacking and fragmented, stretching across genetic lines but unable to fit in anywhere.

Julie McGonegal observes pervading notions about "the indivisibility of racial identity." An interracial subject is often perceived as "a biological combo concocted from the synthesis of previously pure racial parts."[12] The struggles of Wah's father, a Chinese-Scots-Irishman raised in China, exemplifies the problem as he is not fully accepted, either "by the Chinese because (he's a half-breed, he's really a white man, he's married to a white woman) or by the Wasps (he looks Chinese, he can talk Chinese, and he runs the café, right?)"[13] But McGonegal also quotes Mary Pratt's concept of the contact zone—zones in which intercultural relations occur among people who are otherwise divided.[14] Contact zones are not only cultural and geographical, but the interracial subject—a genetic intersection—is also a contact zone. Wah's father navigates the constraints and collisions of intercultural spaces. The focus strays away from the breakdown or the incoherence of his interracial identity, but celebrates instead how Wah's father negotiates the established genetic and cultural boundaries while successfully running the town café. His success as a business man shows that the hybrid's emerging sense of selfhood is not just a mishmash of divergent cultural influences. Instead, this emerging hybrid selfhood can be a creative, potent, and unified whole.

Crossing genetic boundaries and new hybrid formations have traditionally been seen as destructive and fragmented. However, possibilities for taking agency could be found in creating a sense of self outside established boundaries. In Larissa Lai's *Salt Fish Girl*, genetic variance symbolizes the breakdown of the limitations imposed upon racialized bodies, and thus signifies the potential of creation apart from hegemonic origins. *Salt Fish Girl* is set partly in Serendipity, a walled city that could be the Vancouver of 2044 C.E. Serendipity lacks a definite nation-state presence and omnipresent corporations overrun the city instead. With the advancement of science and technology, corporations have begun mass-producing hybrid objects and bodies, with processes ranging from genetic modification and interspecies mixes to cyborg assembly. In *Salt Fish Girl*, genetics becomes a way to talk about class and racial inequalities that stem from oppressive corporate and technological impositions.

Miranda, the protagonist, is a witness to the pervasive corporate and scientific control over her city. Not only do corporations control the genomic compositions of consumable objects, but they also interfere in the production and genetic alteration of their cyborg workers, known as Sonias. According to Jan Pieterse, when celebratory hybridity—whether it is genetic diversity or cultural diversity—becomes co-opted under a consumerist bent, hybridity loses its subversive potential.[15] What forms is an alignment between hybridity and hegemonic power relations. The modified factory workers significantly come from the Diverse Genome Project, which means that the workers look like "the peoples of the so-called Third World, Aboriginal peoples, and peoples in danger of extinction."[16] The corporation takes out the ethnic attributes and replaces the cultural and racial markers on the body with the totalizing stamp of ownership under the corporation by means of genetic alterations. A cloned cyborg worker, Evie, reveals her incompleteness: the taint of the 0.03% *Cyprinus carpio*[17] in her genome is a technicality that allows corporations to label hybrid bodies as simply non-human, exempt from human rights and therefore the perfect victims for oppressive conditions. This intrusion equates genetic diversity with "a note of regret and loss—loss of purity, wholeness, and authenticity." By removing the historicity of a new genetically-altered body, what gets emphasized in the identities of the hybrid worker bodies are their roles as labour fodder.

Even though the genetically modified bodies of the workers are brought under the stamp of the corporation as owned objects, their genetic variance can also undermine the hegemonic aims of the corporations which have produced them. Their genetic alterations bring to mind Julia Kristeva's notion of the abject body, wherein abjection is defined as fearsome because it "does not respect borders, positions, rules. The in between, the ambiguous, the composite." [18] The genetic taint of the workers allows them to exceed their role as mere object bodies of consumption, and is therefore threatening in its ability to break boundaries. Evie mentions that it is the 0.03% carp in her genome which is "the unstable factor." Genetic instability is no longer a lack, but a breach that refuses categorization and containment; in this way it is comparable to Wah's interraciality which escapes classification in *Diamond Grill*.

This genetic difference is not just a medium of instability and disruption, but of regeneration as well. According to Kristeva, the disgust of the abject body can be sublimated to channel works of creativity. [19] The cyborg Sonias exceed their roles as mere workers producing objects for the consumption of others; when they discover a hyper-fertile mutation they take up the agency to produce others like themselves. The Sonias' space for revolt against corporate hegemony is located within the womb, which occupies that space of in-between, of liminality and potentiality. Miranda proclaims:

> Once we stepped out of mud, now we step out of moist earth, out of DNA both new and old, an imprint of what has gone before, but also a variation. By our difference we mark the ancient alphabet of our bodies. By our strangeness we write our bodies into the future. [20]

Unlike the Chinese wives from *Disappearing Moon Café* who are coerced into producing offspring, the Sonias are reclaiming their wombs as their own creative space of immaculate conception, without any outside control. Also, unlike the disastrous insistence of genetic purity in *Disappearing Moon Café*, the Sonias do not reject their genetic variance, despite recognizing that their bodies nonetheless stem from the devastation of scientific and corporate origins. It does not matter where the mutation comes from; the Sonias' regeneration does not rely on an exclusive unstained point of origin, a myth of beginnings which would only revert back to hegemonic reproduction. Instead, the Sonias literally remake themselves. In the end, it is their ability to shape-shift, to transgress boundaries, and to generate life which subverts the hegemonic impositions placed upon them.

While it cannot be denied that genomic interests have previously served oppressive ideologies, emerging Chinese-Canadian literary works show the potential that could arise from the ever-present contestations over genetic diversity. As more biological findings about race develop, they will alter the ways in which we think about race, and with it change the way we think of identities and affiliations. In slowly dissolving the certainty that comes of a singular racial identity, the resulting chaos proves fertile ground for creative overhauls and transgressions across racialized boundaries.

Notes:

1. February, 2009.

2. https://www.23andme.com/

3. Tara Lee, "Promising Transnational Births: The Womb and Cyborg Poetics in Asian Canadian Literature" (Doctorate thesis, Simon Fraser University, 2006), 4.

4. The Chinese Immigration Act, 1923, known in the Chinese-Canadian community as the Chinese Exclusion Act, was an act passed by the Parliament of Canada, banning most forms of Chinese immigration to Canada. Immigration from most countries was controlled or restricted in some way, but only the Chinese were so completely prohibited from immigrating. Before this, Chinese immigration was already heavily controlled by a head tax as a result of the Chinese Immigration Act of 1885. After various members of the federal and some provincial governments (especially British Columbia) put pressure on the federal government to discourage

Chinese immigration, the Chinese Immigration Act was passed. The act banned Chinese immigrants from entering Canada unless they held the title of "Merchant," "Diplomat," or "Foreign Student." The act did not apply only to Chinese from China: ethnic Chinese with British nationality were banned from entering Canada as well.

5. Donald Goellnicht, "Of Bones and Suicide: SKY Lee's *Disappearing Moon Café* and Fae Myenne Ng's *Bone*" *Modern Fiction Studies* 46 (2000): 304.

6. Ibid., 315.

7. SKY Lee, *Disappearing Moon Café* (Vancouver: Douglas & McIntyre, 1990), 30.

8. Ibid., 223.

9. Ibid., 233.

10. Fred Wah, *Diamond Grill*, (Edmonton: NeWest, 1997), 36.

11. Ibid., 54.

12. Julie McGonegal, "Hyphenating the Hybrid 'I': (Re)Visions of Racial Mixedness in Fred Wah's *Diamond Grill*"; *Essays on Canadian Writing* 75 (Winter 2002): 178.

13. Wah, *Diamond Grill*, 39.

14. McGonegal, "Hyphenating the Hybrid 'I':" 173.

15. Jan Nederveen Pieterse, *Globalization and Culture* (Lanham, MD: Rowman and Littlefield, 2003), 55.

16. Ibid., 160.

17. The common carp.

18. Julia Kristeva, *Powers of Horror: An Essay on Abjection*, trans. Leon S. Roudiez (New York: Columbia University Press, 1982), 3.

19. Kristeva, *Powers of Horror*, 21.

20. Larissa Lai, *Salt Fish Girl* (Toronto: Thomas Allen Publishers, 2002), 259.

Ecosystems, Mandalas and Watersheds:
THE DHARMA CITIZENSHIP
OF GARY SNYDER

I pledge allegiance to the soil / of Turtle Island...
—Gary Snyder, "For All"

TREVOR CAROLAN

In the face of a natural world that is crumbling environmentally, the contributions of Pacific Northwest-raised poet, essayist, and generational sage Gary Snyder continue to inform the emotional, philosophical, and activist heart of our current worldwide ecological discourse. Informed by East-West poetics, land and wilderness sustainability issues, cross-cultural anthropology, Mahayana Buddhism, his long years of familiarity with "the bush" and high mountain places, as well as a lifetime of scholarship that has earned him membership in the American Academy of Arts and Letters, Snyder's language and poetic commitment can be understood intimately—from a Pacific Coast perspective especially—as a rethinking of what citizenship might mean in the global age.

Articulated in a series of modern literary classics that include the Pulitzer Prize-winning *Turtle Island* (1974), *Earth House Hold* (1969), *Axe Handles* (1983), his path-breaking translations of Han Shan's *Cold Mountain Poems* (1965), *The Practice of the Wild* (1990), and *Mountains and Rivers Without End* (1996), for more than fifty years Gary Snyder's principles have engaged themes of transformation and responsible planetary ecological stewardship. At the root of his vision is a non-denominational renewal of reverence for the authentic, interconnected sacredness of creation, and from the declarations of his first published works *Riprap* (1959) and *Cold Mountain Poems,* his works have consistently spoken to the essential, life-sustaining relationship that he argues must exist between individual, "place," and community psyche.

In discussing "Four Changes," an essay written in 1969, Snyder describes—with an echo of Emerson resonating in the background—his idea of the ecstatic, the mystical nature of this relationship:

> *At the heart of things is some kind of serene and ecstatic process which is beyond qualities and beyond birth-and-death.*[1]

Of this psychic awareness, or "interrelatedness," he has written that, "if humans are to remain on earth, they must transform the five-millennia-long urbanizing civilization tradition into a new ecologically sensitive, harmony-oriented, wild-minded, scientific-spiritual culture."[2] And as root prescriptions for the overarching global crisis of the age, he offers as remedies the quintessential ideas of an "etiquette of freedom" and a "practice of the wild."[3]

Developing these protocols out of what he terms a "Turtle Island view" of the intrinsic value of nature—a phrase referring to traditional widely-held North American aboriginal depictions of the continent, in which "[humanity] and all of nature are represented by a single continuum of life, strong and virile, emerging from unrecorded ages to the present"[4]—any paradigm for a truly healthy culture, Snyder argues, must begin with surmounting narrow conceits of personal identity and finding a commitment to place, as in, for example, a commitment to Turtle Island, or Arizona's Painted Desert, or British Columbia's West Coast temperate rainforest, or North Beach in San Francisco. For this reason, critics from the period of his 1975 Pulitzer

Prize laureate onward have regarded Snyder as holding himself accountable, "not to laws, but to a higher authority, the earth."[5]

From the humanist position, the Turtle Island view binds man, not to man, but to his environment, to the strong, rhythmic wholeness of individual being. It follows that responsibility to self is also concern for the earth which is humanity's physical and spiritual home. Yet, as a former logger in the U.S. Pacific Northwest's conifer rainforest, Snyder also manifests a sensible concern for the need to harvest, as well as conserve the environment's natural fruits. Snyder's poem "Why Log Truck Drivers Rise Earlier Than Zen Students," an homage to the dignity of labour in the resource extraction industries, is a perfect illustration of this philosophy: while it is necessary for the logger, and for communities, to cut and chop, Snyder implies, it is vital that it be done mindfully and with integrity. As Betty Pickett contends, what Snyder cannot accept is the unfeeling despoliation of all that is Turtle Island. In the poem's concluding line, "there is no other life," she sees the poet's affirmation that even in reducing the extent of the natural state there is a rightness, for the men who do the harvesting—rising earlier than students of Zen Buddhism who might typically presume for themselves the high moral ground in ecological discourse—do so as "whole, contented, unified beings,"[6] and as such are themselves bona fide citizens of Turtle Island, and planetary citizens of Mother Earth.

The Native American mythological origins of Snyder's Turtle Island view expand further, however. He comments:

> *The twentieth-century syncretism of the "Turtle Island view" gathers ideas from Buddhism and Taoism and from the lively details of world-wide animism and paganism. There is no imposition of ideas of progress or order on the natural world—Buddhism teaches impermanence, suffering, compassion, and wisdom. Buddhist teachings go on to say that the true source of compassion and ethical behavior is paradoxically none other than one's own realization of the insubstantial and ephemeral nature of everything. Much of animism and*

paganism celebrates the actual, with its inevitable pain and death, and affirms the beauty of the process. Add contemporary ecosystem theory and environmental history to this, and you get a sense of what's at work.[7]

Extending his analysis further, and borrowing from deep ecology to remake the shopworn literary concept of "sense of place" into something fresh and vital, Snyder refers to the sensibility of fully "inhabiting" a place spiritually, economically, and compassionately as a "bioregional consciousness"; one that is equally powerful in embracing urban, suburban or rural living environments. Bioregionalism, he explains in "The Rediscovery of Turtle Island,"

Calls for commitment to this continent place by place, in terms of bio-geographical regions and watersheds. It calls us to see our country in terms of its landforms, plant life, weather patterns, and seasonal changes—its whole natural history before the net of political jurisdictions was cast over it. People are challenged to become "reinhabitory"—that is, to become people who are learning to live and think "as if" they were totally engaged with their place for the long future. This doesn't mean some return to a primitive lifestyle or utopian provincialism; it simply implies an engagement with community and a search for the sustainable sophisticated mix of economic practices that would enable people to live regionally, and yet learn from and contribute to a planetary society.[8]

Here, Snyder returns to watershed imagery by explaining that while a watershed flows "through" each of these places, it also includes them. "That's why I talk about watersheds," he explains in an interview, bringing in an iconographic image to cement the association:

Symbolically and literally they're the mandalas of our lives. They provide the very idea of the watershed's social

enlargement, and quietly present an entry into the spiritual
realm that nobody has to think of, or recognize as being
spiritual. But there it is. The watershed is our only local
Buddha mandala: one that gives us all, human and non-
human, a territory to interact in. That is the beginning of
dharma citizenship: not membership in a social or national
sphere, but in a larger community citizenship. In other
words, a sangha; a local dharma community. All of that
potentially is in there, like Dogen when he says, "When you
find your place, practice begins."[9]

Thirteenth century master Dogen Zenji is a classical Asian voice
that Snyder has discussed frequently. Snyder himself trained as a lay
Zen monk for ten years at Daitokuji temple in Kyoto, Japan. He
observes of Dogen:

There are several levels of meaning in what Dogen says.
There's the literal meaning, as in when you settle down
somewhere. This means finding the right teaching, the right
temple, the right village. Then you can get serious about your
practice. Underneath, there's another level of implication:
you have to understand that there are such things as places.
That's where Americans have yet to get to. They don't
understand that there are "places." So I quote Dogen and
people say, "What do you mean, you have to find your place?
Anywhere is okay for dharma practice because it's spiritual."
Well, yes, but not just any place. It has to be a place that
you've found yourself. It's never abstract, always concrete.[10]

Snyder has explained how one of the models he uses to present his
ideas is that of an ecosystem. "An ecosystem is a kind of mandala in
which there are multiple relations that are all-powerful and
instructive," he notes in "A Village Council of All Beings." Presented
as an address to the Ladakh Ecological Development Group conference
in Leh, Northern India in 1992, Snyder's essay observes,

> *Each figure in the mandala—a little mouse or bird (or little*
> *god or demon figure)—has an important position and a*
> *role to play. Although ecosystems can be described as*
> *hierarchical in terms of energy flow, from the standpoint of*
> *the whole, all of its members are equal.*[11]

This is the core teaching of equanimity and interdependence. In the mandala visualization, the small as well as central figures are all essential. As Snyder states elsewhere, "the whole thing [the Hindu-Buddhist mandala or *thangka* image] is an educational tool for understanding—that's where the ecosystem analogy comes in. Every creature, even the little worms and insects, has value. Everything is valuable—that's the measure of the system." [12]

For Snyder, value also translates as responsibility. Within his approach to committing to a place is the acceptance of responsible stewardship. It is through this engaged sense of effort and practice—participating in what he salutes as "the tiresome but tangible work of school boards, county supervisors, local foresters, local politics," and all the manifestations of contemporary community and regional activism—that individuals find their real community, their real culture. "Ultimately, values go back to our real interactions with others," he emphasizes. "That's where we live, in our communities." [13]

"Living in place" then, is a process that redefines one's personal stake in the community, for in the larger Buddhist sense, community includes all the beings—the "ten thousand things" of everyday existence. Joan Halifax, a former research assistant to Joseph Campbell, and teaching Director of the Upaya Zen Buddhist Centre in Santa Fe, notes additionally how "in contemporary Buddhism the term *Sangha* refers to the community that practices the Way together." [14] Individually, one's job as citizen member is to develop community networks that extend beyond the obvious political divisions of age, class, race, gender, and employment—boundaries that keep us apart, and which Snyder believes are reinforced through the media. With the growing importance of community coalition-building, however, Snyder explains that he has found it expedient to narrow his ideas concerning bioregionalism, or his notion of a practice of the wild, down to a shared neighbourhood level, arguing that even urban dwellers can and must learn, as U.S. agricultural conservationist Wes Jackson says, to "become native to this place."[15]

It is within this stressing of local involvement at the tangible community level that Snyder sees convergences arising between political activism, social justice issues, and East Asia's traditional Buddhist and Taoist wisdom paths that find increasingly wide acceptance in Western culture. North America's West Coast has long been a fertile ground for the mingling of these cross-cultural forms of energy and practice, and in a letter from 1985, Snyder speaks of a "new world" culture that he identifies arising from the West Coast of North America and the Asia-Pacific region.[16] A Canadian term from this period imagines this as the Trans-North Pacific Rim. Locally, it extends roughly from the Alaska Panhandle through the B.C., Washington and Oregon littoral, and into Northern California. For a poet who from 1958 onward has also been accorded a leading international lay spiritual teacher's role, this area has proven itself a cultural ecology increasingly sympathetic to the Zen Buddhist idea of "waking up" to one's individual home-place.

Having experienced this Zen-style awakening or *satori*, individual commitment to the principle of upholding creative stewardship for its protection and continuance becomes an inherent spiritual obligation within the consciousness of "wild mind." By way of clarification, Snyder confirms that "wild" in this context does not mean "chaotic, excessive or crazy":

> It means self-organizing. It means elegantly self-disciplined, self-regulating, self-maintained. That's what wilderness is. Nobody has to do the management plan for it. So I say to people, let's trust in the self-disciplined elegance of wild mind. Practically speaking, a life that is vowed to simplicity, appropriate boldness, good humour, gratitude, unstinting work and play, and lots of walking, brings us close to the actually existing world and its wholeness.[17]

Unsurprisingly, for a poet, the practices of waking up, stewardship, and cultivating the path of the spirit find a nexus in language. Snyder's poetics have long been rooted in the tradition of Whitman, W.C. Williams, labour ballads, and the vernacular. With its clear language, sharp imagery and spare line, his work has long enjoyed a sizeable B.C. audience, in part for the astringency and plain taste at its core—another legacy of his engagement with Zen Buddhism. In *Mountains and Rivers Without End*, a collection that begins "Clearing the mind and sliding in/ to that created space," the third poem, "Night Highway 99," offers the reader an illustration of Snyder's style. Following an epigraph on poverty and mindfulness by friend and fellow poet Lew Welch, it reads:

> We're on our way
>
> man
> out of town
> go hitching down
> that highway 99...

As the poem travels down the old West Coast highway that once ran from Alaska to Chile, references to Puget Sound, Bellingham, Ferndale, Marblemount, Mt. Vernon, and various Canadian border-hugging locations punctuate the long sequence, situating it in immediate geographic context, leading toward an Everett citation where even "BC Riders gave hitchhikers rides." Anyone who ever thumbed long distances in the West or down the Pacific Coast to San Francisco has these same places and images engraved on their heart. What is edifying in these poems is how their metaphors and images pay homage to the commonplace, the typically overlooked—this precious territory we call home. A few examples suffice: "Gray wharves and hacksaw gothic homes / Shingle mills and stump farms / weary Indians...strawberry pickers speaking Kwakiutl / snag papermill / tugbooms in the river."

It goes on: the Tatshenshini River, Naikoon Beach at northeast-end Haida Gwai, travelling down the dry-side eastern trench of the Rockies with a "lovely but dangerous girl with a dusky voice." This is Gary Snyder's "wild medicine," where a glass of buttermilk in Portland becomes an epiphany reminiscent of Gautama's enlightenment, where snow on the evergreens around Lake Shasta evokes a Chinese landscape, and a tag of coastal slang recalls anecdotes from life in the timber camps and on trail crews. It was precisely this Pacific Northwest referencing of the local, the naming of the particular, that offered a generation of B.C. writers with interests beyond Earle Birney and the poetic traditions of Montreal and Toronto authorization to write in this mode. From the beginning, Snyder's way of carving out a place of individual freedom in the wall of American culture has been founded in a bedrock of insightful seeing practice—a vision honest enough to recognize how both back country and urban metropolis are sacramental, each in their fashion.

In his omitting of the personal in favour of the path, Snyder also exemplifies the basics of the Zen tradition in which he trained. As illustration, he reports:

> *The practice of meditation must have a little to do with getting beyond "wild mind" in language. Spending quality time with your own mind is humbling and, like travel, broadening. You find that there's no one in charge, and are reminded that no thought lasts for long.*[18]

In this, Snyder's East-West ethical orientation is complemented by an older, deeper appreciation of the anthropomorphic richness of the local Native American cultural lore—the rainforest mythological totems of eagle, bear, raven, and killer whale that continue to survive as important elements of regional consciousness in school and community insignias throughout the Pacific Northwest region of Washington State where Snyder grew up, and in adjacent British Columbia and southern Alaska coastal regions. An anthropologist in his early training before transferring into Asian language and literature studies at Berkeley University in the mid-1950s, Snyder wrote a senior B.A. thesis discussing Haida aboriginal mythology entitled *He Who Hunted Birds in his Father's Village, Dimensions of a Haida Myth* (Grey Fox, 1979).[19] Since that time, his etiquette of freedom and responsibility has evolved and crosses ancient cultural—tribal—and even inter-species boundaries. The result, as Joan Halifax explains, has been a recognition that:

> *The encounter between shamanism and Buddhism has something to offer us. Both traditions are based in the experience of direct practice realization, of direct knowing, of communion, of understanding through experience, of seeing through the eyes of compassion.*[20]

In *Danger On Peaks*, his first collection of poetry in more than twenty years that also rests on Japanese *haibun*, or prose/poem journal-style entry technique, Snyder recounts his own moment of direct awakening to the experience of seeing compassionately. Beginning with a section recalling boyhood mountaineering adventures around Mount St. Helens, the site of one of the twentieth century's great explosions in southern Washington State, Snyder combines natural images of the outdoors familiar to anyone raised on family camping journeys. Then, in a poem entitled "Atomic Dawn," he recollects how, on descending from his first major climb up the peak, he learned at age fifteen of the first atomic bombings at Hiroshima and Nagasaki. Horrified by news photos of the destruction, the youthful Snyder appealed to the mountain's huge spirit for help, and he recalls vowing, "By the purity and beauty and permanence of Mt. St. Helens, I will fight against this cruel destructive power and those who would seek to use it, for all my life."

This is what he has done. But there is always the unpredictable. In another poem, "Pearly Everlasting," he recounts, "If you ask for help it comes / But not in any way you'd ever know." In sharing his acquired knowledge of "wild mind," throughout his career Snyder has not hesitated in introducing non-Native American readers to traditional Native myths. Virtually single-handedly he brought the antic, irrational Native tales involving the trickster figure of "Coyote" to popular consciousness.[21] *Danger On Peaks* offers a typical example:

Doctor Coyote when he had a problem
Took a dump. On the grass, asked his turds where
they lay
What to do? They gave him good advice.

He'd say "that's just what I thought too"
And do it. And go his way.
                    —From "Doctor Coyote When He Had a Problem"

   Snyder clarifies the importance of this cross-pollinating influence
in "Reinhabitation," an essential essay from his 1995 collection *A
Place In Space: Ethics, Aesthetics and Watersheds:*

> *Here in the twentieth century we find Occidentals and
> Orientals studying each other's wisdom, and a few people
> on both sides studying what came before both—before they
> forked off... Sometime in the last twenty years the best
> brains in the Occident discovered to their amazement that
> we live in an environment. This discovery has been forced
> upon us by the realization that we are approaching the
> limits of something... We are again, now, in the position
> of our Mesolithic forbears... learning how to live by the
> sun and the green at that spot. We once more know that we
> live in a system that is enclosed in a certain way, that has
> its own kinds of limits, and that we are interdependent
> with it.*[22]

   This demystifying cross-cultural lens into the interdependency that
is important for Snyder points further beyond the human toward the
mana, or living holiness of humanity's precious home-place, Mother
Earth. A Mela-Polynesian term brought to English in the late
nineteenth century by R.H. Codrington,[23] *mana* shares an intimacy
of natural awareness with an equivalent Lakota Sioux cosmological
term from the Great Plains that in recent decades has gained
widespread currency among Native North Americans:

All life is wakan. *So also is everything which exhibits power, whether in action, as in the winds and drifting clouds or in passive endurance, as the boulder by the wayside. For even the commonest sticks and stones have a spiritual essence which must be reverenced as a manifestation of the all-pervading mysterious power that fills the universe.*[24]

Buddhism's transcendent appreciation of this supernatural phenomenon, Snyder relates, reaches its clearest expression in the Avatamsaka Sutra, where its

jewelled-net-interpenetration-ecological-systems-emptiness-consciousness tells us no self-realization without the Whole Self, and the whole self is the whole thing... Thus, knowing who we are and knowing where we are, are intimately linked.[25]

Knowing who we are and where we are implies having, as Snyder adds, "a direct sense of relation to the land." With its overtones to the archaic human past, this literacy of place embodies in the fullest psychic sense, "a spirit of what it [is] to be *there*."[26] In the Taoist perceptual view with which Snyder is familiar, this is consonant with the elemental visualization of that from which all things, temporal and eternal, emanate: with *Tao*, the essential nature of *what is*. Within this accord of self, place, and spirit, the individual self is subsumed by place; and place and self are themselves sublime embodiments of the Tao, which itself serves as both noun and verb.

Similarly, in the archetypal Confucian understanding of this process, when heaven and the individual heart are unified (through *ling*, or meditative purity), then earth and humanity are also in accord (Chinese: *tianrenheyi*). Mencius, heir to the wisdom of Confucius, styles this unity of purpose with elegant economy in the foundational work that bears his name, saying:

For an individual to give full realization to his heart is for him to understand his own nature, and a man who knows

his own nature will know Heaven. By retaining his heart
and nurturing his nature, he is serving Heaven.[27]

Implicit in this appraisal of the attunement of both "self and
sphere" is the cosmic binding of what he terms the "flood-like *chi.*"
This ambiguous concept is an imagistic representation of what in
current interfaith discourse can be understood as compassionate
mind. Mencius acknowledges it may be:

Difficult to explain. [It] is a chi which is, in the highest degree,
vast and unyielding. Nourish it with integrity and place no
obstacle in its path and it will fill the space between Heaven
and Earth. It is a chi which unites rightness and the Way.[28]

In the context of Snyder's appeal, unless such values are grounded
within Right Action in the community itself, they will not last. In this
Buddhist-inflected mode of thinking, perhaps to have a lay spirituality
is a precondition of a more compassionate, dharmic spirituality.
Otherwise, one is left with a cultural void and nobody to share
information with.

Like the character of Japhy Ryder in *The Dharma Bums*, Snyder
left to study Buddhist culture in Japan in 1956—a time when Allen
Ginsberg recalled the young poet was already advising audiences
about the hazards of clear-cut logging and the unnecessary slaughter
of whales. During a ten-year residence in Japan, Snyder cultivated an
intensive Zen Buddhist practice in Kyoto monasteries. Returning to
North America, he began incorporating into his writing the
knowledge gained from his experiences abroad, and in 1969
published *Earth House Hold*. This now-classic document from the
American culture wars of the sixties with its provocative-for-the-time
subtitle, "Technical Notes & Queries To Fellow Dharma
Revolutionaries," is memorable for its inclusion of what has become
one of the most enduring epigraphs of the entire field of Trans-Pacific
Studies. Specifically, in an essay entitled "Buddhism and the Coming
Revolution," he declares:

> *The mercy of the West has been social revolution; the mercy of the East has been individual insight into the basic self/void. We need both.*[30]

Since returning to homestead in the foothills of California's Sierra Nevada range, Snyder has steadfastly championed social changes that bring greater freedom, choice and mobility into individual life—a resistance against what he calls the "Hungry Ghost" culture of modern North American life with its "enormous bellies, insatiable appetites, and tiny mouths."[31] What he has fashioned from his experience has been the Turtle Island view. As Gretel Erlich maintains in a statement that appears on the original North Point edition cover of *The Practice of the Wild*, its influence upon Western environmental and ecosystems thought has provided "an exquisite, far-sighted articulation of what freedom, wildness, goodness, and grace mean, using the lessons of the planet to teach us how to live."[32] Ironically, Snyder's work was initially dismissed by the U.S. East Coast academic establishment and he was tagged as an exponent of the "bear-shit on the trail" school of poetry—a name he recollects that was originally coined humorously by poet Kenneth Rexroth.[33]

Gary Snyder's conceptualization of dharma citizenship rooted in ecosystems, mandalas, and watersheds brings many streams together, and his influence has percolated up and down the Pacific Coast as a critical influence on, among others, Rex Weyler, Robert Bringhurst, Gerry Gilbert, Terry Glavin, Bob Hunter, John Schreiber, Al Neil, Robert Sund, Bill Porter, Mike O'Connor, Tim McNulty, Jerry Martien, Finn Wilcox, and Jim Dodge—a sufficiency that might legitimately constitute a school. Anchoring this citizenship itself is a notion of dharma that is big enough to breath comfortably through a variety of sustaining wisdom practices. As he relates:

> *The emphasis on human rights that is rooted in the Judeo-Christian tradition, the concern for all beings expressed in Buddhism, and the compassionate political savvy of Confucianism...[all] contribute to it.*[34]

In a joyous, ultimately democratic reminder that "we are all indigenous…all members present at the assembly,"[35] Snyder stakes his legitimacy as an heir to the American revolutionary trend manifested in turn by such literary and wilderness sages as Henry David Thoreau and the New England Transcendentalists, Walt Whitman, Ezra Pound, John Muir, William Carlos Williams, and Kenneth Rexroth. One might think here, too, of the older, multilingual Longfellow who could infuse his poem "Hiawatha" with a sharp appreciation of aboriginal tradition, native languages, and local geography. "Ultimately," Snyder affirms, "values go back to our real community, to our real culture, our real interactions with others. That's where we live, in our families and in our communities."[36]

These are the cognate forms of what an arch-modernist like T.S. Eliot could envision as a tradition of "much wider significance," a tradition that by its unity one is obliged to recognize as "the really new,"[37] and that contributes fundamentally to the proposition of a new world dharma. How, though, does one reconcile the contending forces of tradition and "the new" in a practical fashion when, as Eliot insists, "the difference between the present [new] and the [traditional] past is that the conscious present is an awareness of the past in a way and to an extent which the past's awareness of itself cannot show."

For Eliot, likely the chief arbiter of poetry and literary aesthetics in English during the twentieth century, as well as of a new modernism in literary criticism:

> What is to be insisted upon is that the poet must develop or procure the consciousness of the past and that he should continue to develop this consciousness throughout his career…the progress of an artist is a continual self-sacrifice, a continual extinction of personality.[38]

For Snyder, depersonalization has been the meat and bread of his career for more than forty-five years. Having adopted a fine Sino-Japanese poetic aesthetic reaching from the Tang dynasty with its erasure of "the defined subject position of the poem in favour of a malleable one,"[39] and having embraced the anti-anthropocentric philosophical stance in which the reader frequently is unlikely to "meet a subject pronoun"[40] until deep into the unfolding texture of his work, the integrity of his style is a logical extension of the consciousness which informs it.

The judicious word is "style." In early announcement of the postmodernist explication of text, Wylie Sypher assumes a genuine style is one containing...

> an expression of a prevailing, dominant, or authentically contemporary view of the world by those artists who have most successfully intuited the quality of human experience peculiar to their day and who are able to phrase this experience in forms deeply congenial to the thought, science, and technology which are a part of that experience.[41]

This serves as the ethical-aesthetic grounding that is characteristic of Snyder's poetry and essays. Their "mojo," or creative magic, is that which Eliot regards as involving

> in the first place, the historical sense, which we may call nearly indispensable...the historical sense involves perception, not only of the pastness of the past, but of its presence; the historical sense compels a man to write not merely with his own generation in his bones, but with a feeling that the whole of literature of Europe from Homer and within it the whole of the literature of his own country has a simultaneous existence and composes a simultaneous order. This historical sense, which is a sense of the timeless as well as of the temporal and of the timeless and the temporal together, is what makes a writer traditional. And it is at the same time what makes a writer most acutely conscious of his place in time, of his own contemporaneity.[42]

The Beat poetics that swept Snyder, Kerouac, Allen Ginsberg and their colleagues to public attention was informed by Buddhism, and in popularizing this traditional Asian wisdom path for the West, Snyder and his *confreres* nurtured a hybridized "East-West" expression honouring the sacredness of daily existence—what Buddhism understands as "everyday" sacraments. In his recent work, Snyder travels further, extending this compassionate vision to include the victims of early-twenty-first-century terrorist brutality.

Observing that the Mount St. Helens eruption in 1980 would be followed later by other dreadful explosions in Afghanistan and New York in 2001, in the concluding section of *Danger On Peaks* entitled "After Bamiyan," Snyder honours the human victims in New York and the Bamiyan Valley's ancient Gandharan Buddhist statuary destroyed by the Taliban, writing: "The men and women who / died at the World Trade Center / together with the / Buddhas of Bamiyan / Take Refuge in the dust."

It is here that one recalls how like the medieval Benedictines with their mantra *Laborare est orare*—"our work and prayer are one"—Snyder's work has always been a kind of sutra, or prayer. This can also include a hard fraternal boot where appropriate, in this case to utopian journalist and talk-show personality Christopher Hitchens whom Snyder rebuked for his public remarks following the Bamiyan world heritage site destruction.

> *A person who should know better wrote, "Many credulous and sentimental Westerners, I suspect, were upset by the destruction of the Afghan Buddha figures because they believe that so-called Eastern religion is more tender-hearted and less dogmatic...Is nothing sacred? Only respect for human life and cultures, which requires no divine sanction and no priesthood to inculcate it. The foolish veneration of holy places and holy texts remains a principal obstacle to that simple realization..."*[43]

Snyder's response to such unctuous provocation is blunt:

> *"This is another case of 'blame the victim,'" I answered. "Buddhism is not on trial here. The Bamiyan statues are*

*part of human life and culture, they are works of art, being
destroyed by idolators of the book. Is there anything
'credulous' in respecting the art and religious culture of the
past? Counting on the tender-heartedness of (most)
Buddhists, you can feel safe in trashing the Bamiyan figures
as though the Taliban wasn't doing a good enough job. I
doubt you would have the nerve to call for launching a
missile at the Ka'aba. There are people who would put a hit
on you and you know it."*[44]

Amid the *samsara* of confusing and amoral times, Snyder's
straight-talk from the heart has come to be recognized as an oracular
path. Detailing the responsibilities of a true planetary citizen—socially
pluralistic, ecologically holistic in vision and action—through its
synthesis of Western and Asian ideas, a third generation of seekers is
now being inspired to communal action based on respect for the
sanctity of nature it inspires. Honouring community and
commitment to place, from this path has also arisen, as Snyder
articulates, a reconceptualized sense of citizenship—true *dharma*
citizenship. As Snyder explains,

> *Such a non-nationalistic idea of community [and citizen-
> ship], in which commitment to pure place is paramount,
> cannot be ethnic or racist. Here is perhaps the most
> delicious turn that comes out of thinking about politics
> from the standpoint of place: anyone of any race, language,
> religion, or origin is welcome, as long as they live well on the
> land ... this sort of future is available to whoever makes the
> choice, regardless of background. It need not require that a
> person drop his or her Buddhist, Jewish, Christian,
> Animist, Atheist, or Muslim beliefs but simply add to that
> faith or philosophy a sincere nod in the direction of the deep
> value of the natural world and the subjecthood of
> nonhuman beings.*[45]

Newspaper writer Tim Costello argues from Australia that it is precisely this form of "politics with a soul" that speaks to the deep impulse of Green spirituality among many in the West who are currently searching for new expressions of the sacred.[46] Recognizing that our ideas of place and community are implicit forms of social commentary, Costello intimates that in an era of post-institutional religion such ideas may also serve as tangible forms of sanctuary—as new expressions of the perennial human need for an inner serenity based, inevitably, on intangibles.

"Many young people are searching for a fusion of their deepest and truest private aspirations with public meaning," he explains:

> They know that the public secular institutions of government, media, unions and educational institutions like our universities are running on empty because they have little language of interconnectedness or priority for spiritual values.

This where Gary Snyder's language and commitment offer redress. Returning praise and reverence for the simple joys of teaching children, gardening, or for the rewards of individual and communal labour, whether it be through the interconnectedness of poetry, meditation, chanting, labour, or activism, Snyder has shown a way forward. As the late *Ish River* poet Robert Sund contended, his fellow poet has "[known] where to look for what he needed."[47] In a paraphrase of Allen Ginsberg's well-travelled concept of "Aesthetic Mindfulness," he has known how to identify what it is he has seen when he has seen it, and what he has heard when he hears it.[48]

Clarifying what "organic interconnections" between the "natural and human worlds" might mean, Costello points out that spirituality can be reinterpreted as a new, simpler meta-narrative for our age:

> The daily disciplines of meditation, recycling, using public transport, and greening one's neighbourhood are parallels to the rhythms of prayer, Bible reading, witness and love of neighbour in Christian teaching.

Snyder does not disagree. In an essay entitled "Poetry and the Primitive," he relates, "We all know what primitive cultures don't have. What they *do* have is this knowledge of connection and responsibility."[49] This responsibility is seen in the lives of the Australian aborigines of whom Snyder, who has spent time among them, observes how they:

> live in a world of ongoing recurrence—comradeship with
> the landscape and continual exchanges of being and form
> and position; every person, animals, forces, all are related
> via a web of reincarnation—or rather, they are "interborn."
> It may well be that rebirth (or interbirth, for we are actually
> mutually creating each other and all things while living) is
> the objective fact of existence which we have not yet brought
> into conscious knowledge and practice.[50]

Bringing a wider awareness of how benefits may be reaped from the wisdom of "interbeing" lies at the heart of the citizenship Gary Snyder offers the global age. Forged from his roots in the Pacific Northwest, the California Sierras, and the Buddhist-Indic worlds of East and South Asia, it is an ethic easily endorsed by a broadening horizon of seekers that extends from the West Coast's post-sixties, ecologically minded community to enlightened Christians like Tim Costello, who can regard it as the manifestation "of a God who is indeed green."[51]

Among the jobs of poets and shamans is the work of extending new, and renewing good traditional ideas (see "What You Should Know To be a Poet").[52] Bringing these into conscious knowledge and practice, the approach Snyder has traditionally employed is rigorous but uncomplicated. In an interview discussing *Back On the Fire* (2007), a collection of essays, he summarizes his approach by observing simply,

> One of the things I've been trying to do for a long time is to
> find a vocabulary, a way to talk and bring images out that
> will communicate from my rural, backcountry, out-in-the-

woods upbringing and family culture to the intellectual and
literary worlds that I've also lived in on the West Coast, with
the intention of bringing the whole West Coast culture closer
together. That's what I hope…that it makes it possible for
academics, businesspeople, loggers, and Sierra miners to
realize they're together in the same place.[53]

To conclude, advancing the work of building community along more ecologically, socially and economically viable principles can sound remarkably like what Buddhism understands as transmitting the *dharma*. Arising from the Trans-Pacific "new world" culture that Snyder has identified as the West Coast of North America and the Asia-Pacific, a new world dharma that is compatible with the twenty-first century's evolving interfaith and secular learning projects is an idea worth thinking through—a gift of renewed, re-imagined citizenship for our new millennium.

Notes:

1. Gary Snyder, in Robert Mezey, "A Gathering of Poets," *Western Humanities Review* 29 (Spring 1975): 274.

2. Gary Snyder, "Four Changes, with a Postscript" in *A Place In Space: Ethics, Aesthetics and Watersheds* (New York: Counterpoint, 1995), 41.

3. Gary Snyder, "The Etiquette of Freedom" in *The Practice of the Wild* (San Francisco: North Point, 1990), 3-34.

4. Betty Pickett, "A Natural Life," *Prairie Schooner* 49:3 (Fall 1975): 274.

5. Ibid., 275

6. Ibid.

7. Snyder, *A Place in Space*, 246.

8. Ibid., 246-7. Note: Poet-essayist Andrew Schelling notes that the term "bioregion" first appeared formally in the *American Heritage Dictionary* in 1991.

9. Gary Snyder, in interview by Trevor Carolan, "The Wild Mind of Gary Snyder," *Shambhala Sun*, May 1996: 18-26.

10. Ibid., 24.

11. Snyder, *A Place in Space*, 76.

12. Gary Snyder, in interview by Trevor Carolan, 23.

13. Ibid., 23-24.

14. Joan Halifax, "The Third Body: Buddhism, Shamanism, and Deep Ecology" in *Dharma Gaia: a Harvest of Essays in Buddhism and Ecology,* ed. Allan H. Badiner (Berkeley: Parallax), 20-37.

15. Wes Jackson, *Becoming Native To This Place* (Washington, D.C.: Counterpoint, 1996), 87-103.

16. Letter to the author, Dec. 16, 1985.

17. Gary Snyder, in interview by Trevor Carolan, 24.

18. Ibid., 24-25.

19. David H. French, "Gary Snyder and Reed College" in *Dimensions of a Life,* ed. Jon Halper (San Francisco: Sierra Club Books, 1991), 16-23.

20. Halifax, "The Third Body," 34.

21. See "The Incredible Survival of Coyote" in *A Place In Space,* 148-162.

22. Gary Snyder, "Reinhabitation," in *A Place In Space,* 187-188.

23. See Halifax, "The Third Body," 23-24; also Ronald Wright, *On Fiji Islands* (Toronto: Viking, 1986), 44.

24. Leflesche, in Halifax, ibid.

25. Snyder, *A Place in Space,* 189.

26. Ibid.

27. [book of Mencius] Bk 7, A.

28. Ibid.

29. In *Allen Ginsberg and Friends.* Video documentary. Princeton, NJ: Films for the Humanities and Sciences, 1997. Part of the series "Poetry Heaven."

30. Gary Snyder, *Earth House Hold* (New York: New Directions, 1969), 92.

31. Snyder, *A Place in Space,* 208.

32. Gretel Erlich, quoted on the cover of *The Practice of the Wild* (San Francisco: North Point, 1990).

33. In unpublished interview with the author. May, 2007.

34. Gary Snyder, "Exhortations for Baby Tigers" in *A Place in Space,* 208.

35. Gary Snyder, in interview by Trevor Carolan, 26.

36. Ibid.

37. T. S. Eliot, "Tradition and the Individual Talent" in *Selected Prose* (New York: Harcourt Brace Jovanovich, 1975), 38.

38. Ibid., 40.

39. Susan Kalter, "The Path to Endless: Gary Snyder in the mid-1990s," Texas Studies in Literature and Language 41 (1999): 17-46.

40. Ibid., 21.

41. Wylie Sypher, *From Rococo to Cubism in Art and Literature* (New York: Random House, 1960), 50.

42. Eliot, "Tradition and the Individual Talent," 38.

43. Snyder, *Danger on Peaks*, (Berkeley: Counterpoint, 2004), 102. Noted at a public reading in Bellingham, Washington in 2004.

44. Ibid.

45. Snyder, *A Place in Space*, 234.

46. Tim Costello, "Politics with a soul. Yes, it is possible," *Sydney Morning Herald*, December 23, 2002.

47. Robert Sund, "Yes, It's Really Work!" in *Gary Snyder: Dimensions of a Life*, ed. Jon Halper. San Francisco: Sierra Club Books, 1991), 248-251.

48. Allen Ginsberg encouraged his colleagues and students to practice "Aesthetic Mindfulness," explaining it as "paying keen attention to what you see when you see it, and what you hear when you hear it." See Trevor Carolan, *Giving Up Poetry: With Allen Ginsberg at Hollyhock* (Banff, AB: Banff Centre Press, 2001), 15-25.

49. Gary Snyder, "Poetry and the Primitive" in *Earth House Hold*, 121.

50. Ibid., 129.

51. Tim Costello, "Politics with a soul. Yes, it is possible," *Sydney Morning Herald*, December 23, 2002.

52. Gary Snyder, "What You Should Know to be a Poet" in *Regarding Wave* (New York: New Directions, 1970).

53. Gary Snyder, in interview with Trevor Carolan, *The Bloomsbury Review* 27.4 (July/August 2007): 5.

Entering the Forest at Dusk

MARTIN VANWOUDENBERG

Living in what theologian Thomas Berry has called "The Ecozoic Age," increasingly we are becoming accustomed to a literature that is more conversant with the ideas of Deep Ecology. Writers from the B.C. and U.S. Northwest Coast have been engaged for at least the past generation with giving us honest portraits and reflections of the changing ways in which we interact with the world. This investigation is as timely as it is significant. As anyone who follows the daily headlines is aware, the ways that we've traditionally earned a living from the Pacific Coast area and inland as far as the Rockies are changing, especially in working the land, forestry, and the fisheries.

For a long time the jobs in these fields were frequently romanticized, but contemporary writers who have experience in begging and sweating a living out of the soil, the bush, and the sea are giving us new insights into their lives that are far from idyllic. In the face of the modern environmental movement, and its sometimes radical attempts to shock the world into action, a balanced and practical view on ecology and sustainability is sorely needed. That voice does not necessarily come from the offices and headquarters of the great environmental organizations, but from these same men and women out in the wilds every day.

The poet Auden may have claimed that poets and poetry do not change anything, but for three thousand years writers have had the role of bearing witness. As Plato said, "Poetry is nearer to vital truth than history." From the days of Horace and Virgil onward, they have also laboured to address the abstract spirituality of nature and humanity's long association with it. In a contemporary way, poets and writers of prose alike continue to explore our deep-rooted desire to rediscover this spiritual relationship in a postmodern, increasingly secular world. I am thinking of this in relation to a remarkable collection of work published from Port Townsend, Washington, not far from Victoria or Vancouver. Reading it, one cannot fail to be struck by how strikingly similar are the working lives and daily concerns of our neighbours across the monumental divide of the international border.

Edited by Finn Wilcox and Jerry Gorsline, *Working the Woods, Working the Sea: An Anthology of Northwest Writings* (2008), is filled with the reality of life on the West Coast, from a wide variety of perspectives—all of which are intimately familiar with hard work and sweat. In some respects it echoes the "work" poetry of B.C. writers like Tom Wayman, Kate Braid and Calvin Wharton: work and the idea of individual dignity are closely related. The collection is broken down into two main sections, Treeplanting and Working the Sea. The edition itself contains a broad range of poetry, prose, essays, musings and ramblings by such well-known voices as Gary Snyder, Jim Dodge, Red Pine and Mike O'Connor, as well as many other West Coast writers. It also offers memorable work by newcomers like Julia Menard-Warwick ("Treeplanting at Sombrio Creek"). The concerns here are with important environmental issues facing this part of the world, including reforestation, salmon restoration, the defence of old-growth forests, and watershed protection. The perspectives, however, are immediate, honest, raw: in reading them you're likely to feel the grit of the coast in your boots, or the biting cold of the sea on your face. It is a reality not many continue to experience, or one that we quickly forget.

Idealizing something is easy, even within our own memories. After falling trees in the cold of late autumn, or making acquaintance with rugged B.C. destinations like the Bowron Lakes or the West Coast Trail, it's always easier to sit by the fire and reminisce about being at peace with nature—the aches and strains forgotten. It is a testament to the power of the writers here that reading their work sharpened my memories of precisely these kinds of events. Suddenly, I remembered the digging of pack-straps into my shoulders, the dull ache in knee joints that threatened to buckle with every step by the third day of hard slogging. These aren't writers with an idealized longing for simpler times and oneness with the pristine wilderness. The voices here are authentic and I found myself pushed for some B.C. approximations. Howard White, I think, has gone for this same kind of bone and gristle writing with his *Raincoast Chronicles* series from the Sunshine Coast.

It's hard to live and work in the wilderness and there is often little pristine about it. This is best encapsulated in a provoking essay by Richard White that occurs in the sardonically titled third short section, "Are You an Environmentalist, or Do You Work for a Living?" In a powerful way, White brings the purpose and focus of this collection into clear view, taking aim at environmentalists who either do not live near the wilderness, or who take a Marie Antoinette perspective on it. We might remember how that unfortunate queen created her "petit hameau," a mock farm in an idyllic setting complete with farmhouse, dairy, and poultry yard where she and her attendants dressed in satin ribbons played at milking cows and tending docile animals. Sometimes, the fashionable eco-flavoured writing of our day has a similar ring, particularly when the vague epithet of "sustainability" is involved. It's harder to walk the walk than talk the talk. The cold reality underscoring White's essay comes out powerfully in the way that false presumptions can arise in the way we look at nature and work. The viewpoint that the blue-collar worker who grinds out a living through sweat and machinery is somehow in opposition to understanding and loving nature is simply not correct, and White's evidence is compelling on several fronts. As he states,

> Humans have known nature by digging in the earth, by planting seeds, and harvesting plants. They have known nature by feeling heat and cold, sweating as they went up hills, sinking into mud. They have known nature by shaping wood and stone, by living with animals, nurturing them, and killing them.[1]

Anyone who lives in the country knows that living with nature does oblige these things, especially the latter. In the Fraser Valley where I live and work, this is the way things are, although treeplanting is on the wane. Our young people head up north around Prince George in summers to do that.

Whether it is working the lines while treeplanting, with an overloaded bag and an uneven surface that threatens to send the labourer down the mountain, or cutting down the fragrant western red cedar with saw and wedge and hair-trigger nerves ready to run, this is the way of it unless you're home on the farm or working in town. Nature gives, Nature takes, and woe to those who fail to respect her latent power. *Working the Woods, Working the Sea* contains as many failures as it does triumphs, though persistence through labour fills it most of all.

Here a timber examiner loses his partner in the snow, forced to leave him for fear of freezing to death himself, and one can almost feel the ice on the pages of Greg Nagle's "The White Line." There, a Native family heads with drunken father and pregnant mother to the salmon streams, and returns home hungry, as in George Silverstar's "True Indian Modern Story." Here also the fishing boats share the water with the ammo ship that does not carry fish within its belly, but bombs for killing other working men and women, brought powerfully to life in "Ammo Ship" by Clemens Starck. Hippies, labourers, and woodsmen rattle in the backs of pickup trucks, hunkering down inside their coats in the early dawn hours, drowsily downing coffee to ward off the cold and the late-night drinking.

The settings are familiar and unsurprising—often cold, wet, and miserable. Jim Dodge states flatly, "if you aim to plant trees / only two things you really need to know: / Green side goes up, / And ain't no raingear in this world'll keep you dry." Is there a more poignant and powerful disconnect between those who live and work in warm downtown buildings or cozy home-offices while decrying the harvesting of the forests, and those who love the forest for both its beauty and the economic survival it makes possible? "Ah," says the environmentalist with whom White takes issue, "this is proof that the blue-collar worker is simply part of the problem and isn't a deep enough thinker to appreciate the issue in all its complexity." Howard Horowitz tosses that self-righteous idea aside in his poem "The Blue River Highway":

Love
makes impossible demands.
Love for the river
    and the giant trees
has made crusaders of us.

It's just that highways
chainsaws & paychecks
may be stronger than lovers:

    jobs
    are scarce here;
    you can't eat
    trees...

For those like myself who work in a classroom and at a computer and can feel self-secure in the knowledge that no animal or tree has died at my hands, this is compelling, perhaps necessary reading. The computer we use is powered by dams that kill fish, destroy habitats, and exert a devastating impact on the natural environment. The paper we go through in our offices likely destroys far more trees than any logger.

Environmentalist Wendell Berry is one of comparatively few North American authors who write and also work the land. He makes his labour pointedly basic, forgoing modern machinery and using animal power only—a formidable literary man who walks his talk and serves as a potential model for us all. Some environmentalists believe it is modern work, not work itself, that has damaged our relationship with nature. The machine is opposed to the handheld tool, and degrades our symbiotic relationship with the soil. Yet White observes that it is only his writing (and its income) that allows Berry the luxury of his convictions and the ability to forgo modern machinery. In a curmudgeonly way, it is not far removed from Marie Antoinette's idyllic experiment. The peasants in her time, and the blue-collar workers in ours, do not have that opportunity. Not if they want to eat. As White says, environmentalists need to come to terms with work for a number of reasons: Its effects are so widespread that it provides a fundamental and intimate way of knowing the natural world, and any attempted separation creates a dualism where nature can only come into focus during play. In this reality, White argues, Environmentalists themselves "...reach a point where they seem trivial and extraneous and their issues politically expendable." In White's world, and in our own, men and women labour out of need. Any forced attempt to disengage love of the land from the need to till the soil in a practical way that allows people to survive is simply "self-righteous, privileged, and arrogant." White does not discount or discredit Berry's efforts. It is simply not born out of reality, and therefore not a viable model to put forward as a practical alternative.

And so men and women in the woods work, and work hard. The best days are those in which they get paid, not the ones in which they see the most vibrant sunrise. Always open to the natural beauty, it takes on a different perspective when it can harm you, starve you, or kill you. Paul Thomas' "Best Day" is all about finding the perfect fishing spot with the help of a native partner, and for one day owning it. They bring in more fish than they can count, going back again and again until the other fishermen get suspicious and motor over themselves. And while he speaks of "the big kings who almost always died instantly and regally," he is under no illusions. To fish is about eating and surviving.

This, White argues, is the problem in the modern environmental movement. Somewhere along the line "true" environmentalists got into their heads the notion that only an untilled garden is a good one. White points the finger at a Judeo-Christian belief related to the fall from grace in Eden. Before the fall, he argues, there was no work.

Therefore, the ideal is a return to that condition. This is a limited understanding though, or is incorrect. Even in Eden, prior to the fall, the first humans were instructed by God to work the garden and change it. Here too, in a world before sin and human weakness, there was work. White's point however, is not what historical worldview is to "blame" but how to correct it. And though White did not write his essay specifically for this collection, it is hard to imagine a better way for him to make his point than to let it speak in a volume of this kind.

In poems and essays like "Montana," "Treeplanter's Journal," and "Below the Falls" by Howard Horowitz, Jerry Gorsline, and Jerry Martien, we encounter the voices of the day workers, the natives, the drifters, the lovers, the women, the men, and the bosses. The images and experiences they portray speak through the daily events they describe—hiking into the bush with saplings slung over a shoulder, gauging which direction a giant redwood will fall, or hauling nets from the saltchuck and onto the boat deck. There is a persistent and honest rhythm one can almost feel pulsating through the pages. "All day in the rain on summer solstice / Wet hands, cold feet. / Finally, the hot tea I've been dreaming of for hours / is in my hand" (Chuck Eason, 37).

Other events presented are more frantic, such as the re-imagined last thoughts of a logging trucker who loses his brakes on a mountain hill, in "Elegy for a Log Truck Driver" by Mike O'Connor, or the wiper "riding the rope-slung scaffold, dangling in fuel-oil fumes…while he ignored 'Abandon Ship!' and stayed behind and scrubbed," as in Richard Dankleff's "First Trip." Here too, in Bill Shepher's "The Bridge," the cutter's saw is ripped from his hands as he is tossed and "swallowed in a twisting chaos that strikes and batters him, breaking bones on the way down." It's an uneasy, precarious existence for the working men and women who both dismantle and rebuild the forest, and those who fight the seas while simultaneously blessing it for the bounty it gives.

In and amongst this action, noise, and sweat, are the still and quiet voices as well. These are not detached and distant, but born from the same labour and energy as the rest. In "The Best Day" by Paul Thomas we feel the quiet after the engines stop and the saws are silenced. We find the reflections on a perfect day on the ocean, when "the decks were awash in silver and the scuppers gurgling red, when leaping dolphins led us to silky smooth seas." And again, in Tom Jay's "The Salmon of the Heart," we find peace and meaning through an Estonian folksong, and in "The Mountain Poems of Stonehouse", the serenity communicated by a Buddhist monk after a lifetime on the mountain. Again and again, White's point is made for him: the uncultured blue-collar worker is capable of a deeply profound understanding of nature and her needs, outshining many professional environmentalists and armchair eco-theoreticians.

The best proof of this is Tim McNulty's ingenious parable "Coyote at the Movies." To summarize it would be to belittle and spoil it. Suffice to say, it contains traces of the idyllic and the magic, mixed with the salt of reality. It needs to be read for itself. And there are many others like this, mixing and becoming a myriad of voices that seem at first discordant for all their variety, until we settle into their rhythm and hear their quintessential West Coast harmony. These are Pacific Northwest neighbour writers who are neither artificial nor idyllic, but deep, broad and rich, like the earth and sea that inspire them. Their work is meaningful and it calls us back to our true home in nature and asks us to see it in all its complexity. Wilcox and Gorsline offer a lot with their view of writing about work, dignity and place, but like nature itself their compendium needs to be engaged with actively. Enter it as you would enter the forest at dusk—with your heart among the treetops, and your eyes upon the path.

Notes:

1. Richard White, "Are You an Environmentalist, or Do You Work for a Living?" in *Working the Woods, Working the Sea: An Anthology of Northwest Writings*, eds. Finn Wilcox and Jerry Gorsline (Portsend, WA: Empty Bowl, 2005).

CONTRIBUTORS

MICHAEL BARNHOLDEN is the managing editor of *West Coast Line*. He is also the author of *Circumstances Alter Photographs* (Talon, 2009), Reading the Riot Act (Anvil, 2005) and editor of *Writing Class: the KSW anthology* (New Star Books).

JOSEPH BLAKE is a journalist living in Victoria. His music columns appeared in the *Victoria Times Colonist* for over two decades, and he still writes for the paper, reviewing recordings and previewing the city's cultural life. His travel stories are also widely published in the *Globe & Mail, Vancouver Sun, Edmonton Journal, Calgary Herald, Montreal Gazette* and *National Post*. He also contributes to CBC Radio.

FRANCES CABAHUG completed her BA in English Literature at the University of British Columbia. She writes book reviews for *The Pacific Rim Review of Books*, among other publications. She originally hails from the Philippines.

TREVOR CAROLAN teaches English and Creative Writing at University of the Fraser Valley. He has been Coordinator of Writing programs at the Banff Centre, and has published 14 books of poetry, translation, non-fiction, fiction, and anthologies. He has also worked as media advocate on behalf of international human rights, Canadian First Nation land claims, famine relief, and Pacific Coast watershed issues. He holds a Ph.D. from Bond University, Australia, and served as an elected municipal councillor for North Vancouver.

JUDITH COPITHORNE has a B.A. in English and a teaching certificate. Over the years she has worked in a good number of guises including that of being a nurses aide, a writer and a teacher.

RON DART teaches Political Science/Philosophy/Religious Studies at University of the Fraser Valley. He was on staff with Amnesty International in the 1980s. The political science advisor to the Stephen Leacock Museum, he is on the National Executive of the Thomas Merton Society of Canada. His more than twenty books include works on George Grant, Stephen Leacock, Robin Mathews, Thomas Merton, Beat writing and the North Cascades, and mountaineering.

MIKE DOYLE is a poet, critic, biographer and editor (who also writes as Charles Doyle.) He has published books on Wallace Stevens, William Carlos Williams and Richard Aldington. He has written essays on Irving Layton and Al Purdy. Doyle is professor emeritus from the University of Victoria, B.C.

PAUL FALARDEAU is an English major at the University of the Fraser Valley, where he has also studied Biology. He is the Arts and Life editor for the *Cascade* newspaper and is a DJ and programmer for CIVL radio. A regular contributor to *The Pacific Rim Review of Books*, he lives in Aldergrove, B.C.

SUSAN MCCASLIN is a poet, educator, scholar, workshop facilitator, and author of twelve volumes of poetry, including her most recent, *Lifting the Stone* (Seraphim Editions, 2007). She has edited two anthologies of sacred poetry (*Poetry and Spiritual Practice* and *A Matter of Spirit*), is on the editorial board of *Event: the Douglas College Review*, and an editorial consultant for *The Journal of Feminist Studies in Religion* (Harvard Divinity School). She lives in Fort Langley, B.C. After twenty-three years as a professor of English and Creative Writing at Douglas College, she is now a full-time writer. Her most recent project is a new poetry cycle called *Demeter Goes Skydiving*.

GEORGE MCWHIRTER grew up between the Shankill Road in Belfast and Carnalea on Belfast Lough. At the age of twenty-six he left Ulster for Spain, eventually settling in Vancouver in 1968, with frequent sojourns in Mexico. *Catalan Poems* shared the Commonwealth Poetry Prize with Chinua Achebe's *Cry, Soul Brother* and his translation of Mexican poet, José Emilio Pacheco, published by New Directions, won the F.R. Scott Prize for translation. He has recently translated Homero Aridjis's Poemas *Solares/Solar Poemas* for City Lights (2010). He is anthologized in *The Penguin Book of Canadian Verse* and *Irish Writing in the Twentieth Century*. His most recent books of poetry are *The Incorrection* (Oolichan, 2007) and *The Anachronicles* (Ronsdale, 2008). He served as Vancouver's inaugural Poet Laureate, 2007-09. *A Verse Map of Vancouver*, his Poet Laureate anthology with photographs by Derek von Essen and 92 poems on different city locations, is published by Anvil Press.

COLIN JAMES SANDERS was born in Winnipeg in 1954. He came west in 1969 to Gold River, to Prince Rupert, then to Vancouver where he has lived since 1979. He holds an M.A. in Cultural Anthropology, a path influenced by reading Gary Snyder and William Burroughs. A Registered Clinical Counsellor, he has worked since 1989 with City University of Seattle's Vancouver campus where he teaches a course on the sociology of substance use. A therapist with Vancouver Coastal Health's Employee and Family Assistance Program (EFAP), he has also taken a co-lead position on a research demonstration project funded by the Mental Health Commission of Canada. His publications include "A poetics of resistance: compassionate practice in substance misuse therapy" (2007).

CHELSEA THORNTON is a student at the University of the Fraser Valley. She has studied at McGill University and North West Community College. Her research interests in the fields of Ecology and English focus on the overlap between the two. She has been published in *The Pacific Rim Review of Books*.

HILARY TURNER is a teacher of Rhetoric and English literature at the University of the Fraser Valley. She has previously been employed in English departments at a number of universities, including the University of British Columbia.

MARTIN VANWOUDENBERG is the author of three books and regularly writes on literature. He does freelance writing for several technology websites and teaches English and History in Langley, B.C.

CAROLYN ZONAILO has published eleven books of poetry. Born in Vancouver, she received her M.A. in literature from Simon Fraser University, where her papers are now archived in Special Collections and Rare Books at the W.A.C. Bennett Library. She has remained active in literary small press publishing, founding Caitlin Press in Vancouver, in 1977; co-founding The Poem Factory with Ed Varney in Vancouver, in 1990; and Coracle Press with Stephen Morrissey in Montreal, in 2000. Zonailo has served on the executives of The Federation of B.C. Writers, The League of Canadian Poets, The Writers' Union of Canada, and QSPELL, the original English-language writers' association in Quebec. Her works include *The Goddess in the Garden* (2002), finalist for the A.M. Klein Poetry Prize; and *the moon with mars in her arms* (2006).

265

INDEX